THE TWO DUCHESSES

Arthur Calder-Marshall

HARPER & ROW, PUBLISHERS
New York, Hagerstown, San Francisco, London

FIRST U.S. EDITION

ISBN: 0-06-010617-4

LIBRARY OF CONGRESS CATALOG CARD NUMBER: 76-26215

78 79 80 81 82 10 9 8 7 6 5 4 3 2 1

TO ARA, WITH LOVE AND GRATITUDE

Contents

CONTENTS

Illustrations

John Augustus, Lord Hervey, 1757–1796, by Thomas Gainsborough (reproduced by permission of the National Trust, photograph by courtesy of Jeremy Whitaker)

Georgiana canvassing in the Westminster election, after Thomas Rowlandson

Thomas Coutts the banker, 1734–1824, by Sir William Beechey (courtesy of the directors of Coutts & Co.)

Charles Grey, later 2nd Earl Grey, by George Romney (reproduced by permission of Viscount Howick, photograph by courtesy of The Paul Mellon Centre for Studies in British Art (London) Ltd.)

Harriet, Countess of Bessborough at about the time she met Granville, by Sir Joshua Reynolds (reproduced by permission of the Earl of Bessborough)

'Hary-O', Lady Harriet Cavendish, later 1st Countess Granville, 1785–1862, by Sir John Russell (courtesy of the estate of Sir A. Leveson-Gower)

Lord Granville Leveson-Gower, 1773–1846, after Lawrence (courtesy of the Courtauld Institute of Art)

William, 5th Duke of Devonshire at the time of his second marriage (courtesy of the Trustees of the British Museum)

Corisande de Grammont, Viscountess Ossulton and later 5th Countess of Tankerville, artist unknown (courtesy of the National Portrait Gallery)

Caro Ponsonby, later Lady Caroline Lamb, 1785–1828, artist unknown (courtesy of John Murray)

Cardinal Consalvi, 1758–1824, by Sir Thomas Lawrence (by permission of the National Trust, photograph by courtesy of O. G. Jarman)

'Hart', afterwards 6th Duke of Devonshire, 1790–1858, by Horace Hone (courtesy of the Chatsworth Settlement)

'Bess' in 1819, by Sir Thomas Lawrence (courtesy of the Trustees of the British Museum)

Acknowledgements

I thank the Trustees of the Chatsworth Settlement and the publisher, John Murray, for permission to quote documents from the 5th Duke of Devonshire's collection, owned by the former and published in part by the latter. Mr T. S. Wragg, MBE, TD, Chatsworth Librarian, apart from other help, let me see Ann Scafe's journal and introduced me to Professor Franco Crainz, who showed me letters by Dr Richard Croft relating to the birth of Hartington. Lord Dormer and Messrs Methuen, publishers of *Dearest Bess*, gave me similar permission for the journals of Ly. Elizabeth Foster. Thanks are due to the Public Record Office (Granville Papers), the University of Durham (2nd Earl Grey Papers) and to Castle Howard Estate Ltd (Viscountess Morpeth letters).

Acknowledgements for illustrations are made on the previous page. But I must thank Earl Howick, the National Trust, the National Portrait Gallery, the Courtauld Institute and the Paul Mellon Centre for tracking down fine prints.

Mrs Frances Lindley of Harper & Row suggested and greatly assisted the writing of this book. The final draft was kindly read by the Dowager Duchess of Devonshire (without whose enthusiasm the 5th Duke's collection at Chatsworth might never have been so superbly ordered).

I wish to thank my wife for her patience and criticism over five years, her typing of numerous drafts and assistance with the index. At Hutchinson's I am indebted to my copy editor, Mrs Sue Major, and to Mr Harold Harris and Julian Watson who saw the book through the press. My agents, Lady Greene and Mrs Ilsa Yardley, endured the reading of early drafts.

Finally, I am grateful to my old friend Dr Raymond Greene and his colleague Mr Henry E. Hobbs for their diagnosis of Georgiana's eye trouble.

Prelude

For nearly two hundred years people have wondered about the fifth Duke of Devonshire and his two Duchesses. How was it possible for Lady Elizabeth Foster to be at the same time the 'dearest friend' of Georgiana, and the mistress of her husband? By what strange coincidence did Lady Elizabeth give birth to the Duke's illegitimate daughter Caroline St Jules just three weeks before the Duchess gave birth to the Duke's second legitimate daughter Lady Harriet Cavendish? What was the mystery surrounding the birth of Hartington, the much-wanted heir, in Paris in the middle of the French Revolution, when it would have been so much easier for the Duchess to lie in at Chatsworth or Devonshire House? How was it possible for the Duke's children, legitimate and illegitimate, to grow up together, all as members of the Devonshire household? And after the death of Georgiana, his first Duchess, what led the Duke to take Lady Elizabeth as his second Duchess?

These are questions which I have attempted to answer in this book. It is not a composite biography. All the characters who appear had varied and interesting lives of their own. If we were to view any of them in the round, a host of other characters would have had to be introduced. The period during which they lived was one of historical, economic, scientific and social developments of great importance, in which they took an interest great or small. It was the time of the War of American Independence, the Gordon Riots, the French Revolution and the Napoleonic wars which raged through Europe, Africa, Asia and the Americas for nearly twenty years. I have not attempted to describe these events, except in so far as they affected the relationship between the Duke, his two Duchesses and the various relatives and friends who became directly involved in their tortuous affairs.

I cannot pretend that what I have written can be proven. It is based upon five years' study of documents, many of them with the very passages deleted which would have told us what I have had to guess at. I can only say that my account accords with the known facts and seems to me the most plausible explanation of a constantly changing and always intriguing state of affairs.

I

In the summer of 1773 the twenty-four-year-old William Cavendish, fifth Duke of Devonshire, assured his mistress, Charlotte Spencer, that she need not fear for her future or that of the child she was bearing him. Then he left London for Spa, taking the usual route via Sittingbourne, Dover and across the Channel to Belgium.

Of all the European watering places the most fashionable was Spa in the forest of Ardennes. During the season emperors, kings, princes and noblemen came with their families to take the cure either at the thermal spring within the town or at its companion fountain Pouhon Peter the Great in the nearby woodlands. The baths were specific against rheumatism and gout, which latter was considered to attack not merely such extremities as feet, hands and the ear lobes, but also the brain, lungs, heart or blood; in fact wherever there was a distemper which doctors could not diagnose. Taken internally, the waters relieved constipation, a complaint distressingly common when dinners comprised ten to twenty courses. Some physicians even recommended Spa for ladies suffering from barrenness. Whether those ladies conceived owing to the salubrity of the mineral waters or the opportunities for social intercourse afforded by the gaieties of the town will never be determined. But many left with child who came without.

Since bathing and sipping could occupy comparatively little of the day and night, there were twice-weekly dances, concerts and dramatic performances. The gambling houses, the Vauxhall, the Redoute and the Levoz, were open from early morning till late at night. There were tables for faro, hazard, rouge et noir and E.O., games of pure chance in which the stakes ran high; and for those who preferred the exercise of skill, rooms for whist, tric-trac and backgammon.

The Duke of Devonshire was fond of gambling. But he did not come to Spa for that reason. He could have his fill of faro at Almack's Club, in St James's, not three minutes' walk from Devonshire House in Piccadilly. He went to Spa to tell his father's old friends, the Earl and Countess Spencer, that he had decided to marry their elder daughter, Lady Georgiana Spencer, now that she was turned sixteen. The proposal may have been put as a request, but the Duke did not doubt its acceptance. He had only to express a wish for it to be gratified; indeed he expected his will usually to be done without his having to say what it was.

He had had an unfortunate life. When he was aged six and most in need of maternal affection, his mother, Baroness Clifford in her own right, had died. When he was aged sixteen and most in need of paternal guidance, his father died also, leaving him, his sister and two brothers in the perfunctory care of their bachelor uncles, Major-General Lord Frederick and Lord John Cavendish. So, in mid-adolescence, William Cavendish, Marquess of Hartington, Baron Clifford, had found himself fifth Duke of Devonshire. His income was guesstimated at the time of his succession at £36000 a year.[1] This accumulated until he came into his inheritance at twenty-one. The Clifford and Devonshire entails were managed by Mr Heaton, the family solicitor, with the Duke's two uncles as co-trustees. There were properties in England, Devonshire House, Chatsworth, Hardwick Hall, Chiswick House, Bolton Abbey, Londesborough and Compton Place which the young Duke visited from time to time. But he never in his whole life went to see the beautiful Lismore Castle and other estates in Ireland, which brought in £11000 a year.

The fifth Duke grew up cushioned on wealth, burdened with honours and starved of affection. The closest of his relatives was his sister Lady Dorothy Cavendish. But when she was sixteen she had married the third Duke of Portland; and the wealthy young Duke was on his own.

When the Duke had been in Switzerland on the Grand Tour, his uncle Lord John Cavendish wrote recommending him to mix less with his own countrymen and more with foreigners. There was an avuncular hint on how to get on with Italian women.[2] The Duke wanted to be loved for himself, not for his wealth and position. So when he took a girl from the Opéra in Paris, he paid her only modestly, to test her affection. It was a tactic which came naturally to him. He disliked paying bills of any sort; and love should be free.

Worse than women of pleasure were those who wanted to marry him. In France Mme du Barry, the young mistress of the ageing Louis XV, an uncrowned queen of courtesans, tried to trick him into matrimony. She so committed herself that – on the advice of his tutor – the Duke tricked her into bed and escaped a bachelor to England.[3]

In London things proved just as bad. Every designing mother and daughter had her eyes on him. He paid some attention to Lady Betty Hamilton, and even though Lady Betty was in love with the Duke of Dorset, soon society was saying that it would be a scandal if the Duke of Devonshire did not propose to her.[4] He had, it seemed, only to appear at an assembly and it turned into a slave market. He did not like to go with actresses or courtesans; he wanted an accommodating girl for a mistress. But when he attempted the daughter of a City alderman, her mother started clamouring to know the honour of his intentions.[5]

Unlike most of his friends, he was not a lecherous man. He craved affection, rather than sexual satisfaction. In Miss Charlotte Spencer he had found a woman who would have made him a good wife, if his birth had been lowlier. Her father had been what was called 'a brown curate', one of those clerics paid to hold services on behalf of a church-man enjoying a plurality of livings. Mr Spencer had given Charlotte a gentle education, but on his death left only enough for her to travel to London in search of work as a seamstress or milliner. Like the heroine of Hogarth's 'Harlot's Progress', she had been met at the coaching house by a procuress posing as a kindly old lady. She was offered hospitality while looking for work and introduced to 'a field preacher' who would give her spiritual guidance. He proved to be a disguised nobleman, who took her maidenhead and left her pregnant. Faced with the possibility of street-walking, Miss Spencer accepted the pro-tection of an elderly roué, who needed esoteric stimulation. When her protector died, within a matter of months, he left Miss Spencer enough to start her own milliner's shop in Mayfair. There the Duke of Devon-shire noticed her behind the counter, was drawn to talk to her by her physical charms and was so moved by her delicacy of taste and the pathos of her history that he set her up in a villa.[6]

After all she had been through, Charlotte must have felt gratitude, and later even love. The Duke's disabilities, his awkwardness, suspicion and reclusiveness, bridged the social gap between them. In her living rooms she drew him out. In her bed she drew him in. She listened to what he said, interrupting only to ask him to say more. Lovingly she deployed skills she had learnt under duress from her geriatric protector. The Duke's shyness disappeared and with Charlotte Spencer he became a man capable of anything, almost.

We do not know when the fifth Duke of Devonshire decided to

make Lady Georgiana Spencer his Duchess.[7] At the time of her birth he had been eight and his father, the widowed fourth Duke, had been toying with the idea of taking her aunt, Miss Louisa Poyntz, as his second Duchess. Indeed Miss Louisa had gone as far as saying that, having regard to the Duke's kindness and vast fortune she had decided to accept him.[8] But something had prevented the marriage. Perhaps it was illness; or perhaps the fourth Duke found, as a Mrs Calderwood had, that Miss Louisa Poyntz was 'a great hoyden'.*

It may however have been that the person that the fourth Duke would really have liked to marry was the younger Miss Poyntz, the bride of John Spencer and Lady Georgiana's mother. She was 'most captivating and pleasing', Lady Stafford recalled. 'All men liked her and the Beauty of it was that she managed them *all* without their knowing it. Even the late Lord Bath never sat after Dinner or Supper at Wimbledon; he was the first at Skittles, Cards, or whatever Lady Spencer liked to have done.'[9] The fourth Duke of Devonshire remained her obedient admirer up to the time of his death in Spa at the early age of forty-four.

It is possible that before he died the fourth Duke had told his heir, 'You couldn't do better than marry Lady Georgiana Spencer, my boy.' And when he protested that Lady Georgiana was a child, half his own age, his father may have said, 'Nonsense. Wait till she's sixteen. That's the age when I married your mother.'

Certainly the fifth Duke was the most faithful follower of his family traditions; and any such casual remark might have been converted into a virtual command by his father's death. While Lady Georgiana Spencer was still in the schoolroom, the fifth Duke must have sized her up to see whether she was worth waiting for. She was a tall girl, with grey-blue eyes, a blushable complexion and reddish-golden curly hair. The hair created a luminous aura which immediately drew attention. But what fixed it was the way her thoughts and feelings immediately showed in her features. The Duke's face was a mask, through which the eyes peered like a bowman's at a turret arrow-slit. Lady Georgiana's was a crystal ball. In the world of rigid convention (superbly exemplified by her mother) Lady Georgiana was a 'natural', a sort of freak in an age of artificial elegance. The Duke

---

* 'Mrs Spencer is a very sweet-like girl, her sister is a great hoyden. The mother Poyntz commands the party, and she is a deaf, short-sighted, loud-spoken hackney-headed wife, and played at cards from morning till night.' (Sir John Maclean, *Memoir of the Family of Poyntz*, p. 215.)

himself was also a freak, but Georgiana's polar opposite: awkward when she was graceful; introverted when she was extrovert; inhibited when she was spontaneous. They counterbalanced each other.

Let us now view the arrival of the fifth Duke at Spa through the eyes of Georgiana's mother, the Countess Spencer. She was the paragon of eighteenth-century excellence and she had been planning the Duke's proposal of marriage for three years. Her own career was as exemplary of Virtue Rewarded as Samuel Richardson's *Pamela*. Her father, Stephen Poyntz, began life as the son of a City of London upholsterer. By ability, diplomacy, ambition and the use of a family tree rooted in the Norman Conquest, he had raised himself to become a Privy Councillor, adviser to King George I, confidant of his Queen and tutor to their son, the Duke of Cumberland. Early in his career, he had conducted the third Duke of Devonshire on the Grand Tour and he remained the third Duke's lifelong friend. His daughter, Miss Georgiana Poyntz, had married John Spencer, grandson and heir to the estate of Sarah, Duchess of Marlborough, who was at the time of his marriage 'the richest commoner in the land'.* When he was created the first Earl Spencer, Georgiana, now Countess Spencer, looked forward to marrying her daughters upward in the nobility. A religious woman, with a deep sense of the duties towards God and her neighbour laid upon her by rank and wealth, she felt it righteous to increase the rank and wealth in order better to fulfil her duties. Hers was the philosophy of the ascendant aristocrat.

The Earl and Countess Spencer approved the Duke's proposal for dynastic reasons. A union of the houses of Devonshire and Spencer was economically and politically desirable. It helped to consolidate the Whig ascendancy, that tightly knit group of families which had risen to power by siding with William of Orange to depose King James II in the 'Glorious Revolution' of 1688. The fifth Duke of Devonshire did not matter as a human being. His father had been known as 'head of the Whig party' and he could inherit the position if he wanted. He was also the life tenant of the Devonshire and Clifford entails, the head of his family, the dispenser of seats in Parliament and numerous clerical livings. It was obvious that Lady Georgiana Spencer ought to marry

---

* Sarah, Duchess of Marlborough, married three times. The Dukedom of Marlborough and the Blenheim estates went to Charles Spencer, eldest son of her third husband, the Earl of Sunderland. The second son, John Spencer, inherited the estates belonging to the Duchess of Marlborough in her own right, Althorp in Northamptonshire, Spencer House in London and Wimbledon Park in Surrey.

him. Whether or not she loved him did not matter. Rank and fortune were firmer foundations for married happiness. But the time had passed when a daughter could be ordered to marry. Georgiana had to accept the Duke of her own free will.

What of Lady Georgiana herself? Eighteen months before, she had been taken abroad for the first time on a sort of Little Tour of Europe, together with her eleven-year-old sister Harriet.[10] In Belgium they had met a series of royal and noble grotesques: Prince Charles ('a great fat man in a brown coat with a great many ribbands and stars') and the Duchess of Northumberland ('very fat' and with 'a great beard like a man'). They had visited Versailles, met the aged King Louis XV, the Dauphin and his Dauphiness, the future Queen Marie Antoinette. They had been over the luxurious Lucienne Maison, given by Louis XV to Mme du Barry, and learned from Mama the enormous profits that lady earned as the wages of sin. At Montpellier Papa had given a ball on the Queen's birthday and Mama had not gone to bed till 6 a.m. Even little Harriet had stayed up till one in the morning. They had seen corpses swinging from gibbets by the roadside, had been shown the mummified remains of dead children in the crypt of the Cordeliers' church and slept on the floor of a living room opening on to a stable in a crowded inn. In Spa they had met a Mme de Golifet who though not quite fifteen had already been married for two years.

While she herself was still fifteen, Lady Georgiana had received several offers of marriage, but she turned them down, no doubt on her mother's advice. The Duke's was an altogether different proposal. Georgiana did not love him: must indeed have regarded him a, belonging to another generation, half as old again as she was. But loves it was generally agreed in the eighteenth century, was the frailest foundation for a marriage. As Duchess of Devonshire, Georgiana would have a position in society second only to royalty. Of course she had to accept without delay.

But when the date of the marriage was discussed, there was immediate disagreement between the Countess Spencer and the fifth Duke. The Duke wanted an immediate marriage; or at any rate a marriage before Lady Georgiana's seventeenth birthday. His mother had married at sixteen, so had his sister. Why not Lady Georgiana?

The Countess pleaded that her daughter was giddy, had still much to learn before taking on the responsibilities of the Duchess of Devonshire. She herself had waited until she was eighteen before marrying.

The Duke could answer that the Countess's age at marriage had nothing to do with the case. She had married John Spencer on his twenty-first birthday, the very first moment he came into his inheritance: whereas he, the Duke, had waited until he was twenty-four before making his proposal.

If there had been a Dowager Duchess of Devonshire to initiate Georgiana, the Countess might have been less worried. With three great houses, an ailing husband and a younger daughter to look after, she herself could not keep Georgiana under strict surveillance. The Duke did not appear too dependable, lying abed till 3 or 4 p.m. and staying up all night. Nor did she approve of the Duke's bachelor friends, Stephen and Charles James Fox, General Fitzpatrick and Colonel Craufurd. They might be clever, witty, even brilliant. But they were irreligious, spendthrift and dissolute.

While the lawyers haggled over the marriage contract, the Countess Spencer alternately pleaded for time and crammed Georgiana with homilies on the duties incumbent on her birth and elevated status: duties to her Maker, her parents, her sister Lady Harriet, her brother Viscount Althorp, the Duke, her neighbours and herself.[11] Lady Georgiana listened with only one ear. With the other, she hearkened to the blandishments of the future: the good wishes of friends and rivals and advice about her trousseau from Mrs Howe and Miss Lloyd, Mama's cronies.

By early 1774 everyone knew of the forthcoming marriage. Lady Spencer in May confessed herself beaten. She had been caught on the horns of a dilemma. Dynastically the union was a triumph. Temperamentally, now or at any future time, it must be hazardous. What was the point of fighting for delay? She put the rumour about that the marriage would take place on Georgiana's seventeenth birthday, 7 June. But she agreed to let the Duke have his little triumph, on condition that the marriage should be as romantically secret as her own had been.

At a ball given in honour of the King's birthday on Saturday, 4 June, the Duke partnered Lady Georgiana. How well he danced we do not know. He was a clumsy man. It was said that at a rout he had leaned against a precious lustre and sent it crashing to the floor. Moving away from the debris, he had leaned against its companion, which smashed to smithereens. Looking down he had murmured, 'This is singular enough.'[12] Lady Georgiana, luckily, was not as fragile.

The morning after the Royal ball, she was awakened at Spencer House with the news that she was to be married at Wimbledon that day.[13] She had not been told before for fear that once her lady's maid knew, the information would spread via servants' halls to the great houses, the clubs, the chairmen and the gossip writers of Grub Street.

Separately they drove to the Spencer residence at Wimbledon. Lady Cowper, Georgiana's grandmother, drove from Cholmondeley House, Richmond, and the Duke's sister, the Duchess of Portland, came from Burlington House, Piccadilly. They were the only guests at the wedding which was held at Wimbledon parish church between Sunday services. The Duke carried himself as usual and Lady Georgiana behaved like a Duchess. The ceremony was a double triumph: for the Countess, because the secret was kept; for the Duke, because his Duchess was still sixteen. It only remained to re-enact the secret honeymoon, which the Spencers had spent romantically at Althorp Park, Northampton-shire.[14]

But history does not repeat itself. John Spencer had been infatuated with his bride and he had entertained her in the privacy of the magnificent house in which his mother and mother-in-law had become his guests from the moment of his inheritance. The Duke of Devonshire was not infatuated. He was used to living his own sort of life in his own houses. And here he was, imprisoned at Wimbledon with the Countess Spencer in that dreadful house the Duchess of Marlborough had set in a hollow, like a cup in a saucer. Lady Spencer rose with the lark, expected one to attend domestic prayers before breakfast and retire to roost about the same time as the chickens. So used to every man doing what she wanted without telling him, she did not appreciate that the Duke had always had his way. Georgiana, who should have been his Duchess, remained the Countess's daughter and Lady Spencer's bossiness was intolerable. She either told the Duchess what she ought to do or instructed her that she ought to ask the Duke what she ought to do. Furthermore, the young Duchess had no sense of propriety: she had the indelicacy to sit on the Duke's lap in front of the family. The speed with which he rose taught her not to do that again. Old Q., the Marquess of Queensberry, was fond of holding forth at Almack's on the pleasures of deflowering virgins, but the Duke preferred Miss Charlotte Spencer's experience. Charlotte Spencer made love to him whereas Georgiana wanted him to make love to her.

He was glad enough when, ten days later, they crossed the river to his place, Chiswick House. But even there Mama pursued them. She had already pestered them both with instructions about the Duke's attending the Royal *levée* on 15 June and asking Their Majesties' permission to present his Duchess next day. Now, almost the moment they arrived, came a letter with the same instructions; whom Georgiana should visit, what chair to use, what liveries her men should wear, what jewels would be most appropriate. 'I send this to Chiswick,' she had the impertinence to add, 'for fear the Duke of Devonshire should not yet be up, that you might put him in mind of the Levée for which I have some fear he will be too late, and that will make your presentation very awkward.'[15] If, as was probable, the Duke was still in bed, the letter was all the more provoking.

If he had not heard it from Dr Johnson himself, the Duke had probably heard from their mutual friend Topham Beauclerk the Doctor's story of how a husband should begin married life as he meant to end.* He was driven with the Duchess down the turnpike from Chiswick to Devonshire House. He attended the *levée* at St James's Palace. But instead of returning to his bride, he crossed the river to Vauxhall Gardens. He may even have called on Charlotte Spencer to see their little daughter. At any rate, he did not return till early morning.

We do not know what effect his late return had on the Duchess. Perhaps she may have been too concerned with the role she had to play next day to worry about his indifference.

Her reception at the Court of St James's was a triumph. Every eye was turned upon her, the only relief from the Royal tedium. The Duke was not popular with King George III, because of his support for the rebellious American colonists, but Their Majesties were gracious to his Duchess. The lords applauded her beauty and vivaciousness: the ladies her clothes, her headdress, her jewels and the naturalness of her behaviour. Plastered with white and rouge, they envied her ability to blush. Above all, they noted how happy she looked. The Earl and Countess Spencer watched their daughter, now their social superior, with unconcealed pride and pleasure. The only person who appeared utterly indifferent was the Duke of Devonshire.

---

* 'Though Mr Topham Beauclerk used archly to mention Johnson's having told him with much gravity, "Sir it was a love marriage on both sides", I have had from my illustrious friend the following curious account of their journey to the church upon the nuptial morn: – "Sir, she had read the old romances, and had got into her head the fantastical notion that a woman of spirit should use her lover like a dog. So Sir, at first she told me that I rode too fast, and she could not keep up with me: and, when I rode a little slower, she passed me, and complained that I lagged behind. I was not to be made the slave of caprice; and I resolved to begin as I meant to end. I therefore pushed on briskly, so I was sure she could not miss it; and I contrived that she should soon come up with me. When she did, I observed her to be in tears." '[16]

There is no mention of her disappointment in the Duchess's surviving letters. But her bitterness was revealed in *The Sylph*, a novel which she wrote four years later. The narrator here is the heroine, Lady Stanley. Returning from her presentation at Court, she has asked her husband, Sir William, whether she behaved well.

'Like an angel, by heaven! Upon my soul, I never was so charmed in all my life.'

'And upon my honour,' I said, 'I could not discover the least symptom of tenderness in your regards. I dreaded all the time that you were thinking I should disgrace you.'

'You were never more mistaken,' he replied. 'The circle rang with your praises. But you must not expect tenderness in public, my love. If you meet with it in private, you will have no cause for complaint.'[17]

Soon after the presentation, the Duke took his young bride to Chatsworth, the capital of his Derbyshire kingdom.

2

The original Chatsworth House had been built in the sixteenth century by Bess of Hardwick, the foundress of the Cavendish fortunes. During her time, Mary Queen of Scots had been held prisoner there. But of the original buildings the only one surviving was Queen Mary's Bower, a garden house beside the River Derwent in which the Royal prisoner was reputed to have meditated on her fate. On the site of Bess's Tudor residence, the first Duke of Devonshire built two wings of the present house, one facing up the steep hill which ended in the moorland of the Derbyshire Peak, the other facing south. The gardens, vastly extended, were planned in the French manner with a mathematical precision, nature being embellished with fountains and ponds inhabited by sea-gods and dolphins in stone. The grounds fell away in terraces and hedges formed a sort of vegetable architecture which extended the house itself. With its bosquets, its water-wonders, the first Duke's Chatsworth was a triumph of man over careless nature.

But the Chatsworth to which the fifth Duke drove his Duchess in June 1774 was of a different order. His father, the fourth Duke, had called in Capability Brown to make over the grounds in a spirit more consonant with the romantic age, in which mountains from being 'horrid' had become 'sublime'. The formality gave way to elegant disorder. Trees, rocks and lawns broke the monotony of ordered terraces. The house, vastly enlarged, was reconciled with the landscape in which it stood. The course of the River Derwent was straightened to prevent flooding. A new bridge was built across it and the village of Edensor,* which had marred the prospect across the Derwent, was removed from the skyline. There was no intrusion on the privacy of

---

* Edensor was pronounced Ensor. This is one of the many pronunciation traps set by the names of places and people mentioned in this book. Althorp was pronounced Alltrup; Hervey, Harvey; Coke of Holkham, Cook of Hookham; Leveson Gower, Looson Gore.

Chatsworth except on Mondays, the Public Days when the world and his wife were allowed to come and admire the magnificence of Chatsworth, seat of the Duke of Devonshire, Lord Lieutenant of Derbyshire in which he was the largest landowner.

The seventeen-year-old Duchess was not overawed by the splendour. Brought up at Althorp Park, which many connoisseurs of stately houses considered superior to Chatsworth, she had only to behave in her new home with the naturalness and courtesy which Mama displayed in her old. The tenants, the landed gentry, the titled or wealthy neighbours and burghers from Derby, Matlock, Buxton and Bakewell considered that the fifth Duke had found himself a Duchess worthy of his great position. But she discovered that there was a vast difference between the Cavendish family and her own. Her christian name had always been pronounced Georgeena; but the Cavendishes said Georgayna. It subtly distinguished between the two different personalities into which she was being split. Georgeena wanted to please Mama, to hold family prayers, to go to church at least once on Sundays and to confine her play and secular reading to the other six days of the week. But Georgayna wanted to please the Duke, who had little use for religion except for the poor and did not distinguish between Sunday and other days of the week.

He respected not the Christian but the Cavendish tradition. His grandfather had a great fondness for nicknames.* Admission into the inner Devonshire House Circle was signified by initiation into the nickname code. Charles Fox was, for obvious reasons, 'The Eyebrow', Mr Heaton, who handled the business affairs of the Devonshires and the Portlands, was 'The Corkscrew' and Colonel John Craufurd was known as 'The Fish', which was short for 'Selfish'. When Georgayna earned a nickname, it was invidiously 'Mrs Rat'. Earl Spencer was never given a nickname and the Countess had to wait until after his death, when she became for her grandchildren 'La Douairière', the affectionate French for 'Dowager'.

There were a number of private Cavendish jokes, the most famous of which was the copper beech tree at Chatsworth. It was made out of

* See Walpole to George Montagu, 1748: 'I have had difficulties to keep my countenance at the wonderful and uncouth nicknames that the Duke has for all his offspring: Mrs Hopeful, Mrs Tiddle, Guts and Gundy, Puss, Cat and Toe, sound so strange in the middle of a formal banquet! The day the Peace was signed, his Grace could find nobody to communicate joy with him; he drove home, and bawled out of the chariot to Lady Rachel, "Cat! Cat!" She ran down, staring over the balustrade; he cried, "Cat! Cat! The Peace is made, and you must be very glad, for I am very glad." '

real copper and unsuspecting guests were lured into its shade and then drenched with a shower which descended from its leaves at the turn of a tap. No less distinctive a trait was the 'Devonshire drawl'.[1] For the Duchess, who talked as fast as she thought (and sometimes even faster), conversation with the Duke must have been like a hunter in tandem with a drayhorse.

According to Samuel Rogers[2] the Duke told his friend General Fitzpatrick* that his love for Georgiana 'grew quite cool a month after their marriage'. I think it is unlikely the Duke said any such thing. Later in his life James Hare, who was a friend more intimate and trustworthy than Fitzpatrick, waited four months for the Duke to express his feelings towards the Duchess, but he never unburdened himself even in his cups. It is more probable that Fitzpatrick and Charles Fox inferred from his behaviour that the marriage was not proving sexually satisfactory. Both the Duke and the Duchess grew bored.

After a month the Earl and Countess Spencer were invited to stay at Chatsworth. The Duke was more sure of himself on his own ground than he had been at Wimbledon. He and the Earl went hunting and shooting together during the day and during the evening they discussed politics, especially the worsening relations with the American colonists and the forthcoming general election. They both had the same back-stage interest in Parliament, the Duke by temperament reluctant, the Earl forbidden by his grandmother's will, to hold public office. Meanwhile the Duchess was reunited with her beloved mama and her sister Lady Harriet. 'Oh my dearest Mama,' the Duchess wrote the moment her family left for Althorp and the Northampton election, 'how can I tell you how can I express how much I love you and how much I felt at your going. Indeed you are my best, my dearest friend. You have my heart and may do what you will with it.'[3] It was a love letter so fervent that the Countess replied, 'Does the Duke ever see any of your letters? Have you ever wrote anything to him since you married?'

'When one has the happiness of being with a person to whom one is sincerely attached,' the Duchess temporized, 'it is scarcely possible to be enough of oneself to write anything worth setting down. . . .' The truth was, Georgeena loved Mama, Georgiana loved being Duchess

---

* Richard Fitzpatrick (1747–1813), general, politician and wit, was a lifelong friend of Charles J. Fox. In the general election of 1774 he was elected MP for Tavistock in the Duke of Bedford's interest. Though, like Fox, he was opposed to the American War, he did not resign his commission when his battalion was ordered abroad but served with credit at Westfield, the battle of Brandywine, the capture of Philadelphia and the battle of Germantown.

of Devonshire, but Georgayna could not write a letter which did not come from her heart and was frightened of exposing herself to a rebuff.

The Spencers and the Devonshires turned their attention to the elections. After the writ was out, Lord Spencer, as a peer, was forbidden to electioneer for his candidates. The Countess took his place. 'I set out on Thursday morning with Mrs Tollemache [wife of one of two Spencer candidates for Northampton] in my Cabriolet and four, in hopes of putting a little spirit into our people who were sadly discompos'd at having neither drink or money offer'd them. I succeeded much beyond my expectations, for I no sooner got to the George than a little mob surrounded us and insisted on taking off the horses and drawing us round the town.'[4] It was an example of ladies 'politicking' which was to have grave repercussions for the Duchess and her sister at a later election. But in 1774 the Duke of Devonshire can only have smiled if he saw Mama's letter. Giving men drink or money was electoral bribery. But it was not illegal to rent a mob to pull a cabriolet round a town.

The Duchess of Devonshire had an equally legal ploy. She gave a ball in Derby. Dressed in a *demi-saison* silk, pink trimmed with gauze and green ribbon, she was met on the stairs by her uncle-in-law, Lord Frederick Cavendish 'extremely drunk'. The 'Musick' was almost as drunk. She stood for ten minutes in the middle of the floor with Mr Coke, the candidate's son, before the musicians could be waked to play a minuet, and then they all played different parts.[5] This again was not corruption because *all* the voters and their families were invited and not a single vote was solicited.

Apart from the election, the Duchess spent a quiet time in Derbyshire. After breakfast she rode and then wrote, read or walked in the park. In the evening they played whist or its two-handed variation, All Fours. Giardini, the famous violinist and director of the London Opera Company, came to stay at Chatsworth to instruct the Duchess; they had music after dinner. Georgiana strove to emulate Lady Spencer. She reported as a little triumph that 'the Duke of his own accord beg'd Mr Wood to read prayers in the Chapel' at Chatsworth, 'which has not been done for many years'.[6] She also asked advice about a little blind boy to whom she proposed to give ten pounds a year. At a time when a farm labourer had to keep his whole family on seven shillings a week, this was very generous. Lady Spencer advised her daughter to give ten pounds and then sometime in the next year another ten, but not commit herself to an annuity.[7] In a lifetime of charity she had found occasional gifts inspired more gratitude. Annuities were taken for granted. She recognized her daughter's goodness of heart, but doubted her soundness of judgement.

At the end of the year the Devonshires left Chatsworth for the London Season. Lady Derby, who had been married three weeks after the Duchess, was known to be breeding: but despite the quiet months at Chatsworth, the Duchess expected no *petit paquet*. On coming to London, she dutifully called on Mama's old friends, Mrs Howe, Miss Lloyd and Mrs Delany. When she first heard of the marriage, the seventy-four-year-old Mrs Delany had tartly remarked of Georgiana that 'she was so *peculiarly happy* as to think his Grace *very agreeable*'. But when the Duchess dropped in on her and the blue-stocking author of *Letters on the Improvement of the Mind*, Mrs Hester Chapone, they were enchanted. 'In came the Duchess of Devonshire,' Mrs Delany gushed to her friend Mrs Port, 'so handsome, so agreeable, so obliging in her manner that *I am quite* in love with her . . . I hope she will *illumine* and *reform* her contemporaries.'[8]

Her contemporaries hastened to illumine and inform the Duchess. Of these the most important was Lady Melbourne, living in Piccadilly at Melbourne House,[*] half a mile away from Devonshire House. She had been born Elizabeth Milbanke, the only daughter of Sir Ralph Milbanke, fifth Baronet. In 1769 she had married Sir Peniston Lamb, of whom the best that could be said was that he had inherited a large fortune from his father, a money-lending lawyer. Within a year she had borne him an heir, Peniston, while her husband had become a lavish, if ludicrous, client of the theatrical courtesan, Mrs Sophia Baddeley. Intensely ambitious, Lady Melbourne had her husband created an Irish Baron, Melbourne of Kilmore and by 1775 she had become the leading Whig hostess. She was beautiful in a bold way. Men liked her, because she had no use for coquetry. She was shrewd, forthright and rather vulgar. The Duchess of Devonshire was shocked when Lady Melbourne advised her on the duties of a wife. 'You can do what you please once you have done your duty by your husband, but not till then.'[†] But she was grateful for Lady Melbourne's advice on how to succeed as a political hostess. The Duchess had no ambition to eclipse her. It would be enough to outshine her.

* It had been bought from Henry Fox, the first Lord Holland. It was later presented to the Duke of York and Albany, in exchange for his house in Whitehall (now the Scottish Office). When the Duke of York sold it, it was made over into apartments, called Albany Chambers (now Albany, *tout court*).

† In *The Sylph* the Duchess put this remark in the mouth of Lady Besford. Even if not exactly what Lady Melbourne said, it was what she did.

In March the Duke went to Althorp to hunt with his father-in-law, leaving his Duchess alone in London to enjoy the Season. In this she was aided by the Duke's closest friend, Charles James Fox, for whom she developed a devotion amounting to hero worship. 'The great merit of C. Fox is his amazing quickness in seazing any subject,' she told her mother; 'he seems to have the particular talent of knowing more about what he is saying and with less pains than anyone else. His conversation is like a brilliant player at Billiards, strokes following one another piff puff.'[9]

Charles Fox was the younger son of Lord Holland. He had been indulged from birth. As a child he complained one day that he had been promised he could see a wall demolished at Holland House and it had been done in his absence; Lord Holland ordered the wall rebuilt so that Charles could see it fall. While he was still a schoolboy, his father had taken him to Paris so that he could learn the arts of love and gambling. The same age as the Duke of Devonshire, he was his opposite in temperament, believing with William Blake that the path to wisdom lay through excess. He embarked on everything in immoderation. At Oxford he studied trigonometry and read all the Restoration plays, and he walked the fifty-six miles from the university to Holland House in a day, pawning his gold watch at Nettlebed for bread and cheese and porter. Black-browed, blue-chinned, he was no Adonis, but as a dandy, a Macaroni, he was the wonder of St James's. He was said to have driven from Paris to Lyons to buy a waistcoat and to have spent £16000 in ten days at Naples. His father, Lord Holland, had amassed a fortune as Paymaster General and Charles and his elder brother Stephen squandered it. Between them they gambled away £32000 in three nights. One night Charles had lost so much at Almack's that Topham Beauclerk followed him home in fear he would blow his brains out. Topham found him reading Herodotus in the Greek. 'What would you have a man do,' Fox asked, 'who has lost his last shilling?' Knowing, however, that Charles had not lost Lord Holland's last shilling, moneylenders would press money on him at the tables and next morning 'Fox-hunting duns' besieged his apartments. He kept them waiting in a special room which he called his 'Jerusalem chamber', which gave rise to such lampoons as:

> But hark, the voice of battle sounds from far;
> The Jews and Macaronis are at war;
> The Jews prevail, and thundering from the stocks,
> They seize, they bind, they circumcise Charles Fox.[10]

Yet, with it all, he was the most brilliant of orators, in an age of rhetoric: the leader designate of any future Whig administration. No one was more calculated innocently to lead the Duchess astray.

Mrs Delany was the first to see the red light. She wrote to her friend Mrs Port, 'I do hope she will be like young actors and actresses who begin with *over* acting when they first come upon the stage, and abate of her superabundant spirits (that now mislead her) and settle into a character of applause and of the station she possesses; but I *tremble* for her!'[11]

Nobody had ever warned the Duchess about gambling. Her grandmother, Mrs Poyntz, had played at Spa from morning to night. Her father had depleted even more of his fortune at the tables than by sponsoring parliamentary candidates.[12] Her mother could not resist a flutter and the Duke spent more of his time at Almack's than anywhere else. Almack's, which later became Brookes's, was not a London club as now known, a decorous male reserve in which members eat, drink, read, talk, snooze and snore. It was an exclusive gambling club, where fortunes were won and lost.

With such examples, it was understandable that the Duchess should put up for Almack's Ladies Club, in King Street, just round the corner from its male counterpart in St James's. The ten-guinea subscription entitled members to a weekly supper and ball. The Committee, headed by the Duchess of Argyll and Hamilton, its foundress, was selective. But the young Duchess of Devonshire was accepted and given entry to the gambling rooms where cards and faro were played for high stakes. There she often met the Countess of Derby, the daughter of the Duchess of Argyll and Hamilton, who, though pregnant, seemed to be anxious to revenge herself on her unloved and ugly husband by dissipating his fortune as fast as she could.[13]

Lady Derby threw open her house in Grosvenor Square, which Robert Adam had 'filigreed to puerility',[14] to balls and supper-parties which scandalized the town with the lateness of the hours and the size of the stakes laid at the tables. In company with Charles Fox, the Duchess went to Lady Derby's; and that lady, soured with her own marriage, may very well have wanted to sour the Duchess of Devonshire's. But the Duke, writing from Althorp to chide his Duchess on her lack of correspondence, referred to a ball of Lady Derby's without any sort of disapproval.[15]

Two years before, Lord Spencer had given a *louis d'or* on behalf of each of his daughters to a man who claimed to have an infallible system for winning at faro, and had laughed, saying that he himself had always lost.[16] There had been no parental warnings about the dangers of play. To the Duchess her allowance of £2000 a year had seemed an inexhaustible fortune, and this may have been the period to which Charles Fox referred when he talked of her sobbing her heart out as they drove away from a house of play.

'I begin to grow very uneasy about money,' she wrote to Mama on 13 April 1775, 'for I don't think I can well tell the Duke, and if any of his family was to know it they could be very angry about it. If it was possible to borrow the money just to get out of the scrape now, I think I could better tell him next year at anytime than at present.'[17] It was the first of hundreds of similar letters which she was to write to different people during the next thirty-one years. The variations differed, but the themes remained the same: the desperation, the impossibility of confiding in the Duke just now, the need for a loan till later. Her mother replied by return. She had her sources of information. She had been suspecting this for weeks, but she could not interfere without being asked. Her letter made no mention of debts. It was a long, careful exposition, which she had possibly been composing during her waking hours and as she went to sleep. She began with the advantages Georgiana had enjoyed from birth, her natural talents and her elevation by a marriage of her own choice. In this position she could exercise every virtue to benefit others as well as herself. 'Reflect a moment on your position . . . and what conduct was reasonably to be expected of you. Compare it to the way of life you are in; if you think they agree – 'tis well – if not, your own good sense will direct you to examine in what they differ, and to endeavour to be whatever upon reflection you think you ought to be.'[18] Mama saw her under the shadow of eternity. But the Duchess faced a choice in this world: to be Georgeena or Georgayna? She had preferred Lady Melbourne and Charles Fox to Mrs Howe and Miss Lloyd out of loyalty to the Duke. But it had landed her in a 'scrape' from which no sermon of Mama's could extricate her.

When Mama came to Georgiana's duty as a wife, she ventured from the firm ground of moral theology into the quicksands of the Cavendish psychology. 'When a husband will speak his wishes, a wife who loves him will find it by no means difficult to sacrifice her inclinations to his. . . . But where a husband's delicacy and indulgence is so great that he will not say what he likes, the task becomes more difficult, and a wife must use all possible delicacy and ingenuity in trying to find out his inclinations, and the utmost readiness in conforming to them. You have this difficult task to perform, my dearest Georgiana, for the Duke of Devonshire, from a mistaken tenderness, persists in not dictating to you the things he wishes you to do, and not contradicting you in anything however disagreeable to him.'

One can understand why Mama preferred writing a letter to meeting her daughter face to face. She did not want to be interrupted in her sermon on husband-management. 'You must *make* the world in general and particularly those you most live with, see that your husband is your first object, by a constant uniform attention to him in your behaviour . . . if you ask his opinion or consent in such a manner . . . that he cannot well refuse you, it is forcing him to give an assent to what he does not perhaps approve. . . .'[19]

If the Countess had gained the extra years she wanted before Georgiana married, she might have taught her daughter how to manage this difficult Duke. But it was too late. The Duchess read this interminable letter, which ended with an injunction to avoid the pert, familiar, noisy, indelicate and indecent in language: and there was not a word about getting her out of this 'scrape'.

Mama's ultimatum was delivered next day. She would advance no money. The Duke must be told. If the Duchess was too frightened, Mama would speak for her. But Georgiana must disclose every penny she owed.

The Duchess did not know the extent of her debts. During all-night gambling sessions, she had signed promissory notes of which through drink and tiredness she had no clear recollection. She was probably already in the toils of Henry Martindale, who combined the running of crooked gambling tables with lending money at usurious rates. She could not appeal to Charles Fox, whose losses were so colossal that in comparison her own were a trifle. Charles could draw on Lord Holland's cash. But the Duke of Devonshire was the prisoner of the family entails. He could not realize any capital without the consent of his trustees, his uncles and Mr Heaton. The list which the Duchess made of her liabilities can only have been an approximation. Apart from gambling, she did not know how much of the expenses of the first Devonshire House ball she would be expected to pay out of her allowance.

The debts to which she confessed were disclosed to the Duke by Mama and the Duke agreed to take responsibility for them. Georgiana remained outside the negotiations. When it was all over, she told Mama that she had tried to express her gratitude to her 'by her looks'. She wanted to thank the D. of D., but he had had such delicacy to her as not to mention the subject and she could not bring herself to raise it.[20]

Mama stressed the difference between the Duchess's true self and her public self, 'like one of those many flippant daughters to the imperious mothers that glide about the world together and give one so detestable a notion of parental affection and filial duty.'[21] Past debts were paid and forgiven: but to run into debt again would be serious. Lady Derby having been brought to bed of a son, Mama feared that she would start gambling again. Yet to forbid play was inconceivable: everyone in society played. Let the Duchess say she was tied up not to play quinze, loo, brag, faro or hazard: then games of skill, whist, commerce, backgammon, tric-trac or chess were permissible. And not to take too much in one's purse. If that was lost, then not to borrow.

The Countess and her two daughters joined the menfolk at Althorp for the Easter holidays: and a fortnight later the first great ball was held at Devonshire House. 'Nothing is talked of now so much as the ladies' *enormous* dresses, more suited to the *stage* or a *masquerade* than for either *civil* or sober societies,' complained Mrs Delany. 'The three *most* elevated plumes of feathers are the Duchess of Devonshire, Lady Mary Somerset, and Lady Harriet Stanhope, but some say Mrs Hobart's exceeds them all. It would be some consolation if their manners did *not* too much correspond with the lightness of their dress!'[22] The Duchess had already begun to transform elegance into extravagance, and the Devonshire House ball added a touch of comedy.

Devonshire House had a front courtyard protected from the noise of Piccadilly, except when the great gates, designed by Inigo Jones, were thrown back to receive guests arriving in their carriages and chairs. Any such assembly was free entertainment for the London mob who watched unenviously (and without moral disapproval, unless they were Quakers) the conspicuous display: the splendid horses, snorting and farting, the drivers on their boxes, the footmen jumping down to open doors and let down steps for the ladies to descend, the twin flights of stairs which led from left and right to the great doors which gave entry to the reception rooms on the first floor; the long windows through which could be seen vast crystal chandeliers sparkling with the reflected lights of innumerable candles and the throng of ladies with elaborate headdresses, towering coiffures of powdered hair, real and false, and faces, arms, necks and shoulders painted uniformly white.

On the evening of the Devonshire House ball, the Musick, the Dancing, the Play and the Supper were little different from any other given in London during that season: except of course that the public rooms in Devonshire House were finer than most in great houses. What distinguished it was the arrival of the most fashionable ladies, sitting upon the floors of their carriages in order not to crush their plumes. Then they shook themselves, like hens after taking a dustbath, before proceeding decorously, agitating their fans, up the front steps, there to be received by the Duchess of Devonshire towering above them with two plumes sixteen inches long, besides three small ones. It was the first of a feathered ascension which was to reach its peak with an ostrich feather, rumoured to be an ell (four feet) in length, presented to the Duchess by Lord Stormont.

What did the Duke feel about this, to Georgiana important, social occasion? We can only guess. He hated entertainment, but since this had to be done, let it be done magnificently. If the circle rang with praises of his Duchess, he could be proud without showing it; and without showing it, he could be envious that she, not he, was the centre of attention. It was not important. Being a hostess was secondary. The Duchess's primary function was to breed.

In June they all removed to Spa, the same party as when the Duke had joined them two years before to make his proposal. The salubrious waters worked and on 21 July, the Duke and his pregnant Duchess took ship for Dover. The crossing took ten hours, but the moment they landed they both wrote to assure the Spencers that the voyage had no ill effects.

Nine days later Lady Harriet Spencer wrote to her sister Georgiana in schoolgirl French. 'I suppose you noticed Mama played faro as much as she did the last time we were here. She always believes that she has found the right way to win, though she loses all her money.'[23] The Duchess must have smiled, especially when Mama kept up the bombardment of advice: avoid folly and dissipation.

On 1 October three letters went from Chatsworth. The Duchess had miscarried. But, wrote the Duke, 'Mr Denman* tells me that she is surprisingly well . . . he has not often seen women in her situation whose health seem'd to have suffer'd so little.'[24]

In the eighteenth century fathers seldom wrote to their daughters. From Paris, Lord Spencer took up his pen. 'I cannot resist writing . . . to tell you how sorry I am that you have fail'd making me a grand-

---

* Thomas Denman (1735–1815) was the leading gynaecologist of his day. He had been born and educated at Bakewell, only five miles from Chatsworth, but by 1775 he was 'physician accoucheur' to the Middlesex Hospital, London.

father; however what has been may be again, and you will succeed better another time if you will have a little patience.' Having described the new colours – the rage in Paris were variations on a flea's anatomy (*ventre de puce, dos de puce*) – he lamented on having to return to London for 'this abominable meeting of Parliament'.* He could not help lamenting it on the Duchess's account too. 'I am afraid of your having so much more of all that racketting which did you a great deal of harm last year.'[25] Yet in fact the worst harm had been done that March and April, while Lord Spencer and the Duke went hunting in Althorp, leaving the Duchess alone in London to be hunted and fleeced. Wisely Mama saw that they all spent Christmas cosily at Althorp.

But by the spring the Duchess's debts came up with the daffodils. She owed £1692 13s to tradesmen, not reckoning what was due to Gaubert, the ornamental furniture maker, which would bring the total over £2000 according to Lady Spencer's reckoning. Debts at cards? £500. If not more. 'If the Duke could let you have £3000 it would possibly clear you to Lady Day last and then the remaining quarter you might by care during the summer pay off yourself. But less than £2500 will not do even to clear you to Christmas last.'[26]

The extravagance of the Duchess of Devonshire is legendary. But what of the wealth of the Duke? His income had been reckoned at £36000 a year ten years before. In the five years before his inheritance, capital and interest had accumulated. His establishments cost a great deal to maintain,† but if, during the five bachelor years of his majority, he had not made substantial savings, the Duke could only blame himself for negligence and for gambling even more recklessly than his Duchess. Probably he could have settled her liabilities with a word to Mr Heaton, but he wanted value for money. He had married in order to acquire an heir, whom the Duchess had failed to produce. Instead she had, with his money and title and estates, relegated him to being the husband of the Duchess of Devonshire.

---

* A political crisis had arisen because of the bad news from Lexington and Concord, General Howe's losses at Bunker Hill and King George III's wish to bolster the British armies with mercenaries.

† Though not by our standards. Samuel and Sarah Adams in *The Complete Servant* (1806) estimated that a respectable country gentleman with an income of £16000 to £18 000 could maintain a young family with a staff of fifteen female servants and twelve male on a total expenditure of £7000.

3

The common medical advice after an abortion was to wait before attempting another pregnancy. The Duchess was only eighteen when she miscarried. What did a year or two matter?

Moreover the Duke was content to live his life as it had been in his bachelor days. Miss Charlotte Spencer satisfied his bodily urges. Almack's and other clubs gave him the male company he enjoyed during the London Season. The war in America was teaching the King a lesson. Fox, Burke and the active Whigs debated to their hearts' content, but when they appealed to the Duke, they heeded his drawled wisdom, if he chose to utter. He lived his life as separate from the Duchess during the day as during the night. After the King's birthday, they went down to Chatsworth and in August perhaps he went up to Bolton Abbey to shoot on the Yorkshire moors. There were people down to stay, Fox, 'Fish' Craufurd, his brothers Lord Henry and Lord George Cavendish, his uncles, a succession of visitors. Time passed.

The Duchess lived at another tempo. She spent twenty-four hours a day doing nothing with never a minute to spare. Like the Duke, she was always late; but she was late for more things: late for the Opera, the theatre, or Vauxhall Gardens; late for the masquerade, at the Pantheon, for writing to Mama, for the ball or for church. Yet when she arrived she always created a stir, by her appearance and for her appearance. The acknowledged Empress of Fashion, she ridiculed the smart *ton* by a parody which became *haut ton*. She got away with it because her outrage was good-humoured. The Mrs Delanys from the seventies downwards were never angry for long, because she was the Duchess of Devonshire, who at the same time as snapping her fingers at society would dip into her purse or scribble a letter to help a deserving cause. General Sir John Moore would never have risen to fame at the battle of Corunna if she had not given £500 to secure his majority in the Army.[1]

She was notorious. Pamphlets were written by clergymen and others. But they were never written *against* her. The Duchess was notorious for gambling, extravagance and giddiness. But the pamphleteers did not attack her. They begged her to save the morals of her generation by saving herself from herself.[2] In her schoolgirl French the Duchess wrote to Mama in October 1776 about her spiritual quandary. 'My heart has nothing with which to reproach itself. I had only to plumb the bottom of my heart and I found nothing there but ideas which should fill me with happiness. But at present there are thousands and thousands of things the recollection of which saddens me. For I do not believe, without having done anything truly bad, one could have been more imprudent than I have.'[3] The scandalmongers were hovering over the tottering Devonshire marriage, waiting to pounce.

But in March 1777 the attack came, not on the errant and adorable Duchess, but on the furtive Duke. The *Town and Country Magazine*, which ran a spicy series of 'Tête à Tête' articles on the goings-on of the nobility, featured the D—e of D——e and Miss C—— S——r. It ended on 'the paradox that after some years' intercourse with Miss S——r, who was now rather approaching the decline of her beauty, our hero should marry a nobleman's daughter, an universal toast, still in her teens, with every personal accomplishment, who gives the *ton* wherever she goes, and that he should still be fond of his antiquated (by comparison) Charlotte. There is a caprice in mankind, it is true, that cannot be accounted for – whim prevails more than reason – but that the blooming, the blythe, and beautiful D—— should be neglected for C—— S——r is really astonishing'.

How astonished Georgiana and Mama were, we do not know. The correspondence between them has disappeared, burned no doubt for the benefit of posterity. But bearing in mind Lady Spencer's spy system, which for its time and modest purposes was as efficient as the CIA's or KGB's, Mama had probably known about Miss Spencer before the Duke's proposal at Spa and about the birth of baby Charlotte before Lady Georgiana's marriage. Indeed it may have influenced her consent to her daughter's early wedding. If the Duchess had not learned this secret from Mama, it is almost inconceivable that she had not heard it from innumerable men who wanted not merely to escort the Duchess, but also to bed her. The shock was not the news, but its publication.

In society the Duchess had always been regarded as the outrageous one. Now it was revealed that all this time it was the fifth Duke who had been carrying on a squalid affair with a milliner, who had neither the glamour of a courtesan like Mrs Armistead nor even youth and beauty.

What happened between Their Graces when this 'Tête à Tête' article appeared? Clearly the Duke had to make some defence. He could excuse his recent intercourse with Charlotte Spencer either by referring to Mr Denman's advice that the Duchess should not undergo the risk of another conception too soon or by telling the Duchess about his love child, Charlotte, born before their marriage.* It would be wrong, I think, to fancy that the Duchess was unduly shocked. After all, Lord Chesterfield's only amendment of life after marrying the Duchess of Kendal had been to discard his old mistress and take a new one. But she probably suggested that a sufficient time had elapsed for them to attempt another child. There is a passage in *The Sylph* which shows that the Duchess recognized the possibility of a husband taking his wife out of lust for his mistress. Lady Stanley has seen her husband at the Opera with another woman, who, she learns, is a paramour. Lady Stanley goes to supper with friends and, owing to an accident, is not yet in bed when in the early hours Sir William returns home, at first angry at the thought she has waited up for him, then amused at the account of her accident and finally aroused at the sight of her *en déshabille.*

'Come,' continued he, 'will you go to bed?' While he spoke, he pressed me to his bosom; and expressed in his voice more warmth and affection than he had discovered since I forsook the mountains. He kissed me several times with rapture; and his eyes dwelt upon me with an ardour I have long been unused to behold. . . . These caresses, thought I, have been disposed on one whose prostituted charms are more admired than mine.

This reads as if it was based upon a personal experience. At any rate in the spring of 1777 the Duchess may have become pregnant for the second time. After the King's birthday her parents and Harriet went abroad to take the cure at Spa and then to go on to Paris. The Devonshires were to join them there in the autumn; but meanwhile they went to Chatsworth, where Charles Fox and Lord John Townshend were

* The Earl of Bessborough in his introduction to *Georgiana* wrote 'The [*Town and Country*] *Magazine* places the date of the birth [of Charlotte Williams] between 1775 and 1780.' The 'Tête à Tête' article made no reference to any baby, other than the one begotten by the 'field preacher'. I have searched the magazine for later references to Charlotte Williams without success. There is no mention of Charlotte Williams' existence in the Chatsworth Collection until 1780.

among their guests.* 'What makes C. Fox more entertaining now is his being here with Mr Townsend [sic] and the D. of Devonshire, for their living so much together makes them show off one another. Their chief topic is Politicks and Shakespear. As for the latter, they all three seem to have the most astonishing memory for it, and I suppose I shall be able in time to go through a play as they do.'[4]

Mama wrote from Fontainebleau saying how much Queen Marie Antoinette talked of Georgiana and hoped she would come over. But in October the Duchess, if pregnant, had a second, more serious miscarriage and went instead to Brighton to recuperate.† Mr Denman perhaps again prescribed marital abstinence: certainly for the next two and a half years there was no further talk of breeding.

In 1778 the pattern of their lives was changed by France's recognition of the independence of the United States and declaration of war against Britain. As the *eminence grise* of the Foxite Whigs, the Duke of Devonshire opposed the King's policy in America. But as Lord Lieutenant of Derbyshire his patriotic duty lay with the militia, raised to repel the threatened invasion by the French. With the rank of captain, he took his men to camp at Cox Heath, near Maidstone, Kent. Her Grace, accompanied by her maid Betty, followed in his train.

The Duke's quarters measured up to his noble, rather than his military, rank. The dining tent was as large as those erected by Lord Spencer at Wimbledon for summer festivities. The bedchamber was larger still, with two recesses at each end for dining-room, kitchen and servants' quarters. Camping at Cox Heath was one long garden party. The Duchess and other officer's wives established a Ladies' Mess to which no officer was admitted who was not smart on parade, well-mannered at table and adept at the ball. Apart from two or three 'ill looking dogs'[5] some were very handsome and many of the young ones

---

* Lord John Townshend was a great-grandson of Charles, second Viscount Townshend, who had launched Stephen Poyntz on his rise to fortune. In 1787 he married Georgiana's cousin, Elizabeth 'Jockey' Poyntz, after the annulment of her marriage to her first husband, William Fawkener.

† Lord Bessborough (*Georgiana*, p. 32) wrote, 'They had thought of joining Lady Spencer in Paris, but decided against it.' There is no mention of the Duchess's pregnancy and miscarriage in the surviving Chatsworth letters. In *The Noels and the Milbankes* (pp. 76-7) Malcolm Elwin quoted a chatty letter from Lady Melbourne's sister-in-law, Mrs Elizabeth Burges, dated 13 October 1777 and beginning, 'My Br[other]'s disorder was an Abscess on his Bum. . . .' Later it says, 'The D[uche]ss [of Devonshire] I hear has miscarried and gone very ill to Brighton. She was not however so ill that she could not walk, sea bathe, gamble and consider going on to Paris. Walpole may therefore have been right to consider her "illness" an excuse for escaping the boredom of Chatsworth.'

would turn out very well. Although the Duchess and Lady Derby were foiled in their efforts to parade a military band for a ball, by the orders of the General,[6] the camp festivities were giddy compared to election parties in Derby or Public Days at Chatsworth. The variety of military uniforms was gayer than the dull dominoes of most masquerades. Awkward at assemblies, His Grace excelled on parade. Though he had but just learned, he saluted in public better than any fellow officer. Or so said the gallant Colonel Gladwin, kissing Her Grace's hand before gazing into her eyes.

Bored after ten weeks under canvas, the Duchess and Lady Derby struck camp for Tunbridge Wells. 'A vile place,' said the Duchess; 'would have liked camp a thousand times better.' But she billeted herself there until the military exercises ended in November in the company of the beautiful Mrs Crewe, who often hit a thing off very well 'despite her idiotism', and Lady Clermont, newly from France, who rallied Her Grace on her resemblance to Marie Antoinette.

Rusticating at Wimbledon, Mama warned dearest Georgiana against being stand-offish towards the guests at Tunbridge Wells. So down to the Pantiles sallied the Duchess, Lady Clermont and Mrs Crewe to be greeted by the Master of Ceremonies with a speech of welcome to the Assembly Rooms. All very well, wrote Mama, but the dangers of intimacy exceeded those of distance. 'You should especially at such a place as Tunbridge keep up a civility and dignity to men of your own set, and a courteous good humour'd affability to the company in general whom you are little acquainted with, whereas I suspect, if you will examine your own conduct, you put in that killing cold look you sometimes have to those you should be *prévenante* to, and a great deal more familiarity and ease than is either necessary or proper to the men about you.'[7] How much better to come to Wimbledon!

That Mama should have suggested coming to Wimbledon is evidence that any attempt to produce an heir had been postponed. The Duchess answered that the Duke favoured Tunbridge, close enough to Cox Heath to spend his leaves there. But she was obediently *prévenante*. She greeted Mama's old friend, the blue-stocking Mrs Montagu, walking in the Pantiles with the wife of the wealthy brewer Henry Thrale, and went to play whist with them next day. She found Mrs Thrale very clever and entertaining, but at fault in having a vulgarity about her that sought to be fine. There was no parity in those days between the peerage and the beerage.

Mrs Thrale had come from Brighton, where Mr Bowen, the bookseller, had been in ecstasy over an anonymous novel called *Evelina*, published that January by T. & W. Lowndes. 'O ma'am, what a book thrown away was that! all the Trade cry shame on Lowndes, not, ma'am, that I *expected* he could have known its worth, because that's out of the question – but when its *profits* told him what it was, it's quite scandalous that he should have done nothing nothing! – quite ungentlemanlike indeed.'[8]

The Duchess read *Evelina* and decided to try her hand. While the Duke marched and saluted, she sat and scribbled. She chose the same publisher, and Lowndes published *The Sylph* in January 1779, advertising it so close to *Evelina* that Miss Fanny Burney was driven to protest.

Evelina, a masterpiece, took two years to write. *The Sylph*, a *jeu d'esprit*, was dashed down in two months. Its contrivances were ludicrously clumsy. For example, a young heiress as a result of plunging a painful ankle in cold water, dies so rapidly from gout of the head and stomach that she has no time to make a will. But *The Sylph* ran through three editions in four years. The first volume rattled on apace; and when the identity of the author leaked out, it continued to be read as a *roman à clef*. How much was sentimental chaff, how much was wittily and scandalously true? Lady Melbourne was taken to be the original of Lady Besford in *The Sylph*. Within six weeks of publication, she gave birth to her second child, William Lamb, universally regarded as the son of Lord Egremont, and her views on marriage may well have prompted the following:

'Are you not happy?' I asked [Lady Besford] one day. 'Happy! why yes I probably am; but you do not suppose my happiness proceeds from my being married, any further than that I enjoy title, rank and liberty, by bearing Lord Besford's name. We do not disagree because we seldom meet. He pursues his pleasure one way, I seek mine another, and our dispositions being very opposite, they are sure never to interfere with each other. I am, I give you my word, a very unexceptionable wife and can say, what few women of quality would be able to do that spoke truth, that I never indulged myself with the least liberty with other men, till I had secured my lord a lawful heir.' I felt all horror and astonishment. 'Come don't be so prudish,' said she: 'my conduct in the eye of the world is irreproachable. My lord kept a mistress from the first moment of his marriage. What law excludes a woman from doing the same? Marriage now is a necessary kind of barter, and an alliance of families; – the heart is not consulted: – or, if that should sometimes bring a pair together – judgment being left far behind, love seldom lasts long. In former times, a poor foolish woman might languish out her life in sighs and tears for the infidelity of her husband. Thank heaven! they are wiser now; but then they should be prudent. I extremely condemn those who are enslaved by their passions, and bring a public disgrace on their families by suffering themselves to be detected; such are justly our scorn and ridicule; and you may observe they are not taken notice of by anybody. There is a decency to be observed in our amours; and I shall be very ready to offer you my advice, as you are young and inexperienced. One thing let me tell you; never admit your *Cicisbeo* to an unlimited familiarity; they are first suspected. Never take notice of your favourite before other people: there are a thousand ways to make yourself amends in secret for that little but necessary sacrifice in public.'

The Duchess's use of names must have intrigued her readers. Her heroine belonged to a junior branch of the famous Greville family. Her husband, Sir William Stanley, took his christian name from the Dukes of Devonshire and his surname from the Earls of Derby. Lady Besford's name was a conflation of Bessborough and Oxford (or Orford?). There was a minor character called Spencer and the Duchess herself appeared in an amusing passage, when a *friseur*, dressing Lady Stanley's hair for presentation at Court, was outraged at her destroying the monstrous headdress he had contrived from 'curls, flowers, ribands, feathers, lace, jewels, fruit and ten thousand other things', protesting that 'He had run the risk of disobliging the Duchess of D——, but giving me the preference of the finest bunch of radishes that had yet come over from Paris.'

To restore her health after the London Season of 1779, the Duchess went to Spa with her parents and Harriet. There a plan was devised to deprive the Duke of his excuse for continuing to see Charlotte Spencer. Their misfortunate daughter, Charlotte Williams, would face a better future if placed with some respectable woman who could train her for absorption into the Devonshire household as a member of the family, in some recognized but inferior degree. If it was his natural child in whom the Duke was really interested, he would agree; and the ageing mistress could be pensioned off. It remained only to find a suitable respectable woman.

The chance arose from the war still 'raging' between France and England, which prevented the Spencers from visiting Paris to see the dear Duchesse de Polignac and the Queen of France. Instead, they sailed in one of two packet-boats bound from Helvoetsluys to Harwich, convoyed by Captain Garner of the *Fly* sloop.

The convoy had hardly left port, at 7 a.m. on 30 September, when two French privateers attacked. The *Fly* mounted only fourteen guns to the Frenchmen's forty-eight. But Captain Garner held the enemy off to allow the packet-boats to escape and broke off the engagement only when he ran out of gunpowder. Then, pursued by the privateers, he overtook the packet-boat carrying the Duchess and her family. He came aboard a gory sight, covered all down one side with the blood of a man killed in action. When he demanded more powder, Lord Spencer, torn between admiration for courage and dismay at fool-hardiness, begged him to desist. 'It is of no consequence,' he said, 'whether the Duchess, the Countess or myself are carried into France or not.' He did not add that if captured they would certainly be invited to visit the Queen at Versailles before being given safe conduct back to England. 'It may be of no consequence to your lordship,' barked the gallant seadog, 'but it is of the utmost consequence to *me*, and therefore you shall not be taken while I have life, by God!'

Returning to his ship with fresh powder, he re-engaged the enemy. As the packet-boat sailed on towards Harwich, the passengers saw flashes in the gathering darkness and heard the distant booming of guns. When silence fell, they were so anxious for the fate of the *Fly* that the moment they landed, the Earl wrote to 'his connections' in France, begging that, if captured, Captain Garner should be treated as 'his valour merited'.[9]

The plea was unnecessary. Having driven off the privateers, the *Fly* returned to Holland. For his gallantry Captain Garner was made post★ and promised one of the frigates then building. In gratitude for his family's escape, Lord Spencer gave him a silver cup on both sides of which were engraved representations of the engagement: and the Countess and her daughter decided that the wife of such a noble example of the Senior Service must be a paragon. Who better than Mrs Garner to take custody of little Charlotte?

But the Duke had to be persuaded. He was like his family motto, *Cavendo Tutus*, safe by being cautious. He had been promoted to the rank of colonel and was at Warley Camp in the West Country, a position more exposed to French invaders; there he was far too busy saluting and being saluted to think of anything else when his Duchess joined him.

Drake played bowls, awaiting the Spanish Armada. Awaiting the French, Georgiana danced and wrote *vers d'occasion*.

★ i.e. a senior captain, commissioned for a ship of twenty guns or more.

Here the fat dame with hair of shining black
With puckered bonnet and with linnen sack
Swims down the dance, while her pert ensign's run
Has finished ere his partner had begun.
But to revenge her cause a damsel slim
Whose very sleeves hold yards of gauzes trim
With bustling gown and flounces wide and deep,
Whilst from her hat enormous lappets peep
With arms extended trips it down the dance.
Now here now there her frisking steps advance
Whilst the fat major, whom politeness taught
To ask the miss some neighbouring friend had brought,
Sweats through the horrors of the toilsome yoke
To which the longest march appears a joke.[10]

It was not until 1780 that the Duke agreed to put little Charlotte with Mrs Garner. It was the first time the Duchess had seen the child and she reported to Mama, 'She is a very healthy good humour'd looking child, I think, not very tall. She is amazingly like the Duke, I am sure you would have known her anywhere. She is the best humour'd little thing you ever saw, vastly active and vastly lively, she seems very affectionate and seems to like Mrs Garner very much. She has not good teeth and has often the toothache, but I suppose that does not signify as she has not changed them yet, and she is the most nervous little thing in the world, the agitation of coming made her hands shake so, that they are scarcely recovered today.'*[11]

The Countess Spencer found no incongruity between Charlotte's being vastly lively and active and so agitated that her hands shook. She did not speculate on the child's state of mind. What had Miss Charlotte Spencer told her? Did she know the Duke was her father? What did she make of seeing the Duchess or going to live with Mrs Garner? The Countess was only worried at Charlotte's being given the surname 'William'. Might it not lead to confusion with Lord X's natural daughter, Fanny Williams? Wouldn't Charlotte Duke be better? Or Ven from Cavendish?[12]

A change so violent, replied the Duchess, might have a bad effect on a little girl of such intelligence. In the end William was pluralized. Perhaps they thought a confusion between Fanny and Charlotte Williams not a bad idea.

* From this letter Lord Bessborough deduced that Charlotte was born in 1772 or 1773. The central milk incisor teeth fall out during the seventh year. Charlotte's toothache in May 1780 was probably caused by the cutting of her first pair of second teeth. If so, the day of her birth was between 9 May 1773 and 9 May 1774: probably some time after the Duke's proposal to Lady Georgiana.

4

It was the Duchess rather than the Duke who enlarged the Devonshire House Circle, and it was inevitable that the Prince of Wales should join it as soon as he reached the age of indiscretion. All the Royal Georges went into opposition against their fathers; and the Foxite Whigs, wearing the buff and blue of the rebel Americans, stood for everything abominated by King George III. 'Florizel', as the Prince subscribed himself in his infatuated correspondence with the actress Mrs 'Perdita' Robinson, sought the Duchess's aid in his frequent scrapes with women. She was five years his senior and they addressed one another as 'brother' and 'sister'. Their exchanges were rapturous and their friendship lifelong. However fantastically in debt he might be, the Prince always found some money when duns had brought the Duchess to her wits' end. And since in 1779 she was rumoured to have lost £3000 at a single sitting, she needed friends like Florizel. But she properly kept his amorous advances at bay. Notes she made in 1782 on the Prince's person were not uncritical: 'A figure which though striking is not perfect . . . inclined to be too fat and too much like a woman in men's cloaths . . . whether it is in intrigues of state or gallantry, he often thinks more is intended than really is.'[1]

Another recruit to the circle was Richard Brinsley Sheridan, son of an Irish actor-manager, a brilliant playwright and ambitious to be a gentleman, who had eloped with Elizabeth Linley, a great beauty and the finest singer of her day. After marriage Sheridan forbade her to perform in public; but she sometimes sang at Devonshire House. The Duchess, who admired Sheridan's plays, won him the friendship of Charles Fox and nomination to the parliamentary seat of Stafford. But she did not realize how damaging politics would be to his dramatic talent.

But the most important addition to the group was the Duchess's sister, Lady Harriet Spencer. Harriet had not been stampeded into marriage. Once bitten, twice shy, the Countess had kept her younger daughter single, until she felt that Harriet was mature enough to resist the giddy temptations of Devonshire House, and when Lady Harriet married Frederick Ponsonby, Viscount Duncannon, she was all of nineteen. Duncannon's father, second Earl of Bessborough, had married Lady Caroline Cavendish, aunt of the Duke of Devonshire, and Duncannon's uncle, the Right Honourable John Ponsonby, had married Lady Elizabeth Cavendish, Lady Caroline's younger sister. It was thus a triple alliance between the Ponsonbys, Spencers and Cavendishes. Unfortunately the Bessboroughs had no ancestress as shrewd as Bess of Hardwick or the Duchess of Marlborough. From ill-managed estates in Ireland, the Earl of Bessborough could afford only £2000 p.a. for Duncannon, with a jointure of £500 p.a. to Harriet. On this the young couple maintained a house in Cavendish Square and Manresa House at Roehampton, more or less halfway between the Spencers at Wimbledon and the Devonshires at Chiswick.

It was not the marriage Mama would have wished. Ambitious for a prince, she would have settled for a duke. But with Christian resignation, she accepted the heir to an Irish earldom. Watching from Strawberry Hill, Horace Walpole observed, 'I know nothing to the prejudice of the young lady, but I should not have selected, for a gentle and very amiable a [sic] young man, a sister of the empress of fashion, nor a daughter of the goddess of wisdom.'[2]

Harriet loved Mama as much as Georgiana did. But she looked up to her sister in every way. The Duchess was her superior in age, height, rank and *ton*. Lady Duncannon in 1780 was a pocket edition of the Duchess, with the same love of gaiety and wit, the same propensity for alternating between English and French, the same warmth of heart and liability to Hystericks.

The Duchess had promised Mama over and over again that she would see that Harriet came to no harm and throughout her life she did her best. But difference of wealth and rank proved too much. How could the Duncannons with £2500 p.a. avoid running into debt if they associated with the Devonshires whose income was some twenty times as much?

From an early age Georgiana's brother, Viscount Althorp, had been the odd one out of the closely-knit Spencer family. When he was seven, Lady Spencer handed him over to a tutor, Mr (later Sir William) Jones with the admonition 'Make him, if you can, like yourself'. Mr Jones took Viscount Althorp into his house and when the boy went to Harrow he accompanied him as his private teacher. Jones took his duties so seriously that when the boy's father ventured a suggestion, he was told to mind his own business. Even after Jones left Althorp to the other masters at Harrow, he corresponded with his late pupil, assuming the paternal position which Lord Spencer had vacated in his search for health in Continental spas.[3]

In March 1780 Althorp told Georgiana that he wanted to marry the Honourable Lavinia Bingham, eldest daughter of Lord Lucan. The Duchess thought their parents would not approve. Not only were the Binghams Tories but Lavinia's father had been created Baron Lucan of County Mayo only four years before. An Irish barony was no great coup. There was no previous family connection or dynastic advantage. Lady Lucan painted water-colour copies of great and small masters, which sent Horace Walpole into ecstasies. But Lavinia, though smart, good-looking and clever, was in Georgiana's opinion a foul-mouthed girl, whose malice Mama would instantly perceive.

She was mistaken. Lavinia's commonplaceness was a pleasant change for Mama from her own daughters' giddiness, and Lavinia so concealed her contempt for the Countess and so won her over that in March 1781 the marriage was celebrated with blessings from the parents on both sides.

Within nine months of marriage Lady Duncannon presented her husband (nicknamed 'Harum' by the Devonshires) with an heir, named John William Ponsonby. Lady Althorp did nearly as well, an heir in fourteen months. In 1782 Georgiana was the only one of the Spencer children still childless: and that after eight years of marriage. 'How much more than words can express should I be oblig'd to dear demure Dr Denman would he enable me to give little Ponsonby a playfellow or a wife.'[4] The word 'demure' is significant. Dear Dr Denman had clearly said it was safe to try another pregnancy. But since her ill-fated second conception following the exposure of Miss Charlotte Spencer, the Duke had failed to beget. If Dr Denman had been less demure, he might have told her of some aphrodisiac potion or erotic technique which would have cured their sexual problem. The Countess merely answered that if Georgiana were her age there would be some reason why she should suppose she might never have children. There was no reason to despair at twenty-four.

The Countess was right. God moved in a mysterious way. But she was appalled at the rôle she was given in the performance of His wonders. She acted out of charity towards her old friend Lady Bristol.

Lady Bristol's two elder daughters had made unhappy marriages. They were separated from their husbands and were living penuriously in London. Lady Spencer wrote to Georgiana that it would be a Christian act for her to call.

Though the Duchess had never met them, except perhaps in childhood, when their father Frederick Hervey was a poor clergyman, she knew their fabulous history: Lady Mary Wortley Montagu divided the human race into Men, Women and Herveys, a reference to the bisexuality of Lord Hervey,* but with a wider significance. The Herveys were a breed apart. Frederick, for example, as the third son of Lord Hervey, had had no prospect of succeeding to his grandfather's earldom of Bristol. Yet he had married for love Elizabeth Davers, the poor daughter of a Tory baronet who disapproved of the Whig Herveys. For years Frederick Hervey had bred richly on a pittance and then by family influence he had become Bishop of Derry, whose revenues he raised by shrewd, unextortionate management from £7000 a year to £20000. It was at this stage that he had forced his eldest daughter Mary to marry John Crichton, Lord Erne, a middle-aged widower with four strapping children who were almost as old as she, 'a very unexceptionable man, who will have about £9000 a year and possesses a very beautiful seat in our neighbourhood'.[5] Having made this sacrifice to Mammon, he gave Elizabeth, his middle daughter, to Eros. At the age of nineteen, she had married John Foster in Brussels. It was a love match. Little f (as he was called to distinguish him from big F his father) was a member of the Irish Parliament. He spent much time in Dublin while Elizabeth, soon pregnant, was confined, in both senses of the verb, in dreary Dunleer.

When through the fortunate deaths of both his brothers the Bishop of Derry became fourth Earl of Bristol with an estate in Ickworth Park, Suffolk, Bristol House in St James's Square, London, and a further £20000 a year, the strains on his own and his two daughters' marriages became intolerable. It was said that the Earl-Bishop drove out one day in Ickworth Park gaily talking to his Countess and returned never to speak a word to her again. This was not quite true. But power, rank and money had obliterated conjugal and paternal love. Lady Erne

---

* Hervey was Pope's Sporus:

His wit, all see-saw between that and this,
Now high, now low, now Masterly, now Miss . . .
Fop at the Toilet, Flatt'rer at the Board, –
Now trips a Lady, and now struts a Lord.

left her husband, taking with her their daughter Lal Lal; and Lady Elizabeth parted from little f, with her two sons, Frederick aged five, and Augustus aged two. Sharing lodgings with them was a Methodistical lady, Mrs Gordon, a friend of Lady Erne.

The Duchess's compassion was easily moved. The sight of a blind boy at Chatsworth had made her want to give him an annuity for life. Childless after eight years of marriage, with all these empty ducal houses, her heart bled to see these granddaughters of Lord Hervey and 'dear Molly Lepell' so meanly cribbed in a lodging house with their children. They deserved better than that.

She found them both well educated. A schooling in Geneva had grounded them in French and Italian. The Earl-Bishop, mean about money, had been lavish in his lectures on the *Beaux Arts*. They may have acquired a little Irish in their voices, but their knowledge of Continental architecture, sculpture and painting seemed encyclopedic. They were like birds of paradise, but with a wing clipped to prevent their flight from squalor.

At least Lady Erne had the consolation of having Lal Lal. But Lady Elizabeth Foster was soon to be deprived by little f of Frederick and Augustus, the only consolation she had from what she depicted as a forced marriage to an uncouth Irish drunkard and libertine. Both the sisters had had influenza and were woefully debilitated. Lady Elizabeth also had a cough which racked her frail frame. Yet, in the most courageous manner, she made light of this. Her father, the Earl-Bishop, had promised her an allowance, a very small one indeed considering his vast wealth, almost madly mean. But he had not paid it. Nor had little f paid her the allowance which was due. But she did not repine. She quoted from Dante, Molière or Tasso which was vastly to the point. The Duchess emptied her purse and embraced the unfortunate but gallant sisters. Poor little Bess mingled her tears with the Duchess's as she left.

The Duchess returned to Devonshire House in high emotion. Never had she seen such beauty in such distress, a soul so sensitive so insensitively used. To one whose great ambition was to bear a son, what could be more poignant than a mother bereft of two darling boys? With a spontaneity rare in her marriage, she depicted the plight of the two sisters so vividly that the Duke expressed a wish to see them.

The meeting took place on 22 May 1782. By 1 June, the Duchess was writing to Mama that Lady Erne and Lady Elizabeth Foster were 'their chief support, else it would be shockingly dull for the Duke'.[6] When the Devonshires moved to Bath, they invited their new friends. The two sisters, with Lal Lal and Mrs Gordon, took rooms in a nearby house, sharing expenses and breakfasting separately so as not 'to be a clog on each other'.[7] During this stay Lady Erne and Mrs Gordon drew closer together, united by their interest in Methodism.* Lady Elizabeth who soon began to subscribe herself 'your own poor little Bess',[8] went everywhere with the Duke and Duchess, the baths, the Assembly Rooms, Mrs Siddons at the theatre, excursions to see the bluestocking ladies of Batheaston, rides across the surrounding hills. Despite the loss of her children, Lady Elizabeth was bravely gay. With her hazel eyes and delicate features, she possessed an infinity of grace. She reminded many people of a marmoset, that cutest of monkeys, full of pretty tricks. The Duchess was in ecstasies over her new friend, who prattled as fluently in French and Italian as in English. And the Duke was a new man. He laughed, he joked, he smiled, he drawled gallantries.

The Earl-Bishop's promise of an allowance of £300 a year was still in arrears. The Duchess pressed money on her, and 'poor little Bess' gratefully pocketed it, with tears of gratitude in her eyes. When news of the benefaction reached the Earl-Bishop via the Countess of Bristol, he produced a hundred pounds, which Lady Elizabeth rattled in her purse, while the Devonshires continued to pay.

If the Duchess thought that Mama would be pleased, she was soon disabused. Mama had envisaged a visit or two, perhaps the gift of some discarded finery or other charity. For Lady Elizabeth to be adopted almost instantly as a member of the family was going too far. When dear Bess accompanied the Devonshires first to London and then to Plympton (where that season the Duke was resisting the unforthcoming French invasion) Lady Spencer was alarmed. Though pious, she was also a woman of the world. The change in the Duke was proof that he was in love; and Lady Elizabeth was a far more dangerous threat to the Duchess's marriage than the wretched Charlotte Spencer. She could not understand the Duchess's blindness.

The Duchess was not blind. Dearest Bess had succeeded where demure Dr Denman had failed. The Duke's attentions to the Duchess had been renewed. If that was because the Duke loved Bess, gratitude was the emotion the Duchess felt, not jealousy, as they sketched to-

---

* Lady Erne's enthusiasm may have been aided by the fact that her wealthy aunt, Lady Mary Fitzgerald, had been converted to Methodism 'by correspondence'. Any contributions to the upkeep of Lal Lal and herself would be gratefully received by Lady Erne.

gether during the day and in the evening listened to the Duke reading Shakespeare.

Some years later Lady Elizabeth looked back at her position in 1782. She was 'without a guide; a wife, and no husband, a mother, and no children . . . by myself alone to steer through every peril that surrounds a young woman so situated'.[9] Her only assets were 'books, the arts, a wish to be loved and approved; and enthusiastic friendship for these my friends [the Devonshires]; a proud determination to be my own letter of recommendation; these, with perhaps manners that pleased, realized my projects and gained me friends wherever I have been'.

Offspring of a naval family, she liked navigation in all weathers with uncertain instruments. In her frail person was hidden an explorer, in a neutral sense an adventuress. She did not confess that she had married John Foster because she fancied herself in love with him; that she had resented the birth of Frederick, her elder son, because she was confined in Dunleer while little f enjoyed himself in Dublin; that the rupture in her marriage had been caused by her father's succession to the earldom of Bristol, with the opportunities this afforded her to shine in London and Continental society. She was content to stay at Plympton, trusting to Providence and to her 'manners that pleased'. In August, Harriet and Harum Duncannon came to Plympton, having left John William Ponsonby with Grandmama Spencer. The meeting was crucial for Lady Elizabeth. Would Lady Duncannon side with the Duke and Duchess or with the Countess Spencer?

By the time the Duncannons left, the foundation had been laid of a friendship between Harriet and Bess that was to survive the stresses of the next thirty-eight years. Bess's position was immensely strengthened.

So were the Countess's suspicions. She would have launched a full-scale offensive, if the Earl Spencer had not fallen dangerously ill. Georgiana and Harriet rushed to his bedside, and the insidious Lady Elizabeth was momentarily forgotten.

But when Papa recovered, Mama returned to the attack. She had already warned that even if Lady E.F. was not the Duke's mistress, everyone would think she was, which was just as bad. Now she denounced the immorality of a book which she had not read, but which she miscalled Les liaisons du coeur. If Mama meant Les liaisons dangeureuses by Laclos, the Duchess answered, she had read it. Though 'very indecent' the description it gave 'of the too like manners of the world is far from uninstructive'.[10]

When the Plympton Camp disbanded, Mama hoped the Devonshires would come to Bristol Hot Wells, *without* Lady E., since the Earl was still too ill to see a stranger without discomfort. She regarded Bess as a sort of leech, who if burned off would find it hard to re-attach herself. But Georgiana was obdurate. 'Ly. Eliz: comes with us, my Dst Mama, and, poor little soul, it is impossible it should be otherwise . . . she is the quietest little thing in the world, and will sit and draw in the corner of the room, or be sent out of the room, or whatever you please . . .'[11] The Duchess believed that she was pregnant once again, but she did not want to lose her dearest friend. Supposing that she did not miscarry, there was no certainty that the baby would be a boy. Bess's friendship was more important than Papa's convalescence.

Once she was sure that she was with child, the Duchess agreed that Bess could leave them, in order to silence gossip. While they were at Plympton, Lady Elizabeth had developed 'a very alarming pain in her side'.[12] A winter spent at Nice might set her up. What better excuse for defraying her expenses than to send her as governess to Charlotte Williams in company with Mrs Garner? It removed Bess from proximity to the Duke, yet retained her for future services.

On 3 December 1782, the Duchess wrote to Mama that she 'had hopes'. On 29 December Bess set off with Mrs Garner and Charlotte Williams. Horace Walpole, who smelt a rat even when it was a mouse, entirely misread the significance of the journey. In a letter to Sir Horace Mann, the British Minister in Florence, he concentrated his venom on the Earl-Bishop, 'that Mitred Proteus, whose crimes you are infinitely too charitable in not seeing in the blackest light. . . . The mission of his daughter, and the circumstances, are just as you have heard them. You may add, that though the daughter of an Earl in lawn sleeves, he suffers her from indigence to accept £300 a year as governess to a natural child.'[13]

In the eighteenth century it was impossible to suppress gossip. It was enough if it was diverted into the wrong channels.

5

Lady Elizabeth Foster is the most devious character in this history. But she will be misjudged if she is not seen as the victim of her early lack of foresight. If she had anticipated that her father, the Bishop of Derry, would so soon have become fourth Earl of Bristol she would never have married John Foster. Having made that mistake and borne him two children, she had in 1782 to start a new life with appalling handicaps. She was ambitious to succeed in European society. She could not divorce John Foster except by Act of Parliament. If she did so, she might be forbidden to marry again: and even if she was allowed to marry, she would be ostracized from the society which it was her ambition to enter. As a woman separated from her husband and children, she was in a far more vulnerable position than she would be today. She had no income commensurate with her needs; and it did not seem likely that she could honourably acquire any, until she found in the Devonshires protectors who would advance her aims without damaging her reputation. She was an *allumeuse* by temperament. Like her grandmother Molly Lepell[*] she preferred to light a flame, rather than quench it. But she was now warned of the need for foresight. The Duke and Duchess in seven months had become her dearest friends. They had their private names. The Duke was 'Canis', because of his love of dogs. Lady Elizabeth was 'the Racoon' or 'Racky': the Duchess 'Mrs Rat'[1] They swore eternal friendship on their parting. But Lady Elizabeth knew that friendship, like love, could die, unless carefully cultivated. She had to be prepared for anything. If the Duchess produced the heir she needed in order to obtain the settlement of her debts, Lady Elizabeth might have to find other friends. Meanwhile the pretence of acting as governess to Charlotte Williams had its uses. It cast public shame

[*] 'And who would not go to the Devil/For the sake of dear Molly Lepell?' wrote Lord Chesterfield and William Pulteney. John Gay hailed her as 'Youth's youngest daughter, sweet Lepell!' and Pope as 'A Lady I have a true friendship for'.

upon her father, the Earl-Bishop. It preserved the link with Devonshire House and it provided chaperonage in the event of any admirer becoming too importunate.

Lady Elizabeth was aware of travelling under the eyes of posterity. As soon as she embarked upon her travels, she began the first of many journals which she kept at various stages in her career. She compared 'the thoughtful Englishmen walking on the shore' at Dover with 'the confused clack of many voices' at Calais, 'belonging to this happy but petulant people'.[2] She had an eye for dress and behaviour, an ear for anecdote, a turn for philosophizing about the nature of men and women, especially herself.

But she betrayed no sense of the ambiguous situation in which she was placed. She carried letters of introduction from the Duchess to Queen Marie Antoinette and the Duchesse de Polignac. But how did they regard her? Marie Antoinette was supposed to have lesbian relations with her favourite. Did they think that Lady Elizabeth was the lover of the Duchess? Banished by the Duke in custody of his love-child? Or was she accepted as the daughter of the Earl-Bishop, in whose honour every *hôtelier* with pretensions to luxury called his hotel Le Bristol? We only know that she was received graciously by the Queen and her favourite and that Mlle Bertin, the royal dressmaker, designed something which preserved Lady Elizabeth 'from cold *à la Chinoise*'. Lady Elizabeth, who five years before had been Mrs little f confined in Dunleer, took everything as of right, the Hervey luck which had raised Papa from a clerkship of the Privy Seal first to the richest see in Ireland and then the earldom of Bristol.

When she brought Charlotte and Mrs Garner to Nice (then independent from France) she presented Mama's introduction to Lady Rivers,[*] whom she found 'comfortable, notwithstanding her deafness'. Lady Rivers had two daughters, of whom Lady Bristol thought one preferable to the other. Lady Elizabeth seems never to have discovered which. She was satisfied that deaf Lady Rivers believed that beauty was 'essential to one's happiness and advantage, one should almost think to one's salvation'.[3] Lady Elizabeth had only to glance in a mirror to agree.

But the possession of beauty was not enough in itself. It needed homage and admiration. When a public fountain was dedicated in Nice, Lady Elizabeth, crowned with flowers, impersonated the Goddess Flora.

---

[*] Penelope, wife of George Pitt, first Baron Rivers. Walpole described her as 'all loveliness within and without' in contrast to 'her brutal, half mad husband'.

'A rural compliment well turned,'[4] purred Lady Bristol. But the Duchess of Devonshire was appalled at the ridiculous stories made of it. Lady Elizabeth was displaying the exhibitionism of the Earl-Bishop who had appeared at the Maundy Thursday celebrations in the Sistine Chapel wearing his full canonicals of rochet and chimere, to watch the Pope washing feet.[5]

On another occasion Lady Elizabeth, wearing a befeathered hat and a 'white riding uniform habit', rode up a wooded slope beyond Nice to the house of a curé. The priest was out, but when he came home, he was told of the Englishwoman, as pure as an angel, who had dismounted and mounted a beautiful steed with supernatural ease. He pursued this vision to Nice and begged Lady Elizabeth to visit his humble abode. This she did on a number of occasions, eating his figs and raisins, in sentimental fashion drawing out 'his artless thoughts' and admiring 'his venerable mien'.[6]

These phrases are taken from her journal. They throw light on how she saw herself, or wanted herself to be seen. But they are curiously reticent about motives. Although vanity was a failing Lady Elizabeth acknowledged in herself, lone horsewomen were infrequent in the foothills of the Alpes Maritimes, especially when young, beautiful and conspicuously dressed. Such goings-on attracted attention. Gentlemen gallantly offered to escort her. The Duchess was alarmed. Virtue was important, but reputation even more so. A *cicisbeo* or male escort was immediately suspected as a lover. One *cicisbeo* might be dangerous, Lady Elizabeth admitted. But if she was seen in the company of a number of *cicisbei*, what harm could be imputed, especially if she had little Charlotte with her?

Today these niceties of conduct may seem absurd, but in the late eighteenth century they were serious matters. Lady Elizabeth was walking a tightrope. With the salary of a governess, she wished to occupy the position in society to which she felt entitled as the Earl-Bishop's daughter. The Duchess sent chintz and muslin to be made up to Mlle Bertin's modes, bonnet-boxes of chip hats and packets of tea in case she 'should not get good in Nice'.[7] But Poor Bess needed men to accompany her on excursions and pay the expenses.

When spring gave way to summer, she took Charlotte and Mrs Garner to Geneva, where she and Lady Erne had studied French and Italian with such profit. There she found a number of willing escorts. The Duchess of Devonshire's letters began to sound as if they had been written by Mama. 'I think that the innocence of your conduct and intentions does not make you aware enough of the dangers of your situation. You say after all the resolutions you made about not receiving men, you have been living alone with 2.' Bess had driven out to Vevey with a Mr G and a M. P. This in itself meant nothing. 'But supposing at any place you had seen a beautiful young woman arrive, travelling by herself, who, tho' there was nothing against her, had imprudence laid to her charge, both suppos'd to be in love with her – with all yr candour you would think her imprudent.'[8]

Lady Elizabeth professed penitence. 'Their being two blinded me to the imprudence, and as Charlotte never quits me the consciousness of the openness of my actions and conduct deceived me.'[9] But in fact she was exploring the possibilities of grass-widowhood. Mr G. was a sea-going officer, M. P. was melancholy and infirm. Singly they could overbear her: together they were held in counterbalance. She developed a line of patter, as men went down upon their knees to declare their love.* How could she fail to sympathize with the victim of tender passion? Chained to a brutal husband by the bonds of matrimony, deprived of her own beloved boys, compelled to act governess to Charlotte Williams, a nice child but despite appearances not her own, she confessed to an awareness of the vicissitudes of the heart beyond her years. She was flattered to be the object of Chevalier X's, Comte Y's or Principe Z's regard. Alas, she could not reciprocate. And yet . . . and yet . . . there was one thing she could give, and gladly: friendship.

This formula worked in almost every case. She was a delightful companion, intelligent, beautiful, gay and able to flirt in three languages. To be, and be seen, in her company was a reward in itself, compared to which the satisfaction of a sexual urge was comparatively unimportant. She herself was not interested in passionate consummations, so much as in the infinite possibilities of flirtation.

At the same time she was dependent upon the generosity of the Devonshires, who as well as being her 'dearest friends' were also her employers. She was not worried about her duties as Charlotte's governess (though she convinced the Duchess that she was Charlotte's 'guardian angel' and Mrs Garner was 'diabolical'). She had proved the value of her friendship. Without her presence the Duke and Duchess could not have reached that harmony which resulted, on 12 July, in the Duchess's being brought to bed of a daughter, who was christened a month later

---

* It was said that Mr Edward Gibbon had to ask Lady Elizabeth to help him up. But the same story had been told of Alexander Pope and Lady Mary Wortley Montagu.

Georgiana Dorothy. Playfully (but also in some degree truthfully) Bess insisted on pretending that Lady Georgiana was *her* baby,[10] a delicate implication that if there was to be another child, the necessary son and heir, their friendship must continue.

The Duke and Duchess admitted that in letters. But Bess must be careful to preserve her reputation. 'I declare to God, my sweetest Bess I do not fear the *essential* with you one moment, but to you the opinion of the world is of so much importance for every future scheme, and so many of our women lately have gone into Switzerland and Italy when in scrapes, that you should be doubly cautious to shew you are not that kind of person.'[11] If Lady Elizabeth lost her reputation, it might become impossible for her to rejoin them. She begged Bess not to follow 'the Chevalier' to Turin.

But to Turin, Bess went: and stayed there because she had run out of money. Brilliant evening parties were given in her honour. The King and Queen stayed to receive her at Court and she was invited by the cream of the nobility, and the heads of the diplomatic corps. She was rising rapidly, when one thinks of the visits to the curé outside Nice and the excursions across Lac Léman with the sea-going Mr G and the invalid Mr P.

Lady Elizabeth's debts amounted to £170. 'Good God – Good God – and all from my fault,'[12] lamented the Duchess and despatched £300 to Turin immediately and two or three hundred more to follow in three weeks. 'God bless you, my angel love, I adore and love you beyond description, but I am miserable till I know you have read this. Canis sends a thousand loves.'

Lady Elizabeth travelled from city to city, from triumph to triumph. For herself, she protested, she needed no money, except for pens and paper. Everything, she claimed, was laid out for Charlotte Williams. But when news reached her in Rome that Lord Spencer had died at Bath on 31 October, she went into mourning in a suit of sables.[13] Wearing these, she attended High Mass at St Peter's and met the Emperor Joseph attended by two gentlemen-in-waiting and King Gustavus III of Sweden with an entourage of twelve. Among these was Count Axel Fersen, a romantic soldier of fortune who had served with the French forces sent to aid the American 'rebels' in 1779. At Versailles, he had paid such elaborate court to Queen Marie Antoinette that many said he was her lover. If he had been, it is probable that his public attention would have been less marked. Handsome in a feminine way, he was 'a lady's man' rather than a lover.

When Lady Elizabeth went to Naples to extend her triumphs at the Court of the King and Queen of the Two Sicilies, Count Fersen followed. Lady Elizabeth confided to him her anxieties about the rôle her father was playing in politics. He had become too active on the side of Irish nationalism and the emancipation of Roman Catholics. He was under observation and there was talk of his being arrested. She asked if Count Fersen had any inside information, and when he admitted that the King of Sweden had spoken of the Earl-Bishop a good deal, Lady Elizabeth said that 'unfortunate uncertainty of character' influenced her father in everything, even in her own marriage and situation. She was forbidden either to see or write to her beloved sons. Unlike H., another admirer to whom she had made this sad admission, he did not immediately propose that he should compensate for her loss of husband and children by the gift of his own person. Instead, he burst into tears.

Some evenings later he was left alone with her. She was very low, her hands clutching the frame of a chair and her head resting on them. The Count stooped and kissed her hands, and then her cheek. Lady Elizabeth neither started nor was angry. She took his hand and said, 'This must never be again.'

'No,' he said.

He was very melancholy.

So was she.

With tears in his eyes, he continued until they parted to say, 'I only ask you never to forget me, and always do justice to my feelings.'[14]

Thus began the loveliest of the many friendships Lady Elizabeth enjoyed abroad. The Count had money, birth, position and a reputation for gallantry in both fields. He took her by land to the ruins of Pompeii and Herculaneum, up the slopes of smoking Vesuvius; and across the Bay of Naples to Sorrento, Capri and the enchanting isle of Ischia. He paid her expenses and warmed her with compliments which at the same time expressed his ardour and his resignation to its extinction.

The Duke and Duchess were kept fully posted on these sentimental and social triumphs, as well as her regimen for little Charlotte. 'First the cold bath and a little walk. Then breakfast. Then she reads to me . . . Sunday her catechism.'[15] Her letters, despite protestations of affection for them all, especially *her* little baby Georgiana, made it plain that she had fallen on her feet and could survive if the Devonshires withdrew their patronage.

Not that there was ever any question of that. The Duchess was always devising plans for a reunion. Perhaps Canis and she could meet Racky abroad during the summer or autumn of 1783, prior to her *real* return. When she came back to London, Bess must spend at least a month at Devonshire House; and thereafter (since her 'little pride and perhaps circumstances' might make it as well she should not 'live absolutely' with her 'brother and sister') in some little house nearby.[16] The Duke sent messages and occasionally wrote a note, such a 'I have not had a letter from you this great while, but am in *whops** I shall have one soon and shall hear that you are better.'[17]

But Lady Elizabeth's cough continued and it seemed foolish to endanger her health by returning to England, when she was having so enjoyable a time abroad. In January 1784 she received a *cri de cœur* from the Duke, who had gone to Bath with his first attack of gout. 'This place has been very unpleasant to me compared with what it was a year and a half ago. For then I had the Rat and Bess and good health and fine weather, and now I have had none of them till a day or two ago the Rat and her young one came down here. There are many places in Bath that put me so much in mind of you that when I walk about the town I cannot help expecting upon turning the corner of a street to see you walking along it, holding your cane and bending it over your knee, but I have never met you yet and what surprises me likewise very much is that somebody or other has the impudence to live in your house in Bennet Street.'[18]

This was a disquieting letter. Lady Elizabeth knew that the Duke found her amusing, delightful and attractive; but she had never imagined his feelings to be other than what she termed 'sensual': now they appeared to be deeper, affectionate or even loving.

This imposed a strain upon her loyalty to Georgiana. All the gifts of money or in kind, she thought, had proceeded from the Duchess. It was her generosity that enabled Lady Elizabeth to sustain the position of an Earl's daughter, rather than that of a humble governess. It would be doubly disloyal to establish a sexual relationship with the husband of the woman who was at the same time her dearest friend and her generous protectress.

She was relieved when on 8 March 1784 the Duchess confided in her that all the money Bess had received had really 'flow'd from Canis'.[19] Her benefactor was the Duke, and so Lady Elizabeth felt that one reason for guilt was removed. In the same letter the Duchess swore her 'dearest, dearest dst angel love' to secrecy before telling her that she had

---

* 'Whops': a joke for 'hopes'.

incurred 'a very, very large debt'. 'You must neither change any way of living or give the least hint to him [the Duke] unless you will make me wretched.'

Though she was still being begged to return to England, Lady Elizabeth lingered in Naples. Angelica Kauffmann was painting her portrait, the model wearing a beautiful floppy hat with two brushy plumes which aided the waves of hair to frame the pretty face, the pensive eyes and resolute mouth. She loved the *dolce vita*, the courtesy of Sir William Hamilton, the British Ambassador, the classic poses of Emma, his temporarily respectable Ambassadress, the Neapolitan Court, the respectful amorousness of Count Fersen and the blue sea filling the horseshoe made by Ischia and the Sorrentine peninsula. But when she received a letter written by the Duchess at the end of April she knew she could no longer tarry. 'As much as I long to see you,' wrote her dearest friend, 'it is not for me I write. I am certain poor Canis's health and spirits depend upon y^r soothing friendship. Just now he s^d to me – write to Bess, tell her I never have heard from her, won't she come? Why won't she? She shall return for the winter, and Chatsworth is as good a climate for the summer as any. Dr Love, I took it on me to say I thought you w^d return for a few months and then go for the winter abroad again. . . .'[20]

The message seemed plain to Lady Elizabeth. If she returned to the Duke, there would be no recriminations from the Duchess. She had no secrets from either of them. The only secret was the one they shared, against the prying eyes of the Dowager Countess and the gossiping world.

Soon Mr Gibbon was writing to Lady Sheffield that he had spent some delightful hours by the bedside of 'the Eliza' as she passed from Italy through Lausanne to England, 'poorly in health, but still adorable'.

6

While Lady Elizabeth had, in Lady Bristol's words, been acting as a mother to Charlotte Williams 'all over the world',[1] the Duchess had got into a number of scrapes. Money was at the root of all her evils. But she had used one crisis after another to avoid facing her debts. During her pregnancy, she must not worry for fear she might miscarry. If she produced an heir, the Duke would settle everything. When the baby proved to be a girl, she must wait till little G. was weaned, or else her milk might be affected. It was not till September 1783 that she had to confess, what he already knew, that she owed a large sum. The Duke said he would have to talk to Mr Heaton, the Corkscrew.

Mr Heaton disapproved of the Duchess. She did not understand the law of entail or the difference between capital and income. He resented her interference in estate affairs. Still owing the ornamental furniture-maker Gaubert £300 from the time of the first Devonshire House ball, she had, as an *amende honorable*, recommended Gaubert to the Prince of Wales for the decoration of Carlton House. Gaubert had done his splendid best, but the Prince had not paid his bill. She also commissioned Gaubert to make alterations to the south front of Chatsworth without consulting Mr Heaton about specifications or prices. Gaubert was indignant at being brought to the verge of bankruptcy by the Duchess's patronage. Heaton, embarrassed at having to higgle with a tradesman, was not in a mood to accommodate Her Grace.

Soon Georgiana was denouncing the Corkscrew to Mama. He had done her all the harm he could. Knowing the Duke's generosity and forbearance, he dared not accuse her of extravagance, but he had hinted to the Duke at some undesirable connection between Her Grace and the Prince of Wales. What he said Georgiana did not specify. Three months before she had told Bess that the Prince had kissed her publicly at the Court of St James. '*Je vous assure, mon adorable petite, sans le moindre emotion de ma part*, but you cannot think how uneasy it made me. The Duke, dear Dog, instead of being angry, sd it was not my fault.'[2] The kiss had been in gratitude for the efforts made by the Devonshires and Charles Fox to increase his allowance, but knowing the *tendresse* between the Prince and the Duchess, gossips interpreted the kiss and support for the increase of Florizel's allowance as evidence of a liaison.

From Chatsworth Heaton wrote to the Duke warning him that Her Grace should on no account seem to take Gaubert's part. People were already disposed to say the Duke and Duchess 'liv'd ill together'.[3] When shown this letter the Duchess in turn attacked Heaton's honesty and integrity. The Duke admitted his surprise at 'the freedom (one might say impertinence)' of Heaton, but was sure he did not mean to hurt the Duchess, to which she replied that 'people' (by which she meant the Duchess of Portland) were saying that Heaton was making a fortune out of the Portland and Devonshire estates★ and was keeping the Duke short of cash to force him to borrow. It was also said, she added, that many of the Duke's farms were unlet. The Duchess refused to believe this, because the Duke must know about it, or could easily find out.

This is the only time we know of when the Duchess asked about the Devonshire estates. The Duke's answer is significant. 'Not so easily,' he said. 'I do not look enough into my own affairs.'

'A pity you don't!'

'*If I found out that Heaton was ever so great a rascal,*' replied the Duke, '*I should be mad to quarrel with him for it could quite ruin us.*'†

The Duke meant that if he quarrelled with Heaton, his position as life tenant would be difficult. Heaton and the Duke's uncles, Lord Frederick and Lord John Cavendish, were trustees, and any attempt to remove the only man who understood the vast complexities of the family business would lead to the charge that he was trying to break the entail, and to inquiries into his own gambling debts as well as the Duchess's. His tranquil lethargy would have been shattered.

It is not surprising that the Duke refused to have a showdown with Heaton. But why did he not take the opportunity to explain the economic facts of ducal life to Georgiana? She was, apparently for the

★ As their man of business, Heaton had advance information of his employers' intentions and, like many before and since, he had no doubt profited from this foreknowledge. Though Heaton's retaining fee from the Duke of Devonshire was £1000 a year, his son-in-law decamped with £30 000 some years later.

† The Duchess underlined what she called these 'remarkable words, which I shall never forget'.[4]

first time, trying to understand their financial position. I can think of only one answer. He was as reckless about money as she, but he had no intention of her knowing it. The Duchess was left with the resolution to be prudent in her own expenses and those she might bring on the Duke, and she thanked God for granting her little Georgiana. The birth of a daughter and the prospect of a son prevented awkward enquiries about her affairs.

As a reward, the Duke snubbed Heaton for having grown 'pert' and wanting to manage everybody. Two days later, 3 October, the Duchess announced that she and Heaton were 'good friends'. Her debts were not mentioned until 1 November when Heaton said he must have a full account before he could do anything. Before *she* could do anything she wanted to consult the Duke. But she was glad to be friends with Heaton. Lord George Cavendish was the heir presumptive to the Duchy of Devonshire and Lady George was spreading various malicious rumours. There were 'lies, containing elements of truth' about the Devonshire House Circle; and even hinting at some association between Bess and the Duke of Dorset.[5]

The death of the Duchess's father, an illness of little G. and the need to console Mama provided a succession of reasons for not talking about debts. Mama relinquished the family properties in London, Wimbledon and Northamptonshire to her son, the second Earl and retired to St Albans, where she took Holywell as her dower house. The Duchess was still with her, when the political crisis blew up in December, which was to culminate in the notorious Westminster Election of 1784.

To understand this crisis and the issues of the election, we must briefly go back to April 1783, when Charles Fox had formed a coalition with his enemy Lord North, under the Duke of Portland, with 'the vices of both its parents; the corruption of the one, and the violence of the other'. Fox, who had been elected as the tribune of the people, lost his support among the electorate because of a series of measures aimed at curtailing the King's powers of patronage and increasing his own. The crunch came with his India Bill, designed rightly to reform the powers of the East India Company, but wrongly intended to present Fox with vast powers of patronage by transferring Indian appointments from the East India Company to the government in power. The King secured the defeat of the Bill in the House of Lords and ordered Fox and North to surrender their seals of office. The Duke of Portland and his Cabinet resigned and in December 1783 young William Pitt formed what Fox derisively called his Mincemeat Administration, because he was sure that with his parliamentary majority he could overthrow it the moment the House met after Christmas.

But Fox played his hand so badly that his parliamentary majority diminished at every division. He had advocated annual parliamentary elections a few years before; now he insisted that the seven-year Parliament had still four more years to run. By March 1784 it was plain that Pitt would soon have parliamentary support for calling a general election and even before the dissolution of the old Parliament in March 1784 the first electioneering moves were being made. The Pittite Duke of Rutland distributed between four and five thousand pounds in London, while Parliament was still sitting. A thousand pounds went to the poor, who had no votes; but since the voters had to pay the Poor Rate, they could be relied on in the election to vote for Pitt's candidates out of gratitude. The Duchess of Devonshire threw herself into the pre-election fray. 'I was at the Opera, it was very full and I had several good political fights,' she wrote to Mama. 'L^y Sefton says this is a great *Aria* in the history of England. The Duchess of Rutland said D— Fox, upon which Colonel St Leger with great difficulty spirited up Lady Maria Waldegrave to say D— Pitt.'[6] Georgiana saw the issue simply as an issue between the House of Commons elected by the people and the House of Lords dominated by the King.

To the modern reader used to a six weeks' election campaign followed by an election day when everyone over the age of eighteen long enough resident to be on the electoral roll is eligible to cast a vote, eighteenth-century elections are bewildering. Parliamentary seats bore no relation to population. Growing cities like Manchester and Birmingham had no MPs. The number of voters in the town of Malmesbury amounted to only thirteen. Fox ensured his return to Parliament as MP for the Orkney and Shetland Islands. But he chose also to stand for Westminster, one of the few constituencies where the electors numbered thousands.

Westminster returned two MPs, the one with the most votes being called the Senior Member and the one with the second highest number the Junior Member. There was only one polling booth, in Covent Garden. If a sufficient number of adherents could be collected on nomination day, the members could be returned 'by acclamation' without any election. But if this failed there had to be a poll, which could last for weeks, with the state of the poll being made public each day.

Fox's main opponent was Lord Hood, immensely popular for his victories as Admiral of the British Fleet in the West Indies during the late war with France. As his running mate Fox chose Sir Cecil Wray who had been his colleague in the North–Fox coalition. But at the last moment Wray switched his support to Lord Hood. Hood and Wray tried to get themselves elected by acclamation.

When Fox challenged, an election had to be held, with three candidates contending for two seats. Voting began on 1 April (perhaps appropriately All Focls' Day), and Fox got off to a flying start with 302 votes, compared to Hood's 264 and Wray's 238. But next day Hood went to the top of the poll and by 12 April Fox was bottom, with Wray 318 ahead of him.

As we have seen during the 1774 election, no peer with a seat in the House of Lords could campaign in an election to the House of Commons, but their wives were at liberty to 'politick' for them. The Duchess of Portland headed the Foxite ladies, the Duchess of Rutland the Pittite. The Pittite ladies may have been more upright, but there was no doubt that the Foxites were more beautiful, with the Duchess of Devonshire, Lady Duncannon and the stunning, if 'idiotic', Mrs Crewe sitting in their carriages outside Fox's headquarters at the Shakespear Tavern, Covent Garden, or waving and smiling from the windows within.

In their politicking, as in their gambling, Georgiana and Harriet were merely following Mama's example, but as usual with an enthusiasm which outstripped decorum. To be seen in favour of a candidate was one thing, to canvass for votes was another. In the newpapers appeared the announcement from Fox's HQ: 'The lovely Dss of D. is strong in the interest of Mr Fox. Her Grace canvasses every day and has caused a thousand Coalition medals to be struck on the occasion, one of which she gives to every elector who promises a plumper* for Mr Fox.'

These medals had a commercial value, but as 'souvenirs' they could not be classed as bribes. Yet they could be misconstrued. From the Hood–Wray HQ in Wood's Hotel came the intelligence: 'We hear the D—— of D—— grants *favours* for those who promise votes and interest to Mr Fox.'

The Duchess and Lady Duncannon sallied forth canvassing voters in their shops and houses. They were joined by the notorious Mrs Perdita Robinson, ex-mistress of the Prince of Wales and of Charles Fox, who had granted her a pension of £500 p.a. out of the public purse. They were rumoured to give kisses for plumpers.

Promptly the war of words, hitherto merely acrimonious, turned to

* Each voter could vote for two candidates. A 'plumper' was a vote for only one candidate.

lubricity. *The History of the Westminster Election* (1785), a quarto volume with 574 pages of text and ten cartoons, details this violent, gross and meanly fought campaign. One extract is enough to exemplify what the Duchess had to face.

WESTMINSTER

To be hired for the Day

Several Pair of RUBY POUTING LIPS, of the

FIRST QUALITY

To be kissed by rum Dukes, queer Dukes, Butchers, Draymen,

Dust-men and Chimney Sweepers.

Please to enquire at Devon & Co's Crimson Pouting Warehouse,

Piccadilly.

'Should the unsuccessful Candidate keep behind
on this day's poll – Bulks★ in different markets
may be made to tremble.'

I had rather kiss my Moll than she;
With all her paint and Finery;
What's a Duchess more than woman?
We've sounder flesh on Portsmouth Common:
So drink about to HOOD and WRAY –
Their health – and may they gain the day!
Then fill out Nectar in a glass
As for kissing – kiss my a—.

No Duchess for me, but my sweet Duchess at Portsmouth.

A SAILOR

Huzza! Lord Hood and Sir Cecil Wray for ever!

Mama was appalled. She implored Georgiana to come at once to St Albans, and as the poll for Fox sank each day, the Duchess felt the campaign was as futile as it was filthy. She announced that her mother was ill and went 'to nurse' her at Holywell House. But she was pursued by entreaties. The Duchess of Portland begged her to return. When that failed, the Duke of Portland wrote that the Duchess's presence would assure success, her continued absence defeat.[7] Reluctantly she returned

---

★ 'Bulk': canting slang for a pickpocket's assistant, the one who jostles a person while the other picks the pocket.

to the fray and, sure enough, the day she resumed canvassing for votes the tide turned: Fox 186, Hood 151, Wray 116. On only three of the succeeding days did Wray's votes outnumber Fox's.

Voters were reluctant to go to the Covent Garden hustings. They wanted to be wooed and there was no better wooer than the Duchess. As the last of them were rounded up, a typical daily poll was forty-eight, a dozen each for Hood and Wray two dozen for Fox. Quartering the parishes, St James's, St Martin-in-the-Fields, St Margaret's, St John's, St Clement Dane's, St Mary-le-Strand, the Duchess brought in plumpers for Fox. She even fetched voters from as far away as Hounslow. There had never been so intensive a canvass, nor such an inducement short of bribery as riding beside the Duchess to the polls.[8]

When they saw the way the poll was going, Hood and Wray announced that if Fox was elected they would demand a scrutiny. They alleged bribery and corruption, voting by non-electors and double voting by electors. There was an undignified fracas in which Pitt's carriage was set upon in St James's. Fox was accused of leading the mob, but he had an alibi. He was in bed at the time. Mrs Armistead could confirm that, because she was in bed with him.

The poll finally closed on the fortieth day, 17 May. Lord Hood was elected Senior Member with 6694 votes, Fox Junior Member with 6234. Wray had only 5998. Though a scrutiny was immediately demanded, this did not prevent a victory procession. Fox was borne aloft in a triumphal chair. Bands played for the conquering blue-jowled hero. Outriders in buff and blue cavorted and in the rear came the coaches and sixes of the Dukes of Devonshire and Portland, huzzaing along the Strand, the Mall, up St James's to Piccadilly where the gates of Devonshire House were standing open and the Prince of Wales was waiting at the head of the steps to greet these jubilant Friends of Liberty, who were enemies of his father.

It was a hollow victory. Fox had won in Westminster, but the Foxites had been trounced throughout the country. As MP for Orkney and Shetland, Fox could have been formidable in opposition. But his energies were dissipated first in trying to prove the validity of his election at Westminster and later by the interminable trial of Warren Hastings. It would be more than twenty years before he held public office again.

Though the Duchess was celebrated with a flag emblazoned SACRED TO FEMALE PATRIOTISM, she felt besmirched. She had descended from the Empress of Fashion to the Duchess who Bought a Butcher's

Plumper for a kiss. Perhaps she realized that one motive for her canvassing enthusiasm was to postpone the reckoning of her debts. At any rate she did not dare to face the Duke alone. While she was still canvassing she wrote to Bess begging her to return, for the sake of Canis's health and incidentally to act as an intermediary in negotiating her debts. These had mounted in the six months since she had totted them up for Heaton. She had omitted a matter of £600, run up bills for £700 during the election and lost £1700 at play.*[9]

On previous occasions her 'dearest Brother' the Prince of Wales had been good for a touch. But he now became involved in a scrape which involved the Duchess and their good relations. While she was at supper one evening, two friends of the Prince called at Devonshire House, with the alarming news that the Prince, maddened by Mrs Fitzherbert's hardness of heart, had stabbed himself with his sword. They had visited that lady, begging her to come to Carlton House and save the heir apparent from an untimely death. Mrs F. was in a carriage without, but refused to see the Prince except in company with the Duchess.

As appreciative of melodrama as she was tender of heart, the Duchess could not refuse. Mrs F. was a Roman Catholic widow, who considered it as impossible for her to become the Prince's mistress as for the Protestant Prince to become her husband. With the Duchess's help she might recall the Prince to reason.

Shown into his room, they found Unreason enthroned. He flourished his bandages and swore he would tear them off and bleed to death unless Mrs F. consented to marry him. His hysteria was so royal that they did not dare him to undo the bandages so that they could see how deeply (if at all) the First Gentleman in Europe had pricked himself. To calm him, Mrs F. signed and the Duchess witnessed a promise to wed His Hysterick Highness.

Next day the two ladies met, drafted and signed a letter stating that the promise was invalid because extorted under duress. Mrs Fitzherbert thereupon sought safety across the Channel, leaving the Duchess temporarily without the friendship of a dear brother useful in pecuniary crises.[10]

Somewhere on the Continent the path of Mrs Fitzherbert crossed that of Lady Elizabeth Foster on the way to rejoin her benefactors.

* To Lord Trentham £800, Lady Archer £400, Mr Greville £300, 'Harum' Duncannon £200. Lady Archer was a gambling hostess, whose tables were run by Henry Martindale.

Mr Gibbon, if we trust hearsay, thought Lady Elizabeth could, 'if she beckoned, charm the Lord Chancellor off his woolsack'.[11] But if she had done so, it would only have been to offer sentimental friendship in return for his devotion.

Lady Elizabeth's career as governess was over. The 'diabolical' Mrs Garner was to be dismissed and Charlotte sent to Mrs Belvoir's fashionable school in London. The Devonshires were at the port to meet them. Had not the Duchess assured Bess that 'I am certain poor Canis's health and spirits depend upon y^r soothing friendship'?[12]

Charlotte and Mrs Garner were fussed over and dismissed. Then the three friends were alone to embrace, kiss and rejoice. There was to be such gaiety at Chatsworth as never before. First, of course, Bess must visit her mother at Ickworth Park. Meanwhile the Duchess would go to her uncle, the Reverend Charles Poyntz, rector of North Creek, to pick up little Georgiana whom Mama had taken there for a holiday.

Chatsworth that summer of 1784 was a romping retreat from the world of debts and duns, if we read between the lines of the bread and butter verses the Duchess wrote to thank Mama.

> The bustle at Derby, the races, the Ball,
> The dressing out fine, the jumbling and all,
> The dancing, the racing, the noise of the week,
> Cannot make me forget my beloved North Creek.
> At Chatsworth the riding and flirting all day,
> The drives of the morn, of the Eve and the play
> Still make me in mind, all the happiness seek
> That so cheerful, tho' quiet, I found at North Creek.[13]

Guests came to Chatsworth and departed. Unwary Charles Wyndham was wetted at the copper tree. Love was everywhere, within, without; suggestive glances, protestations, innuendoes – so universal that no one ever knew what was to be taken seriously, what lightly. Lady Elizabeth was at the centre of it all. 'Fish' Craufurd said so many gallant things to her that Canis threw her whip down the steepest part of the bluff and bade him retrieve it. Poor dear Lord Jersey fell quite in love with her. He got very drunk, but as he went to bed they agreed not to tease him about it. Sir William Jones (he who had been tutor to Georgiana's brother) succeeded Lord Jersey as Bess's 'lover'. The Duchess declared she was like Susannah among the Elders.

On one Public Day a clergyman got so drunk that he nearly collapsed on Bess and Miss Lloyd. On another, Dr Taylor brought Dr Johnson over from Ashbourne. Edmund Burke's son Richard asked him if he was quite well. 'Sir, I am not half well,' answered the Dictionary Doctor, 'no, nor a quarter well.' But later when the Duke took him under the lime trees, the Doctor was so agreeable that Georgiana and Bess regretted having to leave him and talk to other visitors. 'He din'd here and does not shine quite so much in eating as in conversation,' the Duchess told Mama, 'for he eat much and nastily.'[14]

August frivolled into September, September to October. Guests came and went but Lady Elizabeth lingered, laughing, fluttering, languishing and alas! coughing. 'She should not stay in such a climate,' observed Mama. 'Every hour may be of the utmost consequence to her.' Lady Elizabeth tried to placate her enemy by adding a postscript to one of the Duchess's letters, describing the beauty of little Georgiana who at fifteen months 'distinguishes letters and aims at words', and professing for the Dowager Countess 'all a daughter's affection'. But the Dowager merely advised that with the onset of November fogs, she would be 'safe in a warmer climate'.[15] Would Charlotte Williams be going abroad again? A foreign education might turn the little girl's head. She did not openly voice her suspicion that the Duchess had not conceived because Lady Elizabeth was the Duke's mistress.

No relationship so crude existed between the Devonshires and Lady Elizabeth. They thrived in a subtler world. 'It has happened to me with people who have influence over me,' the Duchess once explained to Mama, 'to have perfectly seized the reason of their wishing me to do some one thing or other which I did not like to do, and that tho' they did not disclose their real motive, I have been saying to myself all the time that they have been persuading me, "I know what you are at, & why you wish me to do so and so", and yet with this full conviction instead of owning it & in spite of disliking the thing, I have done it because I was desired, & have pretended to believe every word that was said to me, so that I have actually taken more pains to appear a Dupe than most people do to shew that they can't be outwitted.'

The Duke and his two ladies were not out to dupe one another. What they were at did not have to be put into words: the house of Devonshire needed an heir apparent. But after three months together nothing had happened. The insidious November fogs began to creep down from the Derbyshire Peak and they all went south, Lady Elizabeth to stay with her mother at Ickworth Park and the Devonshires to Chiswick and London.

The Duke was worried about his health. His grandfather had died at fifty-seven, his father at forty-four, and his younger brother, Lord

Richard Cavendish, had already died. The Duke himself was plagued with gout. He did not want to die and leave little Georgiana to the generosity of the heir presumptive, his brother Lord George, whose wife had given him an heir in the same year that little Georgiana had been born.

The Duchess shared his anxiety about the succession; and she saw no end to her financial misery unless she produced a son. She had hoped the presence of Lady Elizabeth would effect a miracle. But it had not.

Lady Elizabeth was aware of why she had been recalled from Italy. Her benefactors still professed their love, but how long could she rely upon their generosity? And what would poor little Bess do, if she no longer had 'manners that pleased' them?

In mid-November Bess rejoined her dearest friends, at Devonshire House. They were so intimate that she was as often alone with the Duke as with the Duchess. They were all desperate but there still remained some days and nights before Lady Elizabeth had to leave. We do not know whether the Duchess noticed anything different in the atmosphere. It was not the sort of thing on which one commented.

On 2 December 1784 Lady Elizabeth said goodbye to her dearest friends, telling them not to worry about her journey south. She would go to Paris and await the arrival of her brother John Augustus, Lord Hervey, his wife and their sweet daughter Eliza.

After her departure, the Duke renewed his ardour with the Duchess. She was glad to receive him on any terms.

Interlude One

The Duchess's admission that she actually took more pains to 'appear a Dupe than most people did to shew they couldn't be outwitted' poses the question: how conscious were the Duke and his two ladies of what was happening and of the possible consequences? Since this must be a matter of speculation, conducted not in their idiom but in ours, I have made it the subject of an interlude, rather than part of their story.

The Duchess, I think, knew that the Duke was sexually attracted to Bess and when she found that flirtation was not enough to renew his potency with regard to herself, she was willing that the Duke should take Lady Elizabeth as his mistress. She did not love the Duke any more than the Duke loved her. They had undertaken a family business which they had been unable to conclude without help from outside. In the early stages of their marriage, Charlotte Spencer had been a useful aid. Later, Bess's mere presence had resulted in the birth of little Lady Georgiana. This time something more stimulating was necessary. The Duchess did not *know* what was happening between mid-November and 2 December, but whatever it was she did not mind.

The Duke found Lady Elizabeth charming, sympathetic and sexually exciting. She had an ability to play up to him rather similar to Charlotte Spencer's. She made him the centre of her attention, hung on his lips and flattered his self-esteem. He wanted to have her. I do not think he was in love with her. It is hard to think of him as being more than fond. He was perhaps even more fond of Bess than of the dogs in whose antics they both delighted. But if he possessed her, there was a chance of regaining his potency with Georgiana. And, in this, he was right.

Lady Elizabeth chose to attach herself to the Devonshires in 1782, because it was the only possibility she saw of enjoying the social position of an Earl's daughter, having made a mis-marriage. She knew that it was not merely 'her manners that pleased' that brought her hundreds of pounds. Her future, and that of her two sons Frederick and Augustus

Foster, depended upon Georgiana's producing an heir. She had, so to speak, become a junior partner in the Devonshire business:[1] but, as she had no contract she was liable to dismissal unless she produced results. She had from the first gone out of her way to be not merely useful but essential to both her 'friends'. She had become the intermediary, the confidante of secrets which they could not confide to one another. But by November 1784 matters had reached a crisis. She really was ill. Another winter in England, she feared, might kill her. She had to go south. But would the Devonshires be as generous during her absence as they had been when she took Charlotte Williams off their hands during the Duchess's first successful pregnancy? She must have been aware that she was in some respects the successor to Charlotte Spencer. During her absence, if the Duchess was not pregnant, might not the Devonshires find a successor to her? And in that case, what successor would she find to the Duke? The Duke of Dorset had a *tendresse* for her. He was unmarried and a man of infinite charm. But he was notoriously fickle. He would be delighted to have an affair with her. But what would happen when he abandoned her? He could go on to another conquest without a stain on his character; but she would be left without reputation, a *demi-mondaine* without the financial rewards reaped by other women of soiled reputation. Even if she succeeded in holding the Duke of Dorset off with the promise of marrying him when she was free, what possibility was there of gaining her freedom? Her husband, little f, had committed adultery, but her chance of divorcing him by an Act of Parliament was slender, even if she had the money to pay the costs. And even so, she could not re-marry except by special dispensation. Even if this dispensation was given, the diplomatic career of the Duke of Dorset would be ruined by marriage to a divorcée. The same arguments applied to Count Fersen or any other of her many admirers. She was trapped. Or rather, she would have been trapped, if she had tried to stray out of the Devonshire circle. But within its capacious perimeter, she had freedom and luxuries which she could not have found outside.

All three of them must have recognized the wisdom? the desirability? the necessity? of the Duke bedding Lady Elizabeth in November 1784. Lady Elizabeth had learned to anticipate the future. By becoming the Duke's mistress, she had established a claim upon his generosity. He would support her while she was abroad and he would want to have her back again. Supposing that she suffered 'a misfortune', the Duke would support the child as he had done Charlotte Williams (but in a manner fitting her own more elevated position). When the time came, as assuredly it must, to inform the Duchess, she had no doubt that her dearest friend would show even more kindness than she had to Charlotte Williams. The bond of friendship would be strengthened by the tie of blood. Since it was impossible for Lady Elizabeth to continue to live in the manner to which she had become accustomed without sacrificing her virtue, there was no one to whom she could better surrender it than to the Duke of Devonshire. Considered purely as a business venture, it was the best way in which to invest her manners that pleased

But it would be wrong to regard Lady Elizabeth merely as a woman of business. She genuinely liked the Duke and Duchess. The Duke was not every woman's ideal of manhood; but he suited Lady Elizabeth even better as a lover than he would have done as a husband. She could indulge his whims in private, while in public giving play to her natural flirtatiousness. Vanity she considered to be her vice, but it was a gratifying vice; and she could always explain to the Duke that she was indulging it in order to distract attention from their clandestine love.

When she left London on 2 December, Lady Elizabeth did not know whether or not she was pregnant. If she was, she told him that she would lie in on the island of Ischia. Ischia became a code word. If she was going to Ischia, it meant she was to be confined. If she was enjoying Ischia, all was well. If things went wrong, Ischia had proved a disastrous holiday and so on. It was all rather a gamble for Lady Elizabeth. But the stakes were high and the chances of winning were far greater than those of the Duchess at the faro table.

7

The departure of Lady Elizabeth caused little gossip. The Dowager Countess, it was said, had triumphed in her campaign, and when, early in 1785, Dr Denman confirmed that the Duchess was again with child, it seemed as if history was repeating itself.

The Duchess refused all invitations to spend her time at St Albans, away from the racketing of the London season. The Duke was determined not to pass a night under his mother-in-law's roof; and if Georgiana left her husband and spent weeks or even months at Holywell House so soon after Lady E.'s going abroad, it would set tongues wagging. Mama was welcome at Devonshire House. 'Your reasons for not coming,' Georgiana wrote, 'are only good as far as they concern y^r health, for the Duke w^d be happy to have you and you w^d not interfere with one another. . . . The balls do not affect me, I am never out after twelve, and looking at dancing is a better amusement than play, which, by the bye, I have not entered into yet. . . .'[1]

It was not until 30 April that the Duke wrote to say that they would dine with Mama at Holywell House next day, would stay all night, not troubling her for beds, but sleeping at the inn.[2]

Meanwhile Lady Elizabeth had been allaying suspicion by her behaviour. She placed herself under the protection of the Duke of Dorset, not yet but later to be the British Ambassador in Paris. The Queen and the Duchesse de Polignac hailed her as an old friend. She went everywhere with the Duke of Dorset as her *cicisbeo*. He gallantly pressed her to be his mistress. When she sympathized, aware how ardently she would have felt if she had been in his shoes, but etc., the Duke of Dorset praised, while deploring, a chastity so unusual in the *ton*. Lady Elizabeth felt guilty, as she became more and more convinced that she was bearing the Duke of Devonshire's child. How, when she was in love with the Duke of Devonshire in London, could she take such pleasure in the attentions of the Duke of Dorset in Paris? Married to Canis, or even always in his company, she might have curbed or conquered her vanity. Separated from the one she loved, she needed the adulation of the many who loved her. Or so she confided to her journal.

There was another motive. If she behaved as an *allumeuse*, warming by charms and being warmed by gallantry, no one would suspect her of love for the Duke of Devonshire. She may have hoped that by behaving as if she was not pregnant, the baby would disappear. She dared not consult a doctor.

When she was joined by Lady Hervey and little Eliza, she hearkened to her sister-in-law's complaints about Lord Hervey's infidelity without revealing her own. She sympathized with Lady Hervey, but reflected that her brother might be useful when, and if, occasion arose. He would certainly not cast the first stone.

By the time Lord Hervey reached Paris, Lady Elizabeth knew she was with child. They began the journey towards the sun. As they jolted along the pitted roads, she dreaded what she called 'the overthrow of the fair fabric of fame and character I had raised to myself in the world, of comfort and consolation to my mother and family, joy and pleasure to my friends'.[3]

This is an extract from Lady Elizabeth's second Continental journal. It was, as can be seen, designed to be read by other people, most immediately by the Duke and Duchess in the event of her dying in childbirth, then by her descendants and perhaps ultimately by you and me. The ornate language was in the idiom of the time. One cannot be certain whether her own thoughts and feelings were distorted by such clichés, or had to be presented thus to please her readers. Perhaps it was a muddle of both. Literature has a way of putting life in a straitjacket.

She admitted that she did not want to have the child. Might a broken shaft, a bolting horse, an overturn in a ditch precipitate a miscarriage? Could over-exercise produce an abortion? When she fainted at La Palliasse, had fatigue accomplished what she did not herself dare to do? No, it was her 'misfortune ripening'. The narrative is dramatic, but high-falutin'. No doubt she went through all these emotions. But if given the journal to read, the Duke and Duchess would be overcome by what poor little Bess had suffered in order that the Duchess should conceive. Her journal at the same time afforded the relief of confession and provided evidence for emotional blackmail.

At Lyons she had unspecified business with 'Miss A'.* She toyed

---

* I think that Miss A. was identical with 'Miss Ash' (see D. M. Stuart, *Dearest Bess* pp. 23–4, 28).

with the idea of confessing her misfortune. But instead of that she invited Miss A. to join her at Ischia in June.

The passage of the Alps was agony. The winter snows had not melted and the winds were biting. She had to keep little Eliza amused in the coach and by the time they reached Turin she was so exhausted that a physician was called in to bleed her. She did not tell him she was pregnant. 'It was a miracle so copious a bleeding did not occasion a miscarriage – I half hoped, half dreaded it – Nature as if to torture me more, spoke all a Mother's language to me.'[4]

Despite the insecurity of the mail, she wrote passionately to the Duke (probably care of his bankers), expatiating on her sufferings, physical, emotional and spiritual. He destroyed her letters, after writing to urge her to be of good cheer, not to worry her dear little head, etc. His optimism from the security of Chiswick and Devonshire House made her all the more angry and querulous. She began to be haunted by fear that scandalmongers would guess the reason for her journey abroad. She prayed that her baby's 'too dear, too beloved Father' might never know the pangs that rent her heart.

Yet vanity sustained her in extremity. Her friends in Turin received her 'with joy and every mark of distinction and attention – the English Minister scarcely leaves us and speaks already the language of gallantry'. Milan, Florence, Pisa, Leghorn, Rome and finally Naples provided the mixture as before: the undeserved admiration, guilt at deceiving the Duke of Dorset, remorse, 'still I love Virtue tho' I have wandered from it'.

As her body swelled, she craved solitude. 'Would I could fly the face of human kind – yet I could not bear not to see my loved friend again.★ She has been my comfort and happiness, tho' her unthinking kindness has hurried me down the precipice. Perhaps she thought I was still attached to Count Fersen – I did like him once, never as I do D.D., never was led an instant to what even now I wish I had not done. I then thought D.D. indifferent to me, that his former love had only been a sensual one. Yet even so, the thought of him was a check to my feelings, and the desire of his esteem was more than prudence or principle to me. Oh me – Oh me –'[5]

This is the only passage in which she wrote of herself and the Devonshires. Its inconsistencies are interesting. If she thought the Duke *indifferent* before she went abroad, how could his *love* have been *only sensual*? Blame for Bess's betrayal of her 'loved friend' is placed on 'her unthinking kindness'. And the Duke, who had lain with her in

★ The Duchess of Devonshire.

November out of *sensual love*, was assumed to be as much *in love* with her as she with him. Supposing that the Duchess read this after Lady Elizabeth had died tragically in childbirth, she would see to it that the Duke did justice to their child of love.

By mid-May, Lady Elizabeth's shape increased daily. At dinner with a Mr Morris in Portici, in intolerable heat, conversation turned to the plight of the Countess of Upper Ossory when she tried to conceal that she was with child by her lover. Lady Elizabeth took it as directed towards herself.[6] On 21 June her brother accompanied her to Ischia and left her with her maid and Louis, her manservant, to await the arrival of Miss Ash a few days later.

When Miss Ash arrived, Lady Elizabeth kept postponing the confession that she expected to be brought to bed at the end of July. Somehow a spinster lady from Lyons seemed the wrong person to arrange a confinement on Ischia. On 7 July she confided in Louis, who having seen females of many species, including his wife at Toulon, in advanced stages of pregnancy, responded with alacrity. He took a letter to Lord Hervey and by the time they returned from Naples, they had concocted a plot as complex as any in Restoration comedy.[7]

Bess must leave Ischia. It was insane to think that a lady so conspicuous could drop a baby without its being known all over the island. Neapolitans came over for holidays. News would spread instantly to the mainland, thence post haste to Paris, London, Ickworth Park and Dublin. The only way was for Lord Hervey to announce that he was taking Lady Elizabeth on a protracted sailing excursion, which would lead them wherever the winds should blow. They, like the Earl-Bishop, were interested in classical antiquities, in which the sea coast towns abounded. While her brother returned to inform Lady Hervey and Eliza of the project, Bess broke the news to Miss Ash and her maid, whom she temporarily dismissed.

On 22 July Lord Hervey, Bess and Louis took a small boat, telling the sailors they wished to visit the neighbouring island of Procida. Even today when it boasts a first-class hotel, few people wish to stay on Procida more than a night or so. In 1784 it was no place to be confined in. They took one look and told the crew they had decided to go to Capri.

Lady Elizabeth had only the haziest idea when the baby was due. When a wind rose, she became distraught. The crew said it was impossible to make the cape of Sorrento. Lord Hervey comforted Lady Elizabeth between her bouts of seasickness. She was terrified that nausea would bring on her labour. All night they tossed, the prey to wind and wave. Dawn came at last and they put in at a little fishing village for 'refreshment and repose', before making for Marsa, where the Ischians were paid off.

Lord Hervey's plan was that Lady Elizabeth should pose as the wife of Louis, who would take her to a house of convenience, where Lord Hervey would visit as Louis' master. Since no valet would take his wife to such a place, the inference would be that Bess had been gotten with child by the master and wedded off to the valet. It was a drama which Lord Hervey may have enacted before in his amatory theatricals.[8]

Bess and Louis sailed for Salerno and travelled thence by *calèche* to Vietri, where they were deposited in the *piazza* because the streets leading to the squalid apartment of the '*Archiprêtre des Amoureux*' were too steep and narrow for a vehicle.[9] The Vietrans goggled at her beauty and no doubt giggled at where she was going. She had given her brother all her jewellery, including the medallion of the Duchess of Devonshire which she wore on a chain round her neck. She had also surrendered any documents which would identify her. She had refused to reveal the paternity of her child (an example of discretion Lord Hervey must have hoped would be imitated by any woman he got into a similar scrape). Although a perusal of Lady Elizabeth's journal would have revealed that the Duke of Devonshire was the father, I imagine that the whole bundle had been packaged and sealed with instructions that it should be delivered to the Duchess. The Vietrans do not seem to have recognized Lady Elizabeth's social position by her clothes, but this is not surprising when one realizes that Louis in his livery must have appeared to Italian peasants as a creature from another world and that ladies' maids dressed often in their mistresses' discarded clothes.

They climbed a narrow, dark and dirty staircase to an apartment where they found the *Archiprêtre*, his brother (a doctor), a number of women including the doctor's wife ('wicked, vulgar and horrible'), a woman servant, two young girls who, though pretty, cried all day, the nurse who was to take charge of Bess's child and a number of babies who screamed from morning till night.

Ladies travelling in the eighteenth century were inured to bugs, fleas, lice, rats, mice and the stench of ordure, human and animal. But the apartment taxed even the most hardened sensibilities. Lady Elizabeth reclined on a sofa and, pretending to know no Italian, listened to their comments. She was too delicately beautiful to be a valet's wife: must be his master's lady love. Her features were more royal than the Queen's. What modesty! What sweetness! Even in such squalor, her vanity was gratified. How humiliating if they had believed she was Louis' wife!

No baby had arrived, when her brother, 'dear Augustus', arrived two days later. He stayed a week. There was nothing to do except concoct letters about their supposed sailing excursions, which Augustus could send to Naples. From sheer boredom they invented a shipwreck, an adventure which might have led to questions which would have betrayed them.

When Augustus left, Lady Elizabeth gave him a letter. It was probably to be sent to the Duchess in the case of her death in childbirth, begging the Duchess to befriend her child. 'All my papers were in order,' she noted later. 'I waited patiently for death, regretting only my child, and its father and my friend.'

After two weeks, she was thinking of finding some refuge better than the 'archpriest's' stinkhole, when the pains came on. On 16 August at 9 a.m. after a brief labour she gave birth to a baby girl. The moment she held the babe, she 'felt only a mother's tenderness'.

Meanwhile, in London, the Duke wrote that 'Mrs Rat' was so big that she expected twins, one of which he insensitively suggested would be presented to Bess. Overcoming her hatred of London, Mama stayed at Devonshire House during the last weeks of her daughter's pregnancy. The Duke nipped up to Chatsworth, whence he wrote, 'I am terribly in want of you here, Mrs Bess, and am every minute reminded of the misfortune of your not being here by things that I see, such as the couch you us'd to sit on in the drawing room, admidst all your sighing lovers. The blue bed you slept in, and little Mr Phaon who is at grass in the park. I have some thoughts, if I have time, of going to Bolton to shoot upon the moors, and to prepare the place for you against next summer, for I intend to take you there, whether you like it or not, let the consequence be what it will.'[10]

When Bess received this letter, tender, affectionate, full of future promise, she was filled with resentment and self-pity because it ignored the agonies she had been enduring at the time it was written. In mid-September she heard that all the Duchess had produced in the comfort of Devonshire House was another girl.[11] She tried to bring home to the Duke what she had suffered at Vietri. His reply was complacent. No one could have been more uneasy than he had been for months, but knowing Bess's disposition to look on the worst side, he had thought it wise not to encourage her in exaggerating what with Cavendish phlegm he called 'any disagreeable circumstances'.[12]

In fact Lady Elizabeth was remarkably resilient. In an age when politicians wept in Parliament, it was natural to indulge every emotion. Motherly love urged her not to leave her baby, but the thought of Lady Bristol weeping at her daughter's shame persuaded her to part with the child. There were other reasons which she did not specify: acceptance by society, friendship with the Devonshires and dependence on their patronage. Six days after lying in, she left Vietri for Castella-mare. Though 'quivering and weary', she noted that the peasants would not believe her pretence of being Calabrian, because she was 'too beautiful and too fair'. Vanity was a powerful tonic

Danger of discovery had not been ended by the delivery of the baby, who was named Caroline Rosalie Adelaide, or Caro for short. Louis provided flannels for Lady Elizabeth to conceal her exuberant breasts. He fetched Caro (shamefully neglected at Vietri) and placed her with foster-parents in Naples. Bess took the risk of visiting her, as the 'protectress' of Louis' child. She ordered fine linen to be bought for the baby's chafed limbs. She arranged that Caro should be taken to rendez-vous where Bess could dismount and cradle her.[13] She even toyed with the idea of keeping Caro in Naples for as long as she herself stayed. She might have done so if she had not heard that the Earl-Bishop was on his way to Italy to convalesce from a severe bowel complaint. He was bringing in his train Lady Erne and Bess's younger brother Frederick. If they came to Naples, there was no telling what they might not ferret out between them. The Earl-Bishop might be an eccentric egoist, but he knew his topography and classical antiquities. He had visited the places they had pretended to. That shipwreck they had invented at Vietri might prove her undoing. Louis was given leave to visit his wife at Toulon; he took Caro with him.

The Duke was urging Lady Elizabeth to return to England in the spring and 'We don't allow of any coquetting at Paris on the way'. But a fortnight after parting from her darling Babe, Lady Elizabeth was coquetting in Naples. The Russian Ambassador was paying her violent court. 'Misfortune cannot cure me of my vanity,'[14] she sighed, as she parried his passion with proffered friendship. It was wrong, oh! very wrong. Yet wise! With gallants buzzing round her like wasps in the Neapolitan jamjar, who would suspect her love for the distant D. of D.?

By the end of November she began to feel secure. Only Augustus and Louis knew of Caro and no one knew the identity of Caro's father. On 8 December she ventured to delight Neapolitan society by playing the harpsichord at a concert. She was still sitting at the instrument when a footman brought a letter. It was from Frederick North, the nineteen-year-old son of the Earl of Guildford, another of her admirers. When she read that the nature of Louis' journey was known, she blenched, so faint she could read no further. Imagination pictured her ruin, her mother heartbroken, the Duke of Dorset contemptuous, the Devonshires estranged, the eclipse of her fair fame, ostracism from society.

She recovered enough to read on.

It was generally reported, Fred North wrote, that Louis had with him a baby girl, the love-child of Lord Hervey! This was not ruin but reassurance. John Augustus had no reputation to lose. If he was Caro's father, no one could be base enough to suggest that Bess was the mother.

Her reputation restored, she left her card on Georgiana's brother and sister-in-law, the Earl and Countess Spencer, when they arrived at Naples. She was not received but when the Countess returned the compliment, she *was* received and was introduced to the Ambassadress, Lady Hamilton. Bess wrote to the Duchess, 'Lady S., tho' she had never seen her before, address'd all her conversation to her, almost turn'd her back on poor me, and after a decent time went away without ever enquiring about my health, or saying a common civil thing to me.'[15] Lady Spencer, clearly, had an even lower opinion of Lady Elizabeth than of the Duke and Duchess of Devonshire. When they met again at the British Embassy a few days later, Lord Spencer behaved impeccably but Lady S. 'seem'd to raise herself three feet in order to look down on me'. However, Lady Elizabeth had the satisfaction of being able to tell the Countess that Lady Duncannon had been successfully brought to bed of a daughter on 12 November.* It was evidence that Lady Elizabeth was more intimate with the Earl Spencer's two sisters than the Countess was.

Through the early months Bess nursed her health in the Neapolitan sunshine. The Duke of Cumberland, the uncharming brother of King George III, arrived with his equally uncharming Duchess (née Anne Luttrell). 'He seems to be in love with me,' Bess noted; 'one cannot be suspected of encouraging him.' It was precisely what his Duchess did suspect; nor were her suspicions allayed when Lady Elizabeth also recruited 'Captain B. – clever, entertaining, extremely ugly and *guère dangereux*'.[16]

Lady Hervey was distressed when Lord Hervey turned his attention towards the beautiful young Princess Roccafionta. Lady Elizabeth owed

* Caroline Ponsonby, the future Lady Caroline Lamb.

her brother a debt of gratitude, so when the Earl-Bishop invited her to spend Holy Week in Rome, she accepted with alacrity. As the Earl-Bishop was politically suspect, he could not secure his heir a sinecure in the government or a place at Court, but he might be persuaded to increase his niggardly allowance.

Lady Elizabeth pleaded in vain: and when news came that Lord Hervey was coming to Rome to urge his cause in person, the Earl-Bishop fled the Holy City, taking with him Lady Erne, Frederick and the retinue of painters, sculptors and art critics whom he described as 'the clods I bring with me'.[17]

Lady Elizabeth had done her best and now she began a leisurely progress towards Spa, where it was planned she should rejoin the Devonshires. She had been reluctant to meet the dearest friend whom she had betrayed until she heard from the Duke: 'The Rat does not know the chief cause of your uneasiness and I, of course, shall never mention it to her unless you desire me, but I am certain if she did she could not think you had been to blame about it after I explained to her how it happened.'[18]

Her path passed through Cento, where the Earl-Bishop had ensconced himself. It would be discourteous not to visit him. But, when she called, the seventeen-year-old Frederick was sent with the message that her father would not see her, that the agitation of her presence under the same roof would precipitate a recurrence of his bowel complaint and she must leave at once. How much was illness? how much miserliness? Sir Horace Mann thought the latter. He wrote to Horace Walpole that the Earl-Bishop 'moves from place to place, to avoid his eldest son, whom he leaves in absolute distress at a time when he squanders vast sums in what he calls the Beaux Arts, though he only purchases the dregs of them'.[19]

The meeting did not take place at Spa. Mama insisted that the Duchess's place was with her daughters, little Lady Georgiana and the baby Lady Henrietta Cavendish. They went to stay at Compton Place, Eastbourne, while the Duke journeyed to Southampton to await the arrival of his dearest Bess.

'I landed with transport,' she confided to her journal. 'Alas, my heart, too fondly devoted to the D. of D., forgot all past sufferings and felt nothing but joy. My friend was at Southampton – I fear I was glad. I arrived – he had dined out but left a note; he came; Oh, heavens, such moments do not efface past sorrows! and yet it was happiness mixed with fear and agitation –'[20]

Georgiana, Countess Spencer
1737–1814

William, 5th Duke of
Devonshire, 1748–1811

Lavinia, Viscountess
Althorp, later 2nd
Countess Spencer
1762–1831

George, Viscount
Althorp, later 2nd Earl
Spencer 1756–1834

Henrietta Frances, Viscountess Duncannon, later 3rd Countess Bessborough with her two children

Lady Elizabeth Foster, later Elizabeth 5th Duchess of Devonshire 1759–1824

Frederick Hervey, Bishop
of Derry and 4th Earl of
Bristol 1730–1803

Georgiana, 4th Duchess of
Devonshire and her
daughter Lady Georgiana
Cavendish

John Augustus, Lord
Hervey 1757–1796

Georgiana canvassing in
the Westminster election

ABOVE: Thomas Coutts the banker
1734–1824

ABOVE RIGHT: Charles Grey, later
2nd Earl Grey 1764–1845

RIGHT: Harriet, Countess of
Bessborough at about the time she
met Granville

RIGHT: Lord Granville
Leveson-Gower 1773–1846

BELOW: 'Hary-O', Lady Harriet
Cavendish, later 1st Countess
Granville 1785–1862

ABOVE: William, 5th Duke of
Devonshire at the time of his
second marriage

RIGHT: Corisande de Grammont,
Viscountess Ossulton and later
5th Countess of Tankerville

Caro Ponsonby, later Lady Caroline Lamb 1785–1828

ABOVE: Cardinal Consalvi
1758–1824

ABOVE RIGHT: 'Hart', afterwards
6th Duke of Devonshire
1790–1858

RIGHT: 'Bess' in 1819

8

While Lady Elizabeth had been away, the Duchess's relations with her mother had grown worse. Freed from anxiety about her invalid husband, the Dowager Countess had more time for piety, good works, spying on her daughters and looking after her grandchildren. Mrs Sarah Trimmer, the friend of Dr Johnson and author of children's books, had started a Sunday School at Brentford in emulation of Robert Raikes and had instructed the Dowager Countess how to do likewise in St Albans.[1] Correspondents kept her posted with all the latest news about her progeny. From this scrutiny Lavinia emerged triumphant. She despised her mother-in-law as a stupid, interfering woman, but she toadied up to her whenever they met.

The Dowager's disapproval was reserved for her adoring, high-spirited daughters. The Duchess got into hot water with her mother when the Prince of Wales married Mrs Fitzherbert, bribing a curate imprisoned for debt with £500 and the vicarage at Twickenham.[2] What would Georgiana or Harriet do if they met Mrs F. at the Opera? The Duchess answered that she would treat Mrs Fitzherbert precisely as before: would invite her to large parties but not to small; not go with her to the Opera since she never had done so. But she would not have her plans altered by the Prince. She would keep out of town as much as possible, but 'I cannot entirely absent myself from London without the Duke's wishing it, for my being entirely away from him and his family cannot surely either in the eyes of the world or for my own happiness and interest be a desirable plan'.[3]

Lady Duncannon got into hotter water when she started to put Lady Melbourne's precepts into practice. She had given Harum a brace of sons and now she was having an affair which became a scandal.[4] Harum scolded. Harriet sulked. The newspapers rumoured that Lady Duncannon had run off with an unnamed *inamorato* and the Duncannons were compelled to show themselves together in public to prove the rumours false.

The Dowager was convinced that the centre of all this evil was Devonshire House. If only the Duchess could be forced into retirement, she would have no temptation to gamble, Harriet would have no place of assignation, the Duke would produce an heir and Lady E. would have nowhere to go when she returned from Europe. It was all as simple as the ABC, the Lord's Prayer or a sermon by Blair.

Today 'the generation gap' is an accepted idea. In 1787 it was yawning, but the Dowager Countess could not recognize it. Her *idées reçues* were Divine Revelation. The Duchess and Lady Duncannon, as dutiful daughters, wished that they were, but, as ladies of the *ton*, knew they were not. They had to keep their two worlds in balance: on one side God, Heaven or Hell, on the other the world, debts, love and duty.

In 1785, three months before she was brought to bed, the Duchess had written to Lady Elizabeth, 'The Eyebrow [Fox] has made a general rout amongst my lovers, tho' I have a new one, whom I admire but am not in love with, tho' I think a very dangerous person, from being a very amiable one.'[5] The 'new one' was the twenty-one-year-old Charles Grey, the eldest surviving son of General Sir Charles Grey who had just come down from Cambridge and attached himself to Charles James Fox as a disciple. He was to be famous in history as the second Earl Grey, the Prime Minister who passed the Reform Bill of 1832. But in 1785 he was a brilliant, handsome young man whose admiration for Fox led to an infatuation with the Duchess who the year before had won for his idol the Westminster Election. Of all her admirers, Grey was the only one with whom the Duchess fell in love. He and she were removed from temptation when he was attached to the suite of the Duke of Cumberland for travel in Europe (Lady Elizabeth must have met him when the Cumberlands came to Naples in early 1776) and the Duchess did not see him again until his return the following year when he was elected MP for Northumberland, the county in which his father had his residence. From then on he became a frequent, and to the Duke unwelcome, guest at Devonshire House. When Lady Elizabeth returned to London at the end of July, she must have felt consoled at Charles Grey's presence. It would have indicated to her that by becoming the Duke's mistress she had not deprived her dearest friend of love.

Charles Grey was not the only friend whom the Duchess had made during Lady Elizabeth's absence. There was also the banker Thomas Coutts, to whom she had been introduced by 'Fish' Craufurd. Coutts, born in 1735, was old enough to be her father. A Scotsman of the trading class, he had opened a 'Banker's Shop' in the Strand in partnership with his elder brother, whom he had later bought out. He was a shrewd businessman, with a streak of wild romanticism. The romanticism had showed itself when he married his brother's serving-maid, a folly no ambitious man should commit. By her he had three daughers, whom those who wanted to borrow money from Coutts called the Three Graces. He had, alas! no son to carry on the business which he foresaw would exist, as it does, long after his day. He had become the banker to HRH King George III and Keeper of the Privy Purse. But the Prince of Wales, the future King George IV, had taken his overdraft elsewhere. Coutts was afraid that, when the Prince succeeded, the Banker in the Strand would lose not merely the Royal patronage but the aristocratic clientele which followed. One reason why Coutts begged 'Fish' Craufurd for an introduction to the Duchess was that she was notoriously close to the Prince of Wales. Another was that Mrs Coutts, charming and loyal though she was, was the last person on earth who could introduce the Three Graces to the nobs whom he could buy as husbands. He had to find an aristocratic patroness: and there was no one as *tonnish* and broke as the Duchess of Devonshire. Only third came the reason that is usually put first: he found the Duchess delightfully free from the snootiness of most of his noble clients suffering from pocket-cramp. As a banker, he resented being regarded as an usurer. The Duchess treated him as a father.[6]

We do not know exactly when they met. But the first letter surviving from their correspondence is dated 1786. The Duchess was an 'instant' friend, so it may have been written the day after they met. The Duchess wanted advice on how to invest £400 'for an absent person'. Only £100 of this was immediately available, but the remainder was expected daily. Could Mr Coutts buy the most beneficial stock and not mention it even to her 'best friend Mr Craufurd'? Mr Coutts was only too willing to oblige. How easily Her Grace had swallowed the bait!

Late on the night of 12 March 1787 the Duchess penned a long, unhappy letter (again begging that Mr Craufurd should not be told). The Duke had stepped forth to arrange her affairs. But she found herself four thousand guineas above the amount allotted. A thousand guineas of that was already owing to Coutts. Could he advance the remaining three thousand for a year from that date? She enclosed the £100 stock he had bought for her. 'I had appropriated it for the establishment of a child whose parents were related to me, but it must be better days before I can renew this purpose.'

Canny old Coutts was caught. He had lent a thousand guineas to the Duchess without security and without the knowledge of the Duke. If he refused to advance another three thousand, the Duchess would be offended and would not further Coutts's business with the Prince of Wales or take the three Misses Coutts under her protection. He could not recover by law the money he had lent. The Duke could deny the responsibility and it would ruin the Banker's Shop in the Strand if Coutts took the Duchess to court.

The Duchess may have been reckless in extravagance and the Duke reluctant to bother about anything as sordid as money, but between them they were a dodgy couple. Two years before, Martindale had been pressing for payment of the Duchess's notes of hand. On the advice of the Duke and Bess, the Duchess had handled negotiations herself, threatening Martindale with the awful rage of the Duke if he became embroiled. 'I had a tolerable letter from Martindale,' she had told Mama. 'We are certain of paying but 10, and, I hope, only six. *Voila quinze mille de gagné.*'[7] By her arithmetic, the reduction of a debt from £21 000 to £6000 was a *gain* of £15 000. In a similar way, when by July 1787 she had raised the total of her unsecured debt with Coutts to £7000, she wrote to Mama, 'I am very rich now' and sent her £20 to be distributed charitably in Brighton.[8]

In return for the banker's generosity the Duchess had already despatched letters of introduction for Susannah and Sophia Coutts[*] who were going to Paris to further their education. The Duchesse de Polignac would no doubt be happy to see them at Versailles. In Paris, among the valuable introductions for two young ladies being groomed for the marriage market, were letters to the Maréchal de Biron, the Duchesse de la Vallières and the celebrated Mme de Genlis.[9]

The only chance Coutts saw of safeguarding his money was to make the Duchess promise to borrow from no one but him. This she did readily enough, though by January 1788 she was in debt to her Derbyshire neighbour, Sir Richard Arkwright, inventor of the spinning frame, to the tune of £4239 3s.[10] In the thirteen years of her marriage, the Duchess had not lost her charm and naturalness, but she had gained in cunning and mendacity. She confided in Lady Elizabeth, but chiefly what she wanted to be relayed to the Duke.

When Lady Elizabeth returned to England, she confined her journal to cursory notes. She met Lady Melbourne and liked her, perceiving

[*] Susannah was born in 1771, Sophia in 1775. Fanny, the middle daughter (b. 1773) was kept at home for the time being, because her health was frail.

that Lady M. could be useful as a friend and a source of intelligence. She had a flirtation with General Fitzpatrick, which provoked the Duke to jealousy. But after a lover's tiff they came closer together than ever. She tried to placate the Dowager Countess, writing to apologize for any apprehension she might have caused by a recent illness and adding that dear little Georgiana on her lap was 'laughing and amusing herself as usual'. The Dowager was worried, not by Lady Elizabeth's ill-health, but by her very existence. She refused to stay under the same roof as Lady E. and spent months at Chatsworth dandling little Georgiana on *her* lap.

The moment Mama left, Bess joined the Devonshires in Derbyshire. She found the Duke half-persuaded that it would be wise to rusticate the Duchess, having realized that Georgiana's feelings towards Charles Grey were as sensual as his towards Lady Elizabeth. The Duchess's brother, Lord Spencer, offered to give her a home at Althorp, but the thought of living with the malicious, foul-mouthed Lavinia was too much. If she had to part from the Duke, the Duchess insisted, let her go to Mama at St Albans.

It was a shrewd move. If the Duke wanted to get rid of her, then he would have to give up Bess; or to put it more strongly, Bess would have to give up the Duke. And who else would pay for her to live in a manner befitting an Earl-Bishop's daughter? Lady Elizabeth recalled the Duke to their common purpose, the necessity of producing an heir. '*Depository of both their thoughts, I have sought, when her imprudences have alienated him, to restore him to her, and when my heart has mourned over her avowal of his returning caresses, I have checked and corrected the sensation.*'[11] I have italicized this extract from her journal because it encapsulates her character and her rôle. James Hare, even though he was attracted to Bess and became an ally in her schemes, told the Duchess some years later that nothing would ever induce him to say that Lady Elizabeth was not affected, though it had become so much second nature that it suited her. Stripped of genteel affectation, this extract could read: 'Both the Duke and the Duchess confided in me. When the Duke told me that he was so infuriated by the Duchess's extravagances that he felt he could not go on living with her, I pointed out that unless he was prepared to let the title and estates pass to his brother Lord George he had to beget an heir by the Duchess: and when the Duchess told me that the Duke had resumed sexual intercourse, I as his mistress was upset but suppressed my feelings.'

Eighteenth-century language was more oblique than ours, especially among ladies. But what Lady Elizabeth was writing was not a private journal to be read by herself alone. It was an intimate document, intended to be shared with her two dearest friends. If one re-reads the sentence above, its phrasing reveals diplomatic subtlety. The Duchess herself confessed to imprudences and, at least at times, considered that the Duke's coldness was due to his moral disapproval rather than sexual incompatability. In thawing the Duke's frigidity to the Duchess, Bess was acting as Georgiana's friend. In mourning her success, she was attesting her love for Canis. In checking and correcting the sensation, she was recognizing that her personal feeling must be subordinated to the interests of them all, including little Georgiana Cavendish (and, as the Duke would realize, also Caroline Rosalie Adelaide).

At Chatsworth, that late summer, there was a comparatively small party, of which Lady Elizabeth was the life and soul. Sheridan, to her dismay, taxed her with being in love with the Duke. General Fitzpatrick was his witty, flirtatious self. James Hare* called Lady Elizabeth's bluff by saying in front of everybody, 'I wish you would fall in love with me.' It was so out of tune with their arch innuendos that the others were shocked until he said, 'Tell me, because I must be in town the 29th.'[12]

While Lady Elizabeth strove for 'togetherness', Mama continued to press for separation. What about the Duchess retiring to Londesborough House? If she lived there, there could be no gossip about her parting from the Duke. But the Duchess fought back. She *would* be parted from the Duke, unless he could live at Londesborough House with her. But he had to be in London for the Warren Hastings trial; in Bath for his gout, at Chatsworth and Hardwick for the hunting and Bolton Abbey for the shooting. And *she* had to be in London to settle her debts. The solution was not Rustication, but Retrenchment. By then she had tapped Coutts as a new source of credit; and retrenchment was whittled down to the dismissal of two men servants.

Meanwhile Lady Elizabeth added a third Duke, His Grace of Richmond, to her retinue of admirers. Learning from him that Sir Horace Mann was retiring from the British Ministry at Florence, she secured the post, worth £3000 a year, for her brother Lord Hervey in August 1787.[13] The debt incurred for services rendered at the birth of Caro two years before was thus repaid.

---

* James Hare was MP for Ludgershall in the Duke of Devonshire's interest. He was described by Sir Augustus Clifford as 'the tallest, thinnest man I ever saw: his face like a surprised cockatoo, and as white'.

That same month the Duke of Devonshire fulfilled his promise to take Bess to Bolton Abbey for the shooting. For three weeks the Duke and his two ladies were alone together. Perhaps the Duchess could conceive again. She did not.

On 26 August Lady Elizabeth went south again to stay with her mother at Ickworth Park. While there she recognized the symptoms of pregnancy. This time she took no chances. A doctor in London confirmed her fears. She wrote guardedly to the Duke, who replied inviting her to her 'warm room' at Chatsworth. There she would be 'safer from catching cold than going down to Drury Lane Theatre with the coach glasses down'.[14] She accepted with alacrity. The time had come for a showdown. The Duke must reveal the existence of Caroline Rosalie Adelaide and this second misfortune.

The news came as no surprise to the Duchess. She must have been pleased to be told what she already knew. She had accepted Charlotte Williams, an awkward child. Caroline was altogether different. The same age as little Harriet, or 'Hary-O' as she had nicknamed herself, Caroline would be an ideal playmate if anything, which God forbid, happened to Bess in her misfortune. The Duchess would cherish her as a child of her own.

Georgiana was naturally generous. But in welcoming the Duke's daughter by her dearest friend she may have hoped that this acceptance would help them both to do their duty and produce an heir. The three of them went to Bath, taking with them the Ladies Georgiana and Harriet and their nurse, Mrs Smith.

Now that there were no secrets between them, Lady Elizabeth emerged openly as their planner. Perhaps thinking that the presence of the children at Bath was inhibiting, she suggested that the Duke and Duchess should accompany her abroad when she went south, 'as if for her health' but actually to avoid detection of her pregnancy. The Duchess wrote to Mama that the sea voyage and the change of climate might encourage her breeding.* The Dowager Countess smelt a rat and when the Duke was forced to remain in London for the Warren Hastings trial, she became still more suspicious. The Duchess still wanted to go abroad with Bess, saying in one sentence that it would be a great *comfort* to her and in the next reiterating that the sea voyage might occasion her *breeding* (even though the Duke was staying at home!).

* Though Lady Elizabeth was far too delicate to say openly that the Duchess might conceive if in some French posthouse all three of them shared the same bed, the two ladies may have considered the possibility.

Georgiana's desire to be with Bess had a secret purpose. Having made the existence of Caro known to the Duchess, Lady Elizabeth wanted them to meet 'just in case'. But Mama had her way. The Devonshires got no further with Lady Elizabeth than Dover. To part from the Duchess, wrote Bess, was 'bitterness of grief'. As for the Duke, 'his last embrace – his last look drew my soul after him. . . . Oh, why could I not love him without crime? why cannot I be his without sin? My soul was made for virtue and not for vice.'[15] It was a passage which she may have given the Duke to read twenty-one years later, when he was reluctant to do what she considered his duty.

Freed from the dithering Devonshires, Lady Elizabeth behaved with expedition. She had sacked her maid in England. In Calais she hired Lucille, a pretty young woman who, having been abandoned by her husband, could sympathize with a lady in misfortune. They made south, avoiding Paris and the Duke of Dorset. At Lyons Lady Elizabeth took Lucille into her confidence. Five weeks were spent in Marseilles, receiving 'distinctions, attentions, marks of regard'.[16] A Comte de St Jules, who had an estate at Aiguesmortes near Aix-en-Provence, consented to give his surname to the as yet anonymous Caroline Rosalie Adelaide, a little Protestant girl in whom the Duchess of Devonshire was interested. In March Lady Elizabeth removed to Bordeaux, where she was unknown. In April, there was a quick trip to Toulon to see her 'Sweetest Innocence' and arrange that Louis and his wife should take 'Mlle Caroline *St Jules*' to spend the summer at Sorège before her going to school in Paris with a family called Nagel.*

Lady Elizabeth had originally planned to return to England for her lying-in. But she was met at Dieppe by Dr G., presumably the physician who had confirmed her pregnancy in London the previous year. The Duke of Devonshire had left London in order to avoid suspicion: but it was considered too risky for one so well known as Lady Elizabeth to have her baby in England. Dr G. found her rooms in Rouen, introduced her to a doctor as his 'niece', and on 26 May, after three hours' labour, she was delivered of 'a dear, dear little boy whom I pray God to preserve'. In naming him there was none of the furtiveness there had been about Caroline Rosalie Adelaide. The future Admiral, Baronet and Gentleman Usher of the Black Rod was called Augustus after his uncle Lord Hervey, William after his father, James after James Hare,

* James Hare, who was in Paris and had been told about Caroline and Lady Elizabeth's new expectation, probably made the arrangements with the Nagels. The stay at Sorège was necessary to establish Caroline in her surname of 'St Jules'.

and surnamed Clifford after the barony which the fourth Duchess had brought into the Devonshire family. He was left in the care of a foster mother in Normandy.

'I have heard nothing of that abominable Scimia,' the Duke of Dorsct complained to the Duchess of Devonshire. 'She is playing her monkey tricks, *perdu dans quelque coin*'.[17] He had mail for Lady Elizabeth, which he hoped she would collect from him in person. But it was not long before he heard that she was staying with her mother at Ickworth Park and, by July 1788, she was back at Devonshire House, sorting out the mess that had accumulated during her absence and planning for the future.

9

Lady Elizabeth had strengthened her position during her absence. Caro St Jules had been recognized by the Duchess and was launched on a course which her mother was determined would end in Devonshire House, though she did not yet see how that was to be accomplished. James Hare had been enlisted as an ally in Paris, who could come to the aid of both the children if necessary. Augustus Clifford, the Duke's only male issue, was fostered in Normandy, either by Lucille or some recommended trustworthy woman. The next step was for the Duke to meet his natural children. This would be best arranged by a trip abroad via Paris to Spa, where the Duchess was convinced she would be able to breed.

But in the meantime the Dowager Countess's hatred of Lady Elizabeth had become still more intense, perhaps because she knew or guessed about Caro and Augustus Clifford. The Duchess begged Mama's sympathy for Lady Elizabeth who had suffered a terrible attack of illness for which the Duchess prescribed 'a chicken's gut clyster'.[1] But the bowels of Mama's compassion were not moved. 'You know how anxious I am to make you happy, and to show my regard and gratitude to the Duke. . . . I always avoid naming Lady E.F., and if anybody is injudicious enough to mention her name to me, I endeavour to give such answers as will show them I am determined not to enter into the subject. My behaviour was not premeditated, it arose at Chatsworth out of scenes I was unfortunate enough to be witness to.'[2]

Mama's conspicuous avoidance of discussing Lady Elizabeth did nothing to stop the gossip about the Duke and his two ladies. How could Lady Elizabeth be the mistress of the Duke and the dearest friend of the Duchess? It appeared to be too monstrous to be true but at the same time impossible not to be true. If only Mama could be seen to accept Lady E., some of the scandal could be silenced, because the Dowager Countess would never countenance impropriety. Somehow or other the Dowager must be forced to act as hostess to Lady Elizabeth.

The Dowager had one weakness. She was worried about the moral welfare of her granddaughters, the Ladies Georgiana and Harriet Cavendish. Little G. was coming up for five, ready to leave the nursery for the schoolroom. The Dowager suggested in August 1788 that a suitable person to take over from Mrs Smith would be Miss Selina Trimmer, a daughter of Mrs Sarah Trimmer* of Brentford, well received by the Royal Family when they were staying across the river at Kew. The suggestion hung fire for some months, partly because Miss Selina's health precluded her taking a permanent post immediately. But there was also the driving of a bargain. If Mama wanted to have Miss Trimmer in the Devonshire nursery, then she must receive Lady Elizabeth at least once in Holywell House. When Mama gave way, the Duchess thanked her and forswore her honour. 'I give you my honour, my Dearest M., that I should not be thus anxious if I did not know all her merits, and *if I was not certain of her virtue as my own*† I would not press you to grant this satisfaction.'³

Her standards were crumbling. Despite the loans from Coutts, her debts snowballed, and there was as always no hope of repaying the principal until she produced an heir. Borrowing money to pay interest on what she had already borrowed drove her near wits' end. Bess kept the Duke informed of all she was told. He took no notice. Let Mrs Rat get out of the hole she had made herself.

In September 1788 the Duchess invited M. de Calonne and his wife to Chatsworth. Calonne had been Controller General of Finance in France, but had been ousted by Jacques Necker, and had chosen exile in England until the tide turned. He accepted the invitation with pleasure. The Devonshire connection was valuable. Through the Duke of Dorset, the Duchess received bulletins on the general situation in France; Mme de Polignac (or 'little Po' as Dorset called her) described how Marie Antoinette saw matters, and Charles Fox was in touch with the anti-Royalists.

The Duke took a liking to the Calonnes and the Calonnes a liking to the Duchess. The Duchess sat talking with Mme de Calonne, who 'without being bright' was 'so good and well meaning that she must please', while the ex-Finance Minister wrote letters 'so full of eloquence they wd delight even more than his study'd works'.⁴ Like Fox, he could

---

* Mrs Trimmer's *Story of the Robins* had appeared in 1785 with a dedication to Princess Sophie, the fifth daughter of King George III.

† My italics.

talk about anything. Even better, he could listen. The Duchess opened her heart to him. Despite her gaiety with her husband, children and dear Bess, she was often tormented. Calonne was flattered to be made the confidant of a duchess, so famous, so charming, so sad; and to be thanked for assistance, rendered by merely listening. When he left for Wimbledon, where he had taken a house near the Spencers', Her Grace begged a favour. Her debts (amounting, alas! to £9000) had been disclosed to Mr Coutts. Could M. de Calonne advance Lady Duncannon £500 (coming as if from the Duchess) until the Duchess returned to London?[5] Used to handling the finances of France, Calonne thought nothing of such a trifle: and a few weeks later the Calonnes were back at Chatsworth. The ex-Finance Minister had swallowed the bait and was on the hook.

In October 1788 a crisis occurred for which Coutts had been preparing. The year before, he had written to Charles Fox offering him financial assistance. Fox was frank. 'It is necessary to inform you that in case of my death you would have no security for repayment, and, even if I should live long, a very precarious and uncertain one.'[6] Undeterred Coutts advanced £5000. It was tacitly a bribe for unspecified services to be rendered.

In the spring of 1788 the King fell ill with what he told Pitt was 'a pretty smart bilious attack'. The doctors were baffled when his condition did not improve and, despite the King's moderation in food and drink, they diagnosed the gout and recommended in July that he should drink the purgative waters of Cheltenham. That same month, Coutts lent Fox a further £5000.[7]

In October the fashionable physician Sir George Baker was called in to treat the King for a bewildering variety of complaints; hives, stomach ache, spasms, cramp, swollen feet, bile and rambling speech (to say nothing of the despatch of a blank cheque to Mrs Siddons). Sir George advised the King not to attend a *levée* and sold £18000 worth of stocks. This started a financial panic and sent gilt-edged securities down 10 per cent. 'To stop further lies and any fall in the stocks,' the King did attend the *levée*. His dress was not adjusted. He 'exhibited strong proofs of absence and oblivion' and told Lord Thurlow, 'You suppose me ill, beyond recovery. But, whatever you and Mr Pitt may feel, I, that am born a gentleman, shall never lay my head on my last pillow in peace and quiet so long as I remember the loss of the American colonies.'[8]

Coutts had been in Paris since the beginning of October. He was worried about his daughters. Few of the ladies to whom the Duchess

had given letters of introduction had received the girls. Mme Dauben-
ton, in whose care they had been put, proved an undesirable character.
General Moss, who had promised to stand *in loco parentis*, asked to
resign his charges to the Duke of Dorset. Though Coutts had intended
staying only a week, by mid-November he had not managed to secure
the entry of the girls to Penthémont, the fashionable Benedictine
convent. The news of the King's malady alarmed him. 'If the King
dies, I lose a good friend,' he wrote to the Duchess, 'but I am in hopes
I may still be employ'd by his successor, for I was his *first* banker and
he has always approved my conduct. I should wish Your Grace would
speak to the Prince in case the melancholy event proves true. My house
is so much interested in being continued banker to the King's Privy
Purse at least, if not to other branches of his employ. . . . Mr Fox, I
believe, Your Grace will find much my friend, and I beg you to consult
with him upon it.'[9]

The Duchess could not consult Charles Fox because he was in Italy.
She herself had first heard of the King's 'insanity' at Chesterfield during
the celebrations of the centenary of the Glorious Revolution on 5
November. If the King went out of his mind who would take his place?
Queen Charlotte? The Prince of Wales? Or both as co-regents? The
Duke of Portland urged the Devonshires to return immediately to
London for political consultations; but the Duke of Devonshire wanted
to visit Buxton,* and they did not reach Devonshire House until 19
November.[10] The prospect of a regency had precipitated a political crisis
and Parliament was adjourned for a fortnight. If the Prince could secure
a *sole* regency *with full powers* to appoint his own ministers, the Foxite
Whigs hoped to oust Pitt and enjoy the fruits of office.

On 20 November the Duchess began her journals of the King's Illness,
covering its progress until 12 January 1789. One was a day-book which
she kept for her mother. The other was 'a kind of incoherent journal',
in the words of Sichel, who published a conflation of both in Appendix
III of his *Sheridan*. This incoherent journal may have been notes for
Thomas Coutts, partly as a sort of interest on the money she had
borrowed and partly in the hope of more to come. She had already
touched Calonne for £2000, but the way the duns were pressing, that
would not last for long.

The Duchess gleaned every item of gossip. For example: on his

---

* In 1784 the Duchess mentioned £30 000 having been spent by Heaton on the
Crescent there: it was one of the various developments by which Heaton increased the
Devonshire fortune.

return from the *levée*, the King 'shew'd his backside to his attendants saying that he had not the gout. He pull'd off Sir George Baker's wig and made him go upon his knees to look at the stars; he begins by beating the palms of his hands, then crying and then howling; he got naked out of bed but Cl Digby threaten'd him back. – As Dr Warren had been the first who had been severe with him; he often says, "Don't speak out loud for Dr Warren will hear you."

'The Courtiers pretend it is nothing; and it is a fashion among them to say that they have been all mad: Lord Fauconberg declares everybody must remember his strait waistcoat. Mr Robinson the same, and Lord Salisbury declares that the King has as much understanding as he has.'*[11]

The King was not, in fact, insane, but suffering from porphyria, an hereditary disease which was not identified until the twentieth century.[12] Lunacy in the eighteenth century was regarded as a joke by the sane. But the Duchess's uncharacteristic delight in the unfortunate King's malady was obviously the product of partisanship. If the Prince became regent, Charles Fox would come into his own.

Her judgement, like Fox's, was wrong. The Prince would have retained the Pitt ministry and Coutts need not have feared for the Keepership of the Privy Purse. Perhaps it was best for the Duchess that the King recovered in January 1789. She had proved herself willing to help, even if she had accomplished nothing. She could at least pride herself that the Misses Coutts had danced at one of the British Ambassador's assemblies, where Mme de Polignac had been 'particularly attentive to them'.[13] It was not as good as going to Versailles and meeting the Queen. But by now the Duke of Dorset had seen to it that at Penthémont they should share the same *gouvernante* as his nieces, the Ladies Caroline and Elizabeth Tufton.

The Duke still wanted to know nothing of the Duchess's debts. Lady Elizabeth was anxious only to advance her plan for visiting Paris and Spa. Their departure was fixed for some time after the King's birthday, 4 June. Bess had placed Caro with the Nagels in Paris and she had the brilliant idea that Charlotte Williams, who had proved disappointing at Mrs Belvoir's, should also go to the Nagels to be finished off. It would make it so much easier for them all to see little Caro without their visiting being too obtrusive. James Hare, who was in Paris, had visited Caro in Sorège and would arrange for Augustus

---

* In *The Royal Malady* Charles Chevenix Trench examines the Duchess's journal and finds it full of spiteful stories without foundation in fact.

Clifford to be brought from Normandy to Paris. Lady Elizabeth was a foresighted planner.

The Duchess could never see further than the next disaster, which would loom up suddenly like an iceberg out of an Atlantic fog. April was a cruel month in 1789. In answer to a request for a further £6000, Thomas Coutts wrote her a very long letter, which took him five days to compose. He had sworn to keep his transactions secret from everyone, but he had been compelled to consult Mrs Coutts. Her future and those of the three buddingly beautiful Misses Coutts might be wrecked by the improvidence the Duchess requested. Mrs Coutts (no doubt after discussing fully how useful the Duchess could be as a friend and how dangerous as an enemy) thought Mr Coutts should lend Her Grace the money. 'But how can I?' he asked the Duchess, 'with justice to her and my children, especially having as late as last summer given away £10000 in another way?* It is really *romance* what I have done with the money already. . . . Besides, tho' you say it will *save you*, how does it appear that the second £6000† will succeed (in this charming purpose) better than the first; and if not, what satisfaction will ultimately arise from it to me or to Y^r Grace?'

Coutts was not convinced by the Duchess's 'sanguine idea' that the Devonshires could save money by visiting Paris and Spa that summer. Why not better, a year economically at Geneva or Berne? Two years happily at Chatsworth? (As if anyone could spend a winter beneath the Derbyshire Peak when all the *ton* was in town! And what about the Duke's gout?) Why couldn't Lord Spencer give his bond for the second £6000? (As if Lavinia would agree!) It was a tiresome letter, not to say impertinent. Coutts even ended by suggesting, as Calonne had, that she should tell the Duke. Why could His Grace not give his bond for the whole £12000? Probably, before she read through this tendentious nonsense, the Duchess assured herself that Coutts had given instructions to the Banker's Shop in the Strand for her to borrow £6000 more, making £12000 in all, equivalent to her allowance for the next six years.[14]

* The £10 000 was probably the £5000 given to Fox in 1787, plus the £5000 in July 1788. If he had given the correct dates, the Duchess would have realized to whom the money had gone, and that they were freely offered bribes. Though the same was true of the 'loans' to her, he did not want her to realize it.

† Before she borrowed her first £2000 from Calonne she admitted to owing Coutts £9000. But in April she owed only £6000. I do not know whether she had repaid £3000 to Coutts to soften him up for borrowing twice that amount: or whether she exaggerated her loan from Coutts to make her request for £2000 to Calonne appear a less extortionate sum.

This was not enough. A week later she borrowed 'the other £2000' from Calonne, who was advising or threatening that the Duke should be told. 'If I become pregnant,' she assured him, 'I would not hesitate to tell the Duke everything since the birth of a son would probably be the end of all our embarrassments.'[15]

Any actuary would know that after fifteen years of marriage the probability of a pregnancy was small and if the Duchess became pregnant, the chance was even that the child would be a girl. But he took the risk. The Duke was prodigiously rich and Calonne was gambling on a return to power. The Duchess in Paris and Spa could provide him with political intelligence which might be intercepted if it came from agents more suspect.

James Hare seems to have been less in Georgiana's confidence than Bess's. In May he wrote to the Duchess, 'If I believe that you really would be here this month, I should not stay, for I lead a life so unlike yours that I might as well be at Constantinople. Neither my nerves nor spirits are equal to French society, and the very idea of a flock of young Frenchmen, as you and Ly Elizabeth will be surrounded by, throws me into a fever. I have not the least curiosity to see the Court of France, but am quite satisfied with having a good view of the Queen and knowing that she is one of the most disagreeable looking women in the world, as I always imagined her one of the worst.'[16]

Nothing Hare did or said could be taken quite seriously. He did not want to be dragged off to see 'little Po' or 'Mrs Brown' as they called Marie Antoinette. He was on the same side of the barricades as Charles Fox. But he was waiting for the Duke, the Duchess, Lady Elizabeth and Charlotte Williams, when they arrived in Paris in June.

None of them foresaw what was to come. Seven months before they had celebrated the Glorious Revolution of 1688: and they saw the clash between the *tiers état* and Louis XVI as a repetition, at best of the overthrow of James II by William of Orange and their own Whig ancestors, at worst of the Civil War between the Cavaliers and the Roundheads. Their political sympathies lay with parliamentarians, which was how they regarded the States General, which Necker had recalled: but they hoped some sort of composition with the monarchy could be reached. Hare had written of a procession in which the King and his brother the Duc d'Orléans had been applauded very much, while 'the Queen walked by in a dead silence, by which I mean to say, in the greatest noise I ever heard, but without hearing her own name mentioned'.[17] He favoured the continuation of the Bourbon dynasty, perhaps with

Louis XVI abdicating in favour of the Duc d'Orléans. He considered that Marie Antoinette and her favourite Mme de Polignac were responsible for the plight in which the feeble Louis XVI found himself. But the Duchess and Lady Elizabeth were bound to Mrs Brown and little Po by ties of personal friendship. The Duchess admired the Queen of France as a compeer of Fashion whose devoted love to little Po was a close parallel to hers for Bess. Lady Elizabeth had a further interest. She had enlisted the protection of the Duchesse de Polignac for Mlle Caroline Rosalie Adelaide de St Jules.

Interlude Two

The fourteen months (June 1789–August 1790) which the Duke and his two ladies were to spend in France and Belgium puzzled his contemporaries and have bewildered biographers ever since. Why should the Duchess of Devonshire choose to go to France on the eve of the French Revolution? Why, having conceived at Spa, should she remain in Belgium, to which the revolution had spread by then, instead of returning to her native country? And why at the last moment should the whole family uproot themselves from Brussels and make for Paris for the lying-in?

Their behaviour appeared so suspicious that some people conjectured that it was not the Duchess, but Lady Elizabeth who was pregnant. Others thought they both were pregnant and if Lady Elizabeth produced a boy and the Duchess a girl, the babies would be swapped so that the Duke could claim an heir. In one form or another, these rumours circulated for the next century and a half.

In fact, as the next chapter will show, their behaviour was determined by Lady Elizabeth's grand strategy to introduce Caro St Jules as a member of the Devonshire household. The vacillations were caused by the variation in tactics necessary to accomplish that end.

But the question still remains: why should they undertake an operation so dangerous? They were intimate with Calonne, who had been dismissed because he was regarded as the creature of Marie Antoinette, and with her friend and political adviser the Duchesse de Polignac. They had been kept abreast of French politics by the English Ambassador, the Duke of Dorset, and James Hare. There had been a rebellion in the Dauphiné which had only been 'suppressed' by Jacques Necker's legalizing the assembly and summoning the States General to Versailles in May 1789.

But by May the Devonshires had already laid their plans to take Charlotte Williams to join Caro St Jules in Paris and they sensed no danger to themselves. Revolution was not a menacing idea. The Glorious Revolution had deposed the Catholic King James II with the minimum of bloodshed and secured great fortunes for Whigs as rewards for their support of William of Orange. The Americans had had a revolution with which the Whigs had sympathized also, and had founded a republic. It was a civilized way of government, blessed by the ancient Greeks and Romans.

The Duchess of Devonshire and Lady Elizabeth were personal friends of Marie Antoinette and the Duchesse de Polignac. But politically the Duchess, if not Lady Elizabeth, sided with Fox and Hare against the *ancien regime*.* The French theorists, Voltaire, Diderot and especially Rousseau, appeared very convincing. Even Tom Paine's *Commonsense* and *Crisis Papers* had a splendid ring to those who admired eloquence and the cause in which it was used. Since George III abominated Charles Fox, Fox and his followers wanted to espouse the cause of the People against the King, first in France and then, by example, in the United Kingdom. Their sort of revolution was a very gentlemanly thing.

Even so, why were the Devonshires not alarmed by the mob violence which they encountered in Versailles, Paris, Brussels and elsewhere? The answer is simple. A great deal of the violence came from hungry people seizing by force food they lacked money to buy. Throughout the years that the Duchess, Charles Fox and other friends of the people had lost at faro in an hour more than most working people earned in a lifetime, there had been in England countless riots, burning of ricks, breaking of machinery, plundering of granaries and looting of shops. Yet the violence had always been contained. In 1780 the most violent mob outburst of the century had been headed by Lord George Gordon to protest against a bill to relieve Roman Catholics of some of the disabilities laid upon them. For a week London had been terrorized by a burning, looting mob composed at the outset of fanatic Protestants, but soon joined by every rogue, vagabond and almost every convict in London.

Charles Dickens told of that fearful week in *Barnaby Rudge* and Christopher Hibbert more soberly in *King Mob*. Newgate Prison was

* Three years later, when Marie Antoinette was still alive but in prison, the Duchess told her elder daughter that there were four types of government in Europe: the Despotick as in Turkey, the Monarchial such as was in France, the Aristocratical as in Venice and the Democratical as in Switzerland. 'The English government is reckoned the happyest of all,' she wrote, 'being composed of the three last.' Her views in 1789 were probably less precise. She was able to combine an affection for the Queen with intellectual sympathy for 'the People'.[1]

stormed and three hundred prisoners were released. Wine vaults were raided. Drunken gangs ranged the streets in search of Papists and plunder. Bridewell Prison was stormed so easily that it did not have to be burned and the jailers threw open the doors of the New Prison in terror. 'Lord George Gordon's people continue to make a great fracas,' lamented the Duchess to Mama; 'there is a violent mob in Moorfields, and I have heard that five hundred of the guards are gone down there. I could not go to the birthday – my gown was beautiful, a pale blue, with the drapery etc., of an embroidered gauze in *paillons*.'[2] She was a little comforted to hear from Lady Melbourne and the Duke that the Prince of Wales expressed his disappointment at having missed dancing with her for the third time. Four days later it was all over. Lord George Gordon was imprisoned in the Tower of London. 'My pity now begins to be moved for him,' remarked the Duchess, 'but two days ago I believe I could have kill'd him myself.'[3]

The story goes that when, on the afternoon of 14 July 1789, the Duc de la Rochefoucauld-Liancourt brought King Louis XVI news that the Bastille had been captured, the King said, 'Why, this is a revolt!' 'No, sire,' replied the Duke, 'it is a revolution.' Lady Elizabeth Foster can never have heard this anecdote, or she would have recorded it in her journals. Yet even if the Devonshires had recognized that the 'turmoils' all around them were not sporadic incidents but an upheaval which would come to be known as the French Revolution, they would not have changed their plans. As Professor W. Alison Phillips observes, 'There had been revolutions in Europe before 1789, but these revolutions had been strictly limited in their aims. Before 1789 the words "republic" and "democracy" conveyed no sense of revolutionary peril.'[4]

IO

The Devonshires, Lady Elizabeth and Charlotte Williams reached Paris on Tuesday 23 June. The day before they had met Lord Titchfield, the son and heir of the Duke of Portland at Clermont and he had told them that the King had shut the *tiers état* out of their assembly place. The Queen's dressmaker, Mlle Bertin, had driven out to meet them at Chantilly. The Duchess of Devonshire was an important customer But Mlle Bertin was too agitated about the Queen to talk much business. They had scarcely settled in the Hôtel de l'Université before Lord and Lady Camelford called and said that civil war was expected any moment. The King had addressed the States General, told them he disapproved their measures and dissolved their assembly. But the moment he left the hall, the *tiers état* passed a resolution not to leave until they had carried every point. They declared the King's dissolution invalid.[1]

Next day the Duchess was 'Overwhelm'd with stay makers etc.'.[2] But on Thursday she and Lady Elizabeth ventured a morning visit to Versailles. Though 'dejected and agitated', the Polignacs pressed them to stay to dinner. The *tiers état* was gaining consequence every day. Forty of the nobles, including the King's brother, the Duc d'Orléans, 'Philippe Egalité', had gone over to them. Every five minutes people came in with the latest news. To the Duchess and Lady Elizabeth it appeared like a family crisis.[3]

On Friday Charlotte Williams was taken to the Palais Royal.[4] Picking her up from the Nagels gave the Duke and Duchess their first glimpse of the three-year-old Caro St Jules. The Duke was enchanted. He was equally delighted when Hare took him to see Augustus Clifford at his lodgings. Hare was careful to conceal from the foster-mother the relationship between the Duke and his son. But Lady Elizabeth was less discreet.[5]

The ladies visited Versailles with the Duke. Lady Elizabeth had never witnessed such gloom there, but the Duchess's observations were personal. The King was not as fat as she expected; the Queen 'sadly alter'd, her belly quite big, and no hair at all', but 'with great éclat'. It was a triumph to rouse the Duke for a Royal presentation. 'Only think of him, stuck out in a drest coat, his hair finely drest and a hat and black feather, before twelve, and what's more liking it.'[6]

Thomas Coutts, in London still further removed from reality, was piqued that they had not taken his three daughters to be presented at the French Court. It was 'a very bad moment', the Duchess apologized; 'they are all preoccupy'd and hate to see strangers.'[7] She took them, however, 'sweet girls indeed',[8] to the Comédie Italienne.

It is plain that they did not connect their personal lives with what was happening all around them: even when the two impinged on one another. When they went for example to the Palais Royal, they were presented to the Duchesse d'Orléans who was very pleasing and invited them 'to dish tea with her'. Yet that same evening they were frightened 'as the mob at the Palais Royal were screaming and huzzaing, because the guards, who had been imprison'd, were let out'.[9] The Duchess confessed to Mama: 'I amuse myself at Paris, and have been well the whole time I have been here . . . but I shall not ask the Duke to stay longer.'[10] Lady Elizabeth was anxious to leave. She had introduced the Duke to Caro St Jules and Augustus Clifford: and all she had seen at Versailles and Paris convinced her that the Polignacs had not long to last in power. The sooner Caro joined the Devonshire schoolroom, the better. But first it must be established that she was just a little girl under the protection of the Duchesse de Polignac whom Charlotte Williams had met at the Nagels as a fellow-pensionnaire.

When Bess and the Devonshires left Paris on 12 July, they had no apprehensions for the children. James Hare would keep an eye on Charlotte and Caro at the Nagels, just as the Duke of Dorset would on his nieces and the Misses Coutts at Penthémont.

As they went their leisurely way north, they were overtaken by evil tidings and refugees from the epicentre of the revolution. Jacques Necker had been found guilty of inspiring the revolution and was dismissed by the King on 11 July. News of his flight reached them *en route*. He had escaped in a full dressed coat, Mme Necker in the clothes she stood up in. She did not have time to pack even a nightdress. They had only two servants, the footman travelling within the carriage to avoid attention. They had managed to cross the Belgian frontier without a passport or *laissez passer*. Mme Necker had fainted several times and it was thought she might not reach Brussels alive.[11]

In Brussels the Devonshires learned of the tumult in Paris following their departure: bridges broken down, pavements torn up for barricades, the cruel fate of the Colonel of Hussars cut to pieces and decapitated when his troops refused to fire on the mob; armed bands ranging the streets; convents plundered for grain.

Augustus Clifford was back in Normandy. But what would happen to Caro and Charlotte? The Duchess was more miserable than she could describe. Lady Elizabeth was beside herself. But what checked hysteria like a bucketful of icy water was the sight of the Duke in tears.[12] To weep was not unmanly in the eighteenth century. But in the Duke of Devonshire this lachrymal emotion was shocking. It was from anxiety for Charlotte, the Duchess wrote to Mama. But *she* knew it was for Caro, whom Hare declared the prettiest child he ever saw. For Caro and Augustus Clifford, who promised to grow up a giant, the Duke had conceived a love which he had never shown towards his two Cavendish-looking daughters born in wedlock.

They gleaned general information from the Brussels news bulletins or friends such as Lady Torrington, Prince Esterhazy and Mme de Staël, the daughter of the Neckers.[13] They would get no personal news until they reached Spa. From Liège they wrote asking Hare to place the girls in a convent or send them to Spa, but soon after they reached Spa a letter arrived from M. Nagel, saying that the night of 13 July and the day of the 14th had been terrible, but the family was safe. A letter from Hare crossed theirs. He thought the danger was past. Another from the Nagels contained a note from Charlotte saying she enjoyed playing with 'the little Comtesse'.[14] Caro continued her social rise in the world of her mother's creation, even though her 'patroness', the Duchesse de Polignac, had indeed been forced to flee to Basle where she concealed herself under the alias of 'Mme Herlingerie, *negociante*'.[15]

Danger can galvanize the most sluggish of men. The Duke talked of returning to Paris to fetch the children, but no one was worse equipped to rescue two girls from a mob whose hatred was fixed upon aristocrats and Lady Elizabeth had a better plan. If Mme Nagel brought the girls to Belgium the Duke and Duchess could devote themselves to the business of breeding, which was the purpose of their being in Spa.

Somehow or other that purpose was accomplished in August.*

* The Duchess, according to her doctor Mr Richard Croft, reckoned the date of conception 24 August 1789. In Lady Elizabeth Foster's journal for 25 August there is a passage missing. This *might* have contained some reference to the events of the night before which Lady Elizabeth deleted.

Was it the salubrity of Spa water? the quickening of desire in the presence of danger? the philoprogenitive impulse roused in the Duke by the sight of his love-children? a triple effort of the Duke and his two ladies? How it happened does not matter. On 23 September the Duchess wrote to Thomas Coutts, who was even more worried about his own daughters than about the Duchess's ever-mounting debts, 'The aim of my journey, I hope, is answer'd (this, Dr Sir, must be a secret). I am in hopes I am with child; we propose, if this is the case, stopping at Brussels till it will be safe for me to cross the sea.'[16]

This would have been possible in September or early October. But the aim of Lady Elizabeth's journey had not been accomplished. Somehow or other Caro must be united with her half-sisters, the Ladies Georgiana and Harriet Cavendish. The first idea was that the Nagel family with their two little *pensionnaires* should be settled somewhere near Devonshire House for a twelvemonth, at Chelsea or Brompton. Then Mme Nagel could teach the Cavendish girls (and Miss Trimmer) good French.

But when James Hare wrote to say that he found Mme Nagel unsatisfactory 'in point of manners', Lady Elizabeth asked him what he thought of the possibility of introducing Caro directly into Devonshire House. Hare answered that it would cause scandal, but *that* consideration was outweighed by the advantage of Lady Elizabeth having Caro under her care. The difficulties which seemed to terrify the Duchess certainly existed, but they could not last long. 'Once the little lady has gained a footing, I am not afraid of her being disturbed. . . . It would be pleasanter if no deceit was necessary, but where there is no choice it becomes a duty to consult the interest of poor little helpless wretches, even at the expense of feelings, which may be sometimes distressing.'[17]

Mme Nagel brought her family and two *pensionnaires* to Spa, all suffering from painter's colic, more or less. While they were recuperating, Lady Elizabeth advanced her plan in its third and final form. The Duchess had put the Channel between herself and her creditors but even so the pressure from Coutts, Calonne and others less reputable was disturbing. Back in England, she might be fretted into a miscarriage. How much better it would be if she lay in abroad! In that case, the whole family should be invited to join her, the Dowager Countess, Lord and Lady Duncannon, Miss Trimmer and the Cavendish girls. How natural it would be, in that case, if the Duchesse de Polignac's little protégée joined Miss Trimmer's schoolroom.

At the same time the Duchess was urged to disclose her debts. 'If you are in any scrape about money it will be impossible for you to conceal it from the Duke,' Hare wrote. 'The sooner the Duke knows about it the better, but, for God's sake, if you tell him anything tell him all, or let L^y Elizabeth or let me tell him.'[18]

Of course the Duchess did not know how much she owed. 'Why do you force me, my dear Ca.,' she asked, when even the Duke begged for a disclosure of debts which he had ignored for years, 'why do you force me to an avowal which agitates me beyond measure?'[19]

Nevertheless, she did everything Lady Elizabeth had planned. On 16 October she wrote asking Mama to come over immediately with Miss Trimmer and the children so that they could be together till she lay in next May. London would be too racketty, Derbyshire too troublesome in the pre-election year for her to be confined in England.[20]

In the event Brussels grew too turbulent in November for the family to go there. Even the Duke's party had to spend some weeks in a filthy inn at Lille to avoid the troubles. When they returned in early December things were quieter and the Duke went to London at the end of the month.[21] There were arrangements to be made and rumours to be scotched. Unaware that this stay abroad was a scheme to smuggle Caro into the Devonshire household, people were whispering that the Duchess was not pregnant at all. 'If those who say I am not with child were to see me,' the Duchess wrote to Mama, 'they w^d, I believe, have an *evident* answer to that, as well as to many other infamous lies.'[22]

Since the Dowager Countess refused to spend months in the company of Lady Elizabeth, the Duke arranged that the Duncannons should go to Brussels, followed by Miss Trimmer and his daughters. There, as Bess had planned, Caro and Charlotte Williams became members of the Devonshire schoolroom. But there is no hint of this in the journals she kept from June 1789–August 1790. These were concerned with day-to-day accounts of what she herself had seen or heard, or rumours exaggerated by others. The storming of the Bastille, celebrated each 14 July by the French, was far less an act of liberation than the opening of Newgate Prison had been during the Gordon Riots. Only seven prisoners were freed. What was horrifying was that the Governor, a civilized man as prison governors go, was decapitated and his bloody head borne through the streets on a pike. The jailers were killed and, according to Lady Elizabeth, prisoners incarcerated in secret cells died of starvation with the voices of would-be liberators audible through doors which only the dead jailers had known how to open.[*23]

From the start, the Devonshires had been involved in politics. The Duke of Dorset borrowed one of Bess's servants to carry despatches to England. 'When he left Paris it was with great difficulty he got away . . . at Clermont he was stopp'd & they examin'd his letters. They made him drink to the tiers État, but his guide who thro' fear & amazement seem'd to hesitate they knock'd off his horse & he saw no more of him – he had fortunately hid his letter to Monsr. de Calonne or probably he would have been kill'd.'[24]

Inevitably the Devonshires and Lady Elizabeth came under suspicion. They followed the political upheavals in Belgium move by move, plots to restore the Austrian monarchy, arguments between those who wanted total independence and those content with the establishment of a limited autonomy. The Devonshires provided unofficial intelligence to British government agents and kept up a lively correspondence with the Polignacs and Calonne, who was trying to recruit a counter-revolutionary force to aid Their Majesties of France. Their mail was seized from an intercepted courier and despite the Duke of Devonshire's protests it was not returned to him by the authorities.

This happened on 14 April. On 20 April the *accoucheur* Mr Richard Croft arrived in Brussels, followed by his wife and sister-in-law. Mr Denman, too old and too busy to attend a lengthy confinement abroad, had recommended Croft, his twenty-eight-year-old son-in-law as a sort of wedding present.† At the end of April the Duncannons went to Paris and on 1 May the Dowager Countess left St Albans for Brussels,

* There were in fact only seven prisoners in the Bastille, when it was stormed on 14 July, the Marquis de Sade having been removed to the lunatic asylum of Charenton for having harangued the mob from his cell in the Tower of Liberty on 2 July using a slop-funnel as a loud-hailer. The demolition of the Bastille came to be regretted during the Terror, when Robespierre increased the guillotinings from a hundred a month to two hundred a week. Sade himself, condemned to the guillotine, got lost among the many convents converted to jails, and escaped with his life. The storming of the Bastille was neither as tragic as Lady Elizabeth Foster imagined, or as glorious as revolutionary mythistorians have made it.

† Croft had married Margaret Denman on 3 November 1789. Uncertain whether to specialize in midwifery or surgery, Croft accepted the important assignment without inquiring about fees. Throughout the four months of his stay, he treated the whole Devonshire household, amounting to 100 persons, borrowing money for his upkeep. During this time, he was rewarded by Lady Elizabeth with a ring made from a stone of the Bastille for treating Caro St Jules, and by the Duke with the gift of a horse. As well as treating a number of cases of dysentery caused by bad water, he delivered the Duchess and brought Hary-O and little G. through severe illnesses which in the case of the latter might have proved fatal.

accompanied by her maid, Ann Scafe.[25] They stayed the first night at
Devonshire House, where they were visited by Dr Warren with an
urgent message from a source he would not disclose. The Duchess
must not lie in at Brussels. The Devonshires were no longer *personae
gratae* there. At a time when even the King and Queen of France were
held under house arrest, anything might happen.

When the Dowager Countess arrived in Brussels on 6 May, there
were long discussions about where to go for the *accouchement*.[26] There
was sporadic fighting throughout Belgium and even Spa was unsafe,
because 'tho' in a regular war water-drinking places are respected, in
this flying kind of war . . . no police or discipline c^d be observed.'[27]
Mr Croft was disappointed, because he wanted his sister-in-law to drink
Spa water. Holland was debated as a possibility, but hearing that Paris
was quiet, they decided to join the Duncannons at the Hôtel de
l'Université

They set out on 10 May and reached Paris on 14 May. The accommodation at Valenciennes and Pont St Maxence was tolerable, but bad
at Peronne. The country people appeared quiet. Lady Elizabeth was
surprised. 'The 13th being a Jour de fête there were great crowds
dancing & diverting themselves on the roads, but with perfect harmony
and good humour – one w^d never think that it was a country without
King or Law – & that had been for the last 8 months the scene of discord
& bloodshed.'[28] There was good news awaiting them in Paris. The
Duncannons had attended a National Assembly debate in which the
King's order to equip fourteen ships of the line for employment against
England had been countermanded.

The ducal entourage could not be accommodated at the Hôtel de
l'Université. But the Marquis de Boulainvilliers offered his *hôtel* in
nearby Passy. It was inspected and approved by the Duke, the Dowager
and Mr Croft on 19 May and that night the Duchess complained of
feeling ill.

First thing next morning two maids were despatched to the Hôtel
de Boulainvilliers to make ready the Duchess's chamber. The Duchess
herself arrived at 11 a.m., accompanied by the Dowager Countess and
Lady Elizabeth, at this critical moment drawn closer together than ever
before or after. The Duke followed with his daughters, legitimate and
illegitimate.[29]

In view of the gossip, it was essential to establish the legitimacy of
the birth. Lady Elizabeth Foster drove into Paris and attended the
Opéra, where she displayed herself in the box of Lord St Helens look-

ing 'as thin as a Wrayle': proof positive that she was not with child. Meanwhile the Dowager Countess wrote to Lord Robert Fitzgerald, secretary to the British Ambassador, and to the Dowager Duchess d'Ahremberg, saying that the Duchess's time was approaching and requesting their presence to witness the birth.

Unfortunately the letter to Lord Robert did not arrive until after he had gone to bed: and his servant did not wake him, thinking that it would be time enough to deliver it in the morning. Nor had the Dowager Duchess arrived when Lady Elizabeth returned from the Opéra. The Duke was waiting anxiously in an anteroom. It was as important to establish the legitimacy of the heir to the Duchy of Devonshire as that of an heir to the throne. Lady Elizabeth went through to the bedroom. The Duchess was in the last stages of her labour. Round her bed were her mother, Ann Scafe, the midwife Mrs Bartho and the nervous Mr Croft.

A little after 1 a.m. a baby appeared. A cry signalled it was alive. A glance confirmed it was a boy. As he was placed in Ann Scafe's arms, the Dowager Duchess d'Ahremberg entered the room. As Ann Scafe noted in her journal, 'There never was a more welcome child.'[30]

11

After nearly sixteen years of marriage the Duchess had produced an heir. Provided that he lived, the succession was assured and with it the futures of Lady Georgiana and Lady Harriet Cavendish his sisters. Those of Caro St Jules and Augustus Clifford, if not guaranteed, were brighter. The Duchess herself could take heart. If the Duke had been so anxious to hear about her debts before the birth of the baby Marquis of Hartington, he would surely be only too willing to pay them now.

The Dowager Countess went back to St Albans, but the rest of them were delayed by little Lady Georgiana Cavendish's falling dangerously ill. She was not well enough to travel until August.

Immediately they reached home, it became plain that the birth of Hartington had been merely the curtain to the first act of a longer drama. The old conflicts were unresolved. They simply took a different twist.

At St Albans, the Dowager Countess had had time to think. She now understood why the Devonshires had not returned to England for the lying-in, why Miss Trimmer and the children had been summoned to Brussels and who were the parents of the little Caro St Jules. But she was not prepared to bring the scandal into the open. If forced, the Duchess would side with the Duke, his mistress and their bastard, rather than with her mother. So Mama went more deviously to work.

The Duchess must bring the children to Holywell House for little G. to convalesce. Dr Warren recommended it. Drs Pitcairn* and Croft advised the seaside, replied the Duchess. They were all going to Compton Place, Eastbourne, for some weeks. Why did not Mama join them there?[1]

At this point Miss Trimmer blundered. She hinted that the Dowager Countess would refuse; and when she did refuse, the Duchess seized the

---

* Dr David Pitcairn had been summoned to Passy to give a second opinion on Lady Georgiana Cavendish's illness.

chance of shifting the attack. 'I have, Dst Mama, a great opinion of Miss T.'s principles and talents for education, but if ever I can discover that she interferes in anything but the care of their education . . . I could not submit to have [her] another moment in the house.'[2] Tossing truth to the winds, she defended Bess's virtue and their need for her. 'Good God . . . how cruel it w^d be to expose her to the malignant ill nature of the world and to expose ourselves to all the misery of parting with her for what we know to be unjust and false . . . and the mother whom I adore . . . forgets all the affection her son-in-law has shewn to her, and only says: I will deprive them of their friend or of my countenance.'[3]

Mama was caught. It was unpardonable to discuss with a governess the morals of her employers. She promised in future to mention no topic more hateful than 'a firm resolution not to buy so much as a yard of ribband'.[4] The Duchess pressed her attack home. 'I wrote very pettishly about Miss T. . . . I think she has a want of civility sometimes . . . the other night . . . she did not (or her sister Julia) make the least motion or offer to rise when L^y Elizabeth came into the nursery. . . . If it is meant as a dislike to anybody in my house you must feel it is what I could not put up with in the governess of my children.'[5] Mama retired, defeated. If Selina was sent packing, Mama would lose her spy and the grandchildren their moral teacher.

The reference to 'a yard of ribband' was a flick at Georgiana's tenderest spot, her debts. She postponed the day of reckoning till Christmas 1790. Then she compiled a list of liabilities which she gave Thomas Coutts, not the Duke. The total, omitting sums too small or too numerous to remember, amounted to £61 917.[6] To Calonne she owed £8000; to the Duke's banker, Cornelius Denne (i.e. the Duke himself), £14 448 and to Coutts no less than £16 000.

Though the Duke professed to have no interest in, or knowledge of, money matters, he was shrewd. He and the Duchess had Thomas Coutts over a barrel. Coutts could not recover money he had lent without either collateral or the Duke's agreement: unless he was prepared to ruin his reputation and business. Coutts asked what he should do. The Duchess had received a hint from 'a person well aquainted [sic] with his disposition' (i.e. Bess) that the best thing was to leave the Duke to himself 'so that his kindness and generosity could operate'.[7] What about the kindness and generosity of the other Cavendishes? Not a chance, said the Duchess. Only Lady George Cavendish would speak to her. He must be patient: and she swore she would not run up any more debts.

But meanwhile she must have £500 for Lady Duncannon. 'Shd I

refuse to assist my sister I shd be a monster indeed. How cd I assist but thro' you?'[8] The bullied banker did not suggest that between them the Cavendishes, the Spencers and the Ponsonbys might scrape up £500. He dared not forfeit the kindness and generosity of the fifth Duke.

Lady Duncannon was genuinely ill. She started with giddy fits early in 1791. Soon she developed an abominable cough and began spitting blood. Then she lost all sensation in her left arm and leg.* The Duchess was drawn to Lady Duncannon's sickroom by sisterly love but it also provided opportunities for another sort of love. Charles Grey, the 'very dangerous' but 'very amiable' person whom Georgiana had met in June 1785, had been her faithful follower for six years. Now that at the age of thirty-four she had given the Duke the heir he needed, the Duchess took from Grey the love she desired. But the extramarital holiday did not last long.

Having attended Hartington's christening at St George's, Hanover Square, on 21 May, the Duchess went to Bath with her sister to stay for three weeks. When she kissed her children goodbye in May 1791, she did not realize that it would be over two years before she saw them again.

There was a good excuse for not returning from Bath. Harriet was very ill.[9] She could not move without crutches. That she might become a cripple for life was horrifying to think of. But the Duchess had her private horror. She was pregnant. Fanny Burney met her in Bath. Miss Burney had seen the Duchess once before, when she appeared 'far more easy and lively in her spirits and consequently far more lovely in her person'. How 'she appeared to me not happy, I thought she looked oppressed within'.[10] The novelist was too nice to guess why.

On 17 July the Duchess ironically assured Thomas Coutts that she was 'not likely to give Hartington either a brother or a third sister, which I am very glad of, as I should be sorry to have any impediment to my attendance on my D' sister'.[11] It is plain from this that she, probably with Harriet, had already considered what must be done, unless she miscarried.

Charles Grey must have been informed immediately. There was no chance that the Duke would accept the Duchess's love-child into Devonshire House as she had accepted his. Grey undertook the respon-

---

* Diagnosis of eighteenth-century symptoms is impossible. The spitting of blood was caused either by tuberculosis or bronchiestasis. The giddiness, followed by hemiplegia, was probably caused by a cerebral haemorrhage, unusual in a woman in her early thirties, but having no connection with the lung condition.

sibility. Her inferior in rank and age, he was as proud of his paternity as a mountaineer of scaling a hitherto inaccessible peak. What to call the child? Courtney would be a good name. Georgiana's aunt had been a Miss Courteney before she married William Poyntz of Midgham. Altered spelling would put people off the scent. The Duchess could go abroad, ostensibly to look after Lady Duncannon as she was doing now. They must use code names. Grey could be Mr Black. The Duchess could be Miss Courtney. Grey must never write to the Duchess in his own name except in the sort of terms a young Whig MP would use. As Mr Black, he could write openly to Lady Duncannon about Miss Courtney. Maybe at this point Lady Duncannon suggested that Mr Black should be an *inamorato* of hers. Lord Duncannon would understand and enjoy the joke. Each letter should be numbered, to know if any went astray. The plot was so much in the spirit of Elizabeth Melbourne that they decided on Melbourne House as an accommodation address for letters to Mr Black. A further refinement was the idea of Lady Duncannon's inserting code messages for Mr Black in letters answering her chance correspondents. No one writing to her before she had written to them would dream that her answers would contain information intended for Grey.

In October the Dowager Countess was staying with her two daughters at Bath when a letter arrived from the Duke, hotly followed by His Grace himself. He was too angry to drawl. When the Dowager Countess made to withdraw, he demanded that she should stay. He was as incensed against his mother-in-law who had refused to accept Lady Elizabeth as his mistress as he was against the Duchess for accepting Charles Grey as her lover. No one is so self-righteous as a guilty person discovering guilt in another. The fifth Duke erupted like a volcano. Having erupted, like a volcano he subsided into fuming. This was the end! Something must be done! Something! or other.

Without saying what, he made his exit into Harriet's room. She had overheard everything, but she waited for him to speak. He walked up and down, up and down. Then he went out, without a word.[12] Though Mama may have been appalled by the Duke's accusations, the two sisters were shocked only by Grey's indiscretion. He must have got drunk and said something. But to how many people?

Next day, the Duke announced his terms. Her Grace should go abroad. She must avoid Devonshire House and Chiswick, proceeding directly from Bath to Southampton. This might mean merely that he was reserving the right to present a Bill of Divorcement and wished to avoid a plea of condonation. But it was more vindictive. He refused to allow the children to come to Bath so that she could say goodbye to them.

The Dowager Countess was a woman of God, but she was also a woman of the world. If the Duchess was sent into exile, did his Grace intend to keep Lady E. and Caro under his roof? Would Lady Bristol be prepared to give the little girl houseroom?

The Duke recognized that he could not banish his wife and keep his mistress. Lady Elizabeth would take Charlotte Williams and Caro back to Paris to continue their education there. What Lady Elizabeth did was her concern, but the Duke would see that as the Duchess's dearest friend she would not starve.*

Though the Dowager Countess hated Lady E. she fell in with the plan of allowing her to join the family party when they went abroad. If she was with the Duchess, Bess could not be up to tricks with the Duke. As for Lady Elizabeth, she was delighted with the idea. She sympathized with the Duchess in her misfortune, which incidentally reduced Georgiana to her own moral level. Having given the Duke two illegitimate children, she did not intend to give him any more. But their future and her own depended upon the Devonshires' marriage continuing.

The Duchess was afraid that, leaving her children at such an early age, she would be a stranger to them when, if ever, she returned. She wanted Miss Trimmer and Little Lady Georgiana to keep her memory fresh with Hary-O and Hart during her absence. She began to keep a journal for G. the moment they started in November 1791. It began, 'Left Bath very miserable at leaving my Dear children'. Then, so that the Duke could not accuse her of trying to set the children against him and so that G. could see that she felt miserable only at leaving her children, she inserted before 'my dear children', as if by afterthought, 'the Duke &'.[13]

The main party consisted of Lord and Lady Duncannon, their daughter Caro Ponsonby, the Dowager Countess and the Duchess, crossing via Southampton. A few days later Lady Elizabeth left Dover

---

* This negotiation is not based on evidence. It is a 'factoid'. Lady Melbourne's papers may or may not bear it out. The Earl of Bessborough, when writing *Georgiana*, was allowed to see the relevant papers, but not quote from them. Now that the British Museum MSS library has been taken over by the British Library, this concession has been denied to me, as to Mr Philip Ziegler in writing his *Lord Melbourne*, despite the request of the representatives of the late Mabell, Countess of Airlie, who deposited the papers with the British Museum.

with Charlotte Williams⋆ and Caro St Jules, ostensibly to take both girls back to school in Paris. But when she met the Duncannon party in Paris, she 'changed her mind'. It would be a good idea if Caroline paid a visit to her relatives, the St Jules at Aiguesmortes. They all travelled together as far as Toulon.[14] There they parted; the Duncannons, Caro Ponsonby and Dowager Countess to make their way to Nice, staying *en route* at Hyères, the Duchess accompanying Bess and Caro on their visit to Aiguesmortes.

Communications had been irregular with Mr Black, despite all their planning. Lady Holland was later to describe him as 'fractious and *exigeant*'. Lady Melbourne found him tiresome and indiscreet. One can sense the tension in this extract from a letter[15] written to him by Lady Duncannon.

HIERES, January 29 [1792]

11th letter!!!

Pray my love continue the way you have done some of y‍ʳ letters putting the number of them & the dates you have rec'd of mine. I will do it though it has this bad consequence, of affronting me every letter I write by seeing how many more I have sent to you than you to me. I have receiv'd 4, I have written 11. . . .

I am surpris'd at Miss Courtney's never writing to you, but you must comfort yourself that a friend who could so forget you was hardly worth the keeping. I believe it is a very common misfortune, distance generally brings neglect, but yet I have no right to say this, for I have been remarkably lucky not only in my friends, but even my acquaintance, most of them I mean, the time of my illness & long absence has shewn those who really cared for me & those who affected it . . . Lʸ Melbourne writes constantly. My new acquaintance, Lʸ Mexborough, very often; Lʸ Jersey too, & I must do Mrs Stanhope the justice to say she has never miss'd a post since I left England. . . .

This letter was written eighteen days after the parting at Toulon. The code meaning is indecipherable; but in an age when newsy letters were handed round to friends, Grey was clearly told to call on Lady Mexborough, etc., in whose letters from Harriet he would find news which he would understand.

Previous writers have stated that the Duchess had her baby *chez*

⋆ Charlotte Williams passes out of our story at this point. After an unsatisfactory stay in Paris she returned to England, coughing blood. The Duke found her awkward and was glad when Mr Heaton took her into his house. She married Mr Heaton's nephew and proved a good wife.

St Jules.[16] This is not correct. They travelled from Toulon to Aix-en-Provence. In normal times, their journey might have attracted notice. But the Revolution worked in their favour. Aix was in feud with Marseilles. Everywhere farms and hamlets had been abandoned and people were on the move. For some weeks the Duchess, Bess and Caro stayed undetected in Aix. Afraid that she might die in childbirth, the Duchess made a will. Her 'only possession', an antique ring given her by Bess, she left to the Duke as a mourning ring.[17] She indited a letter to Hartington, to be given to him on his eighth birthday in the event of her death. It breathed her love, enjoined obedience to Papa and Grandmama and commended to his kindness and generosity his sisters, Lady Elizabeth, Caro St Jules and his cousins, especially the Ponsonbys. 'Make piety your chief study, never despise religion, never betray a secret, never tell a lie.' How often she herself had lied and betrayed secrets – not from malice but thoughtlessness! – she may have thought, as she subscribed herself 'Your poor mother, G. Devonshire'. How often had she forgotten Sunday! how far from first had been her study of piety! She turned to reading Blair's *Sermons*.

They called at Aiguesmortes on their way to Montpellier. The Count was dangerously ill, she wrote to G., so they did not stay. At Montpellier she added, they had to see 'some people of business about Caro'. She enclosed three violets for her three darlings and a kiss for each she 'would travel on foot to give' them.

Her father had often visited Montpellier in pursuit of health. Good doctors abounded and on 20 February the Duchess was brought to bed of a daughter, who was named Eliza Courtney and handed over to a wet-nurse until such time as Mr Black arranged for her to be collected and delivered to his parents.*

Toulon was overcrowded when they reached it a fortnight later. They spent the night in the garret of an inn jammed with refugees. Next morning Louis brought the carriage round and that evening they were at Nice, across the border from revolutionary France.[19] When the Duchess examined her letters, there were many from Thomas Coutts but none from the Duke.

In 1790 the Duke had endorsed a bond for four thousand guineas against his wife's debt to Coutts. But he had specified no date for repayment. On the Duchess's advice, the banker left his card at Devonshire House as a tactful reminder. It was not acknowledged. A month

* They raised her as their daughter, a sinister arrangement whereby Charles Grey became his daughter's brother and the Duchess a family friend called Georgiana.

later, meeting Coutts by accident, the Duke cut him. 'I think myself deserving of more civility,'[20] Coutts complained. Two months later Coutts arrived to dinner at 'Fish' Craufurd's to find the Duke among the guests. 'Whether he knew I was in the room was more than could be discovered by his looks or manner. I make every allowance for his habits and his usual silence, yet, everything consider'd, surely he might have somehow notic'd me, as one he had seen before. His Grace however ought to do me the justice to pay the sum he sign'd for (or at least the interest of it) if he will do no more.'[21]

When the Duchess reached Nice, there was a long letter from Coutts putting proposals for repayment which she might lay before the Duke. Messrs Denne had refused the Duchess's draft for £138. 'What a pity Your Grace should suffer such an affront from the Duke of Devonshire's banker, it hurts me tenderly,' commiserated Coutts. 'I have never yet refused a draft of yours, perhaps it would have been quite as well for you, and much better for me, I had never paid.'[22]

The Duchess temporized. She wrote she expected the Duke's arrival any month.[23] She would lay the proposals before him. She was sure His Grace intended no affront. To repay the four thousand guineas she had assured her life for £1000 and would increase the sum gradually. There was no truth in rumours of a separation of the Duke from herself. The excuses were too many to convince.

The ladies at Nice formed a triple alliance against the Duke. Harriet complained to Lady Melbourne of his 'persecution'. Bess called him 'a brute and a beast'.[24] Lady M. would pass such messages on if she met him. But he seldom left Devonshire House except for his clubs and the House of Lords. 'I think the Dss had better remain with Lady Duncannon, whether she comes to London or stays abroad,' he wrote to the Dowager in April. 'I suppose she will be decided on that by her physician. If she stays abroad I mean to meet you abroad sometime in the summer.'[25] The concession was more apparent than real. The Duchess might not see her children, but he would visit Bess and Caro if they stayed abroad.

On 13 April the Duchess asked James Hare for news of the Duke. He did not reply until three months later and then with little cheer. 'I have probably passed this winter for a greater liar, or rather for a more trusty person than I am, for in answer to all the questions that have been asked me about your staying so long abroad without any of your children, and about the time of your return, and upon what footing you are with the D., I have always said what was literally true, but was believed by no person, viz: that I know nothing of any disagreement or separation, and that I have concluded your stay would depend upon your sister's health. I have seen a great deal of him this year, and frequently din'd with him tête à tête. As he never entered upon the subject of your situation I never suggested it. He must be very sure that I am not indifferent about anything that concerns him and his family, and I believe too that he has no doubt of my secrecy, so that his silence must have proceeded from an unwillingness to start on a subject on which I could only partake of his uneasiness without relieving it.'[26]

By exiling his ladies, the Duke had put himself in Coventry; his only satisfactions were being nasty to Coutts and drinking too much. At the end of August he wrote to the Dowager to confirm a letter he had written his Duchess two days before. But he did not say that he and the children missed her. The Duchess could await his arrival in Lausanne, go to Italy with the Duncannons or come home, if it was not too dangerous. She and Bess waited, then went to Italy.

Testy with gout, the Duke was plagued by Coutts, greatly daring. It was eighteen months since he had discussed the Duchess's debts with His Grace. 'I had better see the worst at once,' Coutts wrote, pointing out in the delicate language of the day that it was his four thousand guineas, which had financed the birth of Hartington. He suggested various ways of repaying the Duchess's debts to him which now amounted to £20000.[27]

The Duke was outraged, but on 21 October he gave him a bond (backdated 13 September) for £5610, representing the capital of £4400 plus five and a half years' interest. He did not pay a penny in cash. Acknowledging the *bond*, Coutts pointed out that a further £15000 was due from the Duchess. His Grace did not reply, but at the end of November he paid Jefferys the jeweller the Duchess's debt of £450 in *cash*. Coutts promptly left his name with the porter at Devonshire House without any effect. 'I hope your Grace,' he wrote the Duchess acidly, 'will next year be restored to the bosom of your family.'[28]

His letter crossed one from the Duchess complaining that Coutts's partner, Mr Antrobus, had refused a draft of hers. It arrived when Mrs Coutts and the Three Graces were all ill in bed and Coutts 'in a very weak state of health, not much the better of being ill treated where I least expected to be so'. The sick worm turned. 'I have gone on for years never refusing anything. Your letter says I have been punctual in receipt of £500 a quarter, yet *I would not have a little patience*. I absolutely know nothing of this regular £500 a quarter, any more than I do of my want of patience. . . . I have shown patience beyond example.'[29]

Owing to the French turmoils, letters took even longer than usual. The Duchess had apologized eighteen days before Coutts protested, but the apology did not reach him until New Year's Day 1793. Quarrels rumbled on like summer thunder. A letter of five weeks before renewed at one end an antagonism allayed meantime at the other.

These misunderstandings were sharpened by the Duchess's violent changes of mood. One moment she would be angry, the next filled with self-reproach; sometimes depressed, at others wildly gay. It was not until later that these changing moods would be attributed to anything more than the stresses of separation.

There were two aspects to the Duchess's exile, the maternal and the feminine. Her letters to her children and Miss Trimmer are a delightful combination of gossip and instruction. As described to the children (and read by Miss Trimmer and the Duke), their regimen abroad was innocence itself. On Easter Day at Nice, for example, the Duchess rose at nine, read one of Blair's *Sermons* and attended High Mass at the Cathedral. Back home to listen to dear Grandmama reading prayers. After dinner a ride. 'I have a little pony – very quiet & pleasant and your Aunt rode upon it and gallop'd a little (with two people holding her on).' They met a countrywoman with a long, venomous snake: and in the evening they drew or studied before going early to bed.[30]

When they went to Geneva the great historian Edward Gibbon played with both the Caros. He was very clever but remarkably ugly and when he walked in the garden he wore a green jockey cap to keep the light from his eyes. Caro Ponsonby made him take it off and twist it about. One day she asked one of the footmen who had been jumping her up and down to jump Mr Gibbon too. This was rather difficult as he was one of the biggest men you ever saw.[31] But it was a foretaste of the humour of the future Lady Caroline Lamb. The Duchess picked out the sort of details children adore: four nights in beds without curtains on mattresses like bags of stones; the beautiful Val d'Aosta where almost every man and woman had necks hideous with goitre. There were lots of sketches and presents of the stones collected by the Duchess for her mineralogical collection. Grandmama gathered and pressed flowers, while Lady Elizabeth tirelessly pursued culture and antiquities. In many letters asides suggested the children might plead with Papa for her return. The Duchess seemed to have turned into a model mother.

But the two sisters and Lady Elizabeth were still fabulous beauties, and social lionesses. When they arrived at Nice, they were pounced upon by the twenty-one-year-old Lady Webster. Lady Webster had been born Elizabeth Vassall, a headstrong girl with a great fortune from the West Indies. She disliked her parents so much that, to get away from them, she married at the age of fifteen a man old enough to be her grandfather. Sir Godfrey Webster, Bart., was forty-nine, an MP in the interest of Thomas Pelham,* and owner of Battle Abbey. Elizabeth, a romantic, had married Sir Godfrey more for his abbey than for himself, but she could not get possession. Sir Godfrey's aged aunt refused to move out and the Websters had to squat in a house in the grounds. Elizabeth sent servants to the Abbey to ask 'if the old hag was dead yet'. She arranged haunting parties to rattle chains and make things go bump in the night. The aunt said she would not leave, except in her coffin. Elizabeth then wanted to travel abroad and improve her mind but Sir Godfrey nursed his parliamentary seat, while giving Elizabeth babies to suckle. Only when he was defeated at the polls did she bully him into taking her on a Grand Tour in search of Art, Antiquities, Aristocracy *et l'Amour*. Normally bad-tempered, Sir Godfrey was foulest on mornings after drinking too much and losing at play. When business recalled him to England, Lady Webster remained at Nice, content with the company of a 'grave, married man', Mr Cowper, and 'the learned Dr Drew' until the latter introduced her to the Dowager Countess and the Duncannons. When the Duchess and Lady Elizabeth Foster arrived, Lady Webster pressed herself upon them. These mature beauties had been famous before Elizabeth Vassall left the nursery for the schoolroom.

Though she was brash, they liked her. She had high spirits and she was to be pitied for a marriage even hastier than Lady Elizabeth Foster's. What she lacked in breeding she made up in wealth. And she carried in her train an increasing number of handsome, eligible, young gallants.

The Duchess might be in love with Charles Grey, Lady Elizabeth Foster the mistress of the Duke and Lady Duncannon at times escorted by her husband,† but they all enjoyed the gallantry that flourished

---

* Thomas Pelham (1756–1826) second Earl of Chichester.

† Lord Duncannon left his wife for six months (June–December 1792) to visit his ailing father. When he succeeded to the Earldom of Bessborough on 11 March 1793 he had to return to England, where he found his father's estate, already neglected, threatened by a bank failure. Among the bank's debtors were the Duchess of Devonshire and his wife, now the Countess of Bessborough. He managed to keep their names out of the liquidation proceedings by setting their debts against the Bessborough credits. He was still settling affairs in England and Ireland when the Duchess and Lady Elizabeth returned to London.

round the court of the Kingdom of the Two Sicilies. For them it was not 'see Naples and die', but 'stay in Naples and flirt'. Now in their thirties they still attracted men older than themselves, but they also fascinated younger men, by reason of their fame, experience and understanding. Both sides were delighted: the young men to philander with ladies so experienced; the ladies to dally with the youths who were potential husbands for their daughters still in the schoolroom.

The Dowager Countess urged the Duchess to spend her exile in self-improvement. But in that brilliant sunshine, picnicking *al fresco* in the ruins of Paestum, gazing across the Bay of Baeae, sailing to Sorrento, Amalfi, and the islands, watching Emma, Lady Hamilton, assume her Classic Attitudes, attending the court at Capua, riding up Vesuvius, attending a *ballo in maschera*, it was all too easy to forget the gloomy Duke in dark and dirty Devonshire House, the nightmare of faro at Lady Archer's, Martindale's notes of hand and the persistent Banker in the Strand.

By the summer of 1793 the domestic war petered to an end with an affectionate letter from the Duke. There was no apparent surrender: just an unconditional truce.[32] Perhaps the peacemaker was Caro St Jules. Her pretty ways had softened the heart of the Dowager Countess. She no longer objected to Caro's joining the Devonshire House nursery, and if Caro went, could Bess be far behind? With this concession the Duchess was allowed to return home to her own children.

Leaving Harriet, Mama and Caro Ponsonby to await the return of Harum, now Lord Bessborough, the Duchess set out with Bess and Caro St Jules in August 1793. The nearer they got to England, the graver grew the Duchess. From Maestricht she wrote to Mama, 'I condemn myself . . . for the misuse of time in my *banishment* . . . I ought to have done so much better. . . . I often have given you cause of uneasiness and complaint, tho' I w^d have sacrificed my life for your care. . . .'[33]

On 12 September they landed at last. The family was there to meet them in a new coach, light blue with silver springs. The Duke said he was gouty but otherwise well. G. looked very handsome, Hary-O still fat but with the whitest complexion. The sight of Hartington filled the Duchess with joy. He was like the Duke, pretty blue eyes, fine colour, with a very sensible countenance and a delightful laugh. But when she stooped to take him into her arms, he shrank away from this stranger. He would not look at her or speak a word.

That evening, however, perhaps to please Selina Trimmer, he kissed the strange lady they called his mother 'a little'.[34]

12

During the twenty-two months abroad, relationships had changed. Miss Selina Trimmer had stood by the Duchess. About midway in age between the Duchess and her elder daughter she had become a sort of eldest sister to the children and a youngest sister to their mother; no longer a mere governess, more a loved and loving member of the family. She performed the daily tasks which fell on mothers in lowlier households, but the Duchess never felt her maternal prerogatives threatened. Even Hartington grew to be devoted to his mother.

At the same time Selina still disapproved of Lady Elizabeth. No doubt she stood up, or made as if to stand up, if Lady Elizabeth entered the schoolroom. But when Lady Georgiana and Hary-O made fun of Liz's affectations, her baby talk and gushings, they were not reprimanded, except perhaps by the cautionary wag of a finger which was counteracted by a smile and a twinkle in Selina's eyes. Mockery was better than moralizing. The Duchess may well have known of this without minding. She and her sister must have made fun of grown-ups when they were children. At any rate it did not matter, now that Lady Elizabeth and Caro were accepted as members of the family.

The Duke had suffered more than his ladies from his policy of banishment. In his loneliness he had neglected his health and drunk too much. He was spitting blood and, in the Duchess's opinion, the gout had spread to his heart. Life in London was bad for him. The sooty fogs aggravated his coughing. He stayed at Brookes's too late and found it hard to sleep. After one evening sitting with him in the rooms at Devonshire House, the Duchess confessed to Mama that 'cette chienne de vie me tue".[1] This bitch of a life was not made easier by the news of the execution of Marie Antoinette, after an imprisonment that had been driving her crazy. But the dreariness at Devonshire House was caused initially by the Duke's melancholy. His fear of early death was strengthened when his sister, the Duchess of Portland, died on 3 June

1794, leaving Lord George Cavendish the only one of his siblings still alive. The Duchess urged him to spend more time in the country, but he was hugely bored there because he could no longer hunt. He had his two ladies, of whom Bess was the more attentive, though having produced an heir and five other children in or out of matrimony, he was no longer very interested in sex.

Devonshire House was being repainted and Chiswick House was suffering from dry rot. So the family went to Bath for the waters and then, because the Derbyshire militia was stationed at Bedford, the Duke of Bedford lent them his place at nearby Oakley, 'with plate, linen, wine, garden stuff and fruit'. But the Duke of Devonshire proved too ill to review his militia, and little Hartington deputized for him.*

Mid June they all went to Chatsworth, but for Bess the sparkle had gone out of her flirtation and she left them for Devonshire House, whence she sent news of the latest political developments. She had added current affairs to her enthusiasms, though her taste in politics was less radical than the Duchess's and dear old England appealed to her more than revolutionary France.

From Italy in April 1794 had come the news that Lady Duncannon, now Lady Bessborough, was at last sufficiently improved to make her leisurely way home. To understand the significance of her return that August we must go back to February of that year, and introduce a new and important character in this story.

On 16 February Lady Stafford† wrote an urgent letter to her only son, Lord Granville Leveson Gower. The letter had been prompted by a meeting with the Duchess of Devonshire, whose ideas, she observed, were 'supposed to have changed but were still *Grey*'.

When the tiresome war with France had broken out, Granville had been enlisted in the force defending Plymouth, but since he was designed for the diplomatic corps, he was given furlough to visit Italy. He had to wait for weeks before his squadron finally sailed on 1 December. He took with him Charles Fox's beloved nephew, young Lord Holland, who was excused military service because of a leg

---

* 'You cannot think how pretty it was to see his little figure in the regimentals standing in the middle of the field, and taking off his hat as they saluted him, his little fair locks blowing about by the wind. Of his own accord he desir'd to give the soldiers bread and cheese and ale. They were delighted with him, and the officers gave us a very pretty breakfast.' The Duchess to her mother, 10 April 1794.

† Lady Stafford, third wife of Lord Gower (later Marquess of Stafford). By his second wife Lord Gower had had an heir who became Earl of Sutherland when he married Elizabeth, Countess of Sutherland, *suo jure*.

deformity. Suddenly Lady Stafford realized that Granville was likely to go to Naples, where he would inevitably meet Lady Bessborough, a beauty as bewitching as her sister the Duchess and by all accounts more accommodating. Her darling boy, a mere twenty years of age, with only his ability, his handsomeness and the possibility of making a rich marriage to establish him in a world where the eldest son took all, might be heading for a disaster. 'An artful woman,' wrote Lady Stafford, 'may draw the best disposed into horrible Scrapes, and may outwit a better understanding than her own. Professions of Attachment, Interest in your Happiness, Sincerity of Affection, and a thousand plausible, ensnaring ways which that Sort of Woman possesses are not easily withstood. When once she gets possession of a Young Man's Mind, he thinks that she feels and is what she wishes him to believe her to be. All the flattery which she administers with Art appears to him her genuine, undisguised Thoughts, and the Censures which she bestows on others, and the Satire whetted with a *very little* Wit, operate so forcibly on the Person, on whom she fixes her Claws, that he sets her down in his Mind as the most perfect of Beings, *comme le chef d'oeuvre de la Nature*, and Time and Observation will find it difficult to remove the Film. I did not think of this long Tirade when I began this letter, but a Lady came into my Head and produced the foregoing.'[2]

Could ever a song have been sung by an over-anxious mother so designed to make a Siren irresistible?

Lady Webster collected Lords Granville and Holland in northern Italy. At first she preferred Granville, unaware that when he had met her earlier he had considered her vulgar. But when they reached Naples, she surrendered him to Lady Bessborough, finding the swart, politically passionate and physically encumbered Lord Holland, inheritor of the Fox fortune, more desirable.

Lady Bessborough behaved almost exactly as Lady Stafford had fore-told, but from very different reasons. She was adept at handling lovers for whom she had no deep feeling. Her current *cisisbeo* was Charles Beauclerk* of whom Lord Bessborough was jealous, without cause. Lord Granville frightened her. He was, like Charles Grey, a very dangerous person, because very amiable. Twelve years her junior, he had a beauty which she found fascinating and a self-conceit which she knew would pain her if she fell in love. She refused to take his gallantries seriously. She would gladly be his *gouvernante*, but not his mistress. Rejection enflamed his ardour: holding him at arm's length was a

* Son of Topham and Lady Diana Beauclerk, the artist.

pleasure Lady Bessborough could not forgo. When he was recalled to England she gave him commissions for her sister. If he joined the Devonshire House circle, they could meet again without arousing suspicion.

Lord Granville was welcomed in Devonshire House. Lady Georgiana was only ten and Hary-O eight, but the Duchess was already selecting eligibles. To the Ponsonby and Lamb boys, known from infancy, she had already added Lords Morpeth and Boringdon. Little Lord Ossulton, heir to the Earl of Tankerville, was enlisted later. Lord Morpeth, the future owner of Castle Howard and the Carlisle fortune, would suit little G. very well. For Hary-O, the Duchess and her sister had decided, the eldest Ponsonby boy, John, Viscount Duncannon, would be an ideal choice, strengthening the ties between the houses of Devonshire and Bessborough. Lord Granville, however, of an age with Morpeth and Boringdon, made a handsome attendant lord, one that would do to swell a progress, start a scene or two, but more suitable for the amusement of Lady Bessborough than as a husband for either of the girls. As a younger son, he needed to marry an heiress.

Though Granville was stationed at Plymouth Dock, he was able to slip up to London to see the Bessboroughs when they returned from Italy towards the end of August. Infatuated with the 'keep away closer' tactics of Lady Bessborough, he snatched a few moments with her alone at Cavendish Square and bitterly upbraided her when she sent him away. Her carriage, she wrote from St Albans, came for her two minutes after he left. 'My brother sent to me to beg I would come here to do civilities for him, but more to attend a morning ball and visit some freeholders' wives, whom he wanted to please. Conceive being dress'd out as fine as I could at eleven o'clock this morning, squeez'd into a hot assembly room at the Angel Inn, cramming fifty old Aldermen and their wives with hot rolls and butter, while John and Fred* danced with their Misses, playing at fourpenny Commerce and tradille,† and then visiting all about the gay town of St Albans. Can you boast of anything to surpass this? and, to crown all, a mad Mr Caven-

---

* Her sons, John (Viscount Duncannon) and Frederick Ponsonby.

† Commerce was a game of chance played with cards. Tradille is not included in the Compact edition of the *Oxford English Dictionary* and I suspect that Castalia, Countess Granville, who edited the *Private Correspondence of Lord Granville Leveson Gower*, misread it for quadrille, a card game of which *Hoyle's Games* (1847) says: 'Quadrille, which for upwards of a century held the first rank in all the gambling circles of Europe, is now completely banished from them: and is rarely or never seen beyond the precincts of some antiquated provincial circles.'

dish who lives here, se fait jour [*sic:* probably for *jouer*] parmi la foule, in the midst of the ball room, and after demanding silence, repeated à ma tête, a long copy of verses, in which he compar'd me to Venus visiting her favourite Island, my children to Cupids, the old coach horses to doves, the tea to Nectar, and all the fat Aldermen – my votaries'[3]

One can understand how Granville, himself a stuffy letter-writer, was bedazzled by such wit. To his delight, the Bessboroughs took a house in Teignmouth near Plymouth in November, and the Duchess followed with her children early in December. The Duchess described it as 'really Botany Bay'.[4] Not that she repined: her children would make even the Australian penal settlement delightful to her, 'but after the comfortable habitation of Devonshire House one gets spoilt'. To Granville it was like an English Naples to be with Lady Bessborough, Morpeth and Boringdon, with whom his friendship was being further cemented.

While at Teignmouth, the Duchess received news which she had been expecting and dreading. Charles Grey had married. His bride, Mary Elizabeth Ponsonby, allied him doubly with Georgiana's family. Through her father, William Brabazon (later first Lord) Ponsonby, she was related to the Bessboroughs and through her mother to the house of Devonshire. The Duchess had supped with Grey in company with Sheridan and others only a month before but Grey had not mentioned marriage. It was an abrupt ending to the one romance in her life. They continued to meet in public during the rest of her life, but she only occasionally saw 'Mr Black' alone and in secret, when their principal topic of conversation would be Eliza Courtney, a subject of more concern to the Duchess than to Grey, who was to have ten sons and five daughters by Mary Elizabeth

Not long after Grey's marriage, the Duchess began to complain of blinding headaches and of pain in one eye. This eye had given her some trouble fifteen years before, but the inflammation had cleared up after the eye had been bathed in warm milk. This time it did not yield to treatment. On 2 April 1795 Thomas Coutts sent his best wishes for the Duchess's eye and Lady Bessborough's health. He had learned to associate ill-health, the Duchess's, the children's, the Duke's, Lady Elizabeth's or Lady Bessborough's, with pleas for more money. But the eye trouble was no pretext. It grew steadily worse over the next sixteen months. On 1 August 1796 the Duke wrote to the Dowager Countess that the Duchess had been examined by Dr Warren and three eye specialists, John Gunning, Gustavus Hume and Jonathan W. Phipps, who feared she might lose the sight of the afflicted eye, though there was no danger to the other. But even if she lost the sight, it would not alter much the appearance. Then, in a postscript, he added, 'They have taken some blood from the eye since I wrote this letter and they seem to think more favourably of the case than they did some hours ago.'[5]

Knowing the Duke's lethargy Mama and Harriet hurried to Devonshire House. On 4 August Mama wrote to Selina Trimmer that the inflammation had been so great that the eye, the eyelids and adjacent areas were swelled to the size of her hand doubled, sticking out of the face. The doctors had tried without success to reduce the inflammation with leeches. A small ulcer had formed on the top of the cornea and burst, and the damage thus caused was irreparable. If the inflammation increased and another ulcer formed and burst, the whole substance of the eye would be destroyed and collapse in its socket. Luckily the inflammation was so much abated, the eye so much less swelled and the discharge so diminished that the doctors hoped she would recover a degree of vision and a tolerable appearance. The Duchess was not aware of the damage done. She had prayed earnestly for submission to God's will and this had made her calmer and enabled her to bear the pain of the leeches more bravely. The lids were still swelled and scarred, the little opening between them filled with thick white matter. The Dowager could not bear to examine the eye herself but those who had said it was still more horrible.[6]

Lady Bessborough's account was given to Granville. She had scarcely ever quit her sister's room for a moment, using every effort to keep up Georgiana's spirits and her own, to seem calm and cheerful though her heart was breaking. When she did leave the sickroom, she immediately collapsed in mind and body. After three hours of spasms, she felt equal, with the aid of laudanum, to begin a letter, which she finished next day when the crisis seemed over. 'I am almost dead. I believe another day like some of these I have passed would destroy either body or mind. I could not bear it; but have no uneasiness for my health. Her illness has made me as strong as Hercules; I can bear any fatigue or pain without feeling it. Want of sleep, weariness, anxiety – it is all one.'[7]

Mother and sister stayed on at Devonshire House until they were told all danger was past. In October the Duchess went to Chiswick House to recuperate. Acknowledging her first post-operative letter, the Dowager advised her to be careful. The illness might prove a blessing in disguise, a warning to eschew the world. But the world could not be eschewed. 'Still a great invalid and forbid writing', the Duchess had to pen a letter to Coutts. Harriet, she explained, had not known she already owed Coutts £300 when she had asked for £100. 'She was thrown into violent hystericks and past the day very ill indeed, numbness and cold, as usual being the consequence of agitation. It was receiving a harsh letter from you that hurt her so.' She implored Coutts always to apply to herself, 'but, oh, for God's sake, never, never to her'.[8]

The Duchess's strength did not equal her courage. Before the end of the year, there were two relapses, the first involving what Harriet called 'a dreadful operation which she bore with wonderful courage, and I with wretched cowardice'.[9] The second consisted in 'applying Causticks behind her ears and blister to the back of her neck for four hours. I never saw anything like the agony she suffers, and the exertions I made to hold and soothe her brought on my old complaint of spasms with great violence. I am perfectly easy now, and she seems charmingly well again, but it was shocking to see; only her fortitude and patience really made it something wonderful.'[10]

The Duchess used 'an excellent invention not to strain the eyes'. She did not complain at losing her beauty but she grew shyer daily. She hated going anywhere except to her own boxes at the theatre or Opera in the reclusion of which her disfigurement was not too noticeable. Her only public appearance in the following year was at a masquerade, in which she could mask her eye, and she dreaded the approach of the time when she would have to bring her elder daughter out. Elizabeth Vassall, by then divorced and married to Lord Holland, described her after yet another 'operation': 'The change is painful to see; scarcely has she a vestige of those charms which once attracted all hearts. Her figure is corpulent, her complexion coarse, one eye gone, and her neck immense. How frail is the tenure of beauty.'

Though the world lamented the Duchess's loss of looks, two who loved her were not displeased: Mama and Miss Trimmer. 'I come to the most interesting part of your letter, what regards my dear daughter,' the Dowager wrote to the governess. 'All my consolation from the moment I got over the shock of seeing her poor eye, has been the benefit I have hoped she might derive from it, and for some weeks her sentiments seemed so exactly what I wished that my confidence was very great that this would be one of the happiest epochs in her life, but before I left Chiswick, I feared that the fatal enemy to her peace – the world – was gaining ground perceptibly, and that a barren mortification was all she would reap from what, if properly managed, might produce the richest fruits.'[11]

Interlude Three

Georgiana was aware that the World was a fatal enemy to her peace of spirit. But she could not retire at the age of thirty-nine merely because she had lost her beauty and her health was failing. Sarah Siddons left the stage at the age of thirty-seven when her 'divinity' began to leave her, but the Duchess could not abdicate. Apart from her debts and her rôle in Whig society, she had her duties to the daughters whom she hoped to see married before she died and to Hartington, in whose hands lay the future of the young generation. Alone she turned to prayer; in company she relied on Bess. A poem which she wrote to Lady Elizabeth when she was afraid she would be totally blind testifies to her submission.

> The Life of the Roebuck was mine,
>   As I bounded o'er Valley and Lawn;
> I watched the gay Twilight decline,
>   And worshipped the day-breaking Dawn.
>
> I regret not the freedom of will,
>   Or sigh, as uncertain I tread;
> I am freer and happier still,
>   When by thee I am carefully led.
>
> Ere my Sight was doomed to resign,
>   My heart I surrendered to thee;
> Not a Thought or an Action was mine,
>   But I saw as thou badst me to see.
>
> Thy watchful affection I wait,
>   And hang with Delight on Thy voice;
> And Dependance is softened by fate,
>   Since Dependance on Thee is my Choice.[1]

When they had first met and the Duchess was the patroness with Lady Elizabeth the poor little dependant, Georgiana had proposed various plans to induce John Foster, little f, to part with his children and allow them to be brought up in Devonshire House. But he had insisted on keeping them with a family called Marshall in Dunleer. In 1796 he died and at last Lady Elizabeth found herself a free woman. She could no longer plead to suitors that she was bound in matrimony to an Irish boor. Aged thirty-seven, she was still a very attractive woman. Her health was frail, she was sometimes confined to bed with a high fever, and, like many of her contemporaries she spat blood. But no one knew that tuberculosis was contagious; and, unlike the Duchess's eye complaint, it was not disfiguring. Her cheeks needed no rouge. Her eyes were brilliant, her body slender and her fingers as delicate as a bird's claws. She had a choice of husbands. But Lady Elizabeth did not want to marry. If she did, what would happen to Caro and Augustus Clifford? Either she would have to leave them at Devonshire House or, if she took them with her, the world would recognize her infidelities.

She decided that the time had come for the Devonshires to redeem their promises to Frederick and Augustus Foster. The thought of those two dear boys brought on a 'hemicrania' or migraine, that condition so agonizing to endure and easy to simulate. The Duchess, herself still half-blinded, hastened to write to Frederick telling him that 'appartements' were awaiting him and Augustus at Devonshire House. 'Your dear Mother's heart is so full of anxiety and expectation that any disappointment or delay in the expected moment would be fatal to her health.'[2] They came post haste.

Lady Elizabeth's migraine had been cured by the administration of bark of cinchona in pills with ginger. It was fourteen years since she had waved her sons tearful goodbyes in London. Frederick was now nineteen and Augustus nearly sixteen. She received them in black mourning velvet, wearing on her bosom a miniature of Frederick.[3] The Duchess found Frederick plain but most interesting and sensible, Augustus a very fine boy. But the Cavendish girls thought them a couple of pills. Frederick made jokes which made himself laugh. Both boys assumed a superiority because they were older than the girls, but they talked with an Irish accent, had provincial manners and knew nobody in polite society. Even without these disadvantages, they would have been unwelcome, because their mother was Lady Liz, who was affected, patronizing and the more odious for seeming so sweet and solicitous.

Lady Liz's sons, however, having been brought up in dreary Dunleer on a diet of slander, were already prejudiced in their mother's favour. Her fame, her conquests, her social grandeur had made her fabulous in absence. Her presence in the splendour of Devonshire House entranced them. When she lavished on them the blandishments that had enslaved Count Fersen, the author of *The Decline and Fall of the Roman Empire* and the Dukes of Devonshire, Dorset and Richmond, they might have echoed the Duchess's poem in praise of Lady Elizabeth:

> A la beauté enchanteresse,
>> Elle unit l'attrait de l'ésprit;
> Par un regard elle interesse,
>> Par un sourire elle seduit.*[4]

By this time the Duke had sent them both to Oxford at his own expense, Lady Elizabeth congratulated herself that they had been accepted 'as *enfants de famille*'.[5] Another crisis had been met and mastered.

As the eighteenth century approached its end Lady Elizabeth could look back with satisfaction. Everything had gone as she planned. The Duke had his heir. The Duchess had been delivered of Miss Eliza Courtney without an open scandal. The families had been united. She and Caro St Jules were accepted into Devonshire House. The story that Caro was the *protégée* of the Duchesse de Polignac had been made more plausible by the adoption of a genuine French refugee, Mlle Corisande (or Corise) de Grammont, a connection of the Polignacs. The Duchess of Devonshire had surrendered her heart to Bess. 'Not a Thought or an Action was mine, But I saw as thou badst me to see.'

But what of the future? What would happen, if her dearest friend, who frankly ate and drank too much for the good of her health, should be called to her Maker before poor little Bess? It was not a prospect that Lady Elizabeth wanted to contemplate. But ever since committing the folly of marrying John Foster under the illusion that she was in love, she had realized the importance of foresight.

Perhaps that was the reason why the Duchess had ended her French poem in praise of Lady Elizabeth the enchantress with four warning lines:

> Mortels, craintifs fuyez ses charmes,
>> Fuyez son pouvoir enchanteur.
> La cruelle impose les peines,
>> Au lieu de donner le bonheur.†[6]

---

* Lit.: 'To beauty enchanting she unites/The attraction of the spirit;/By a look she interests,/By a smile she seduces.'

† Lit.: 'Mortals, flee her charms in fear, Flee her power to enchant. Cruel, she inflicts punishment, Instead of giving happiness.'

13

At the end of 1799 Lady Bessborough discharged her debts and recovered her health. In relief she gave herself to Lord Granville and early in 1800 she confessed to the Duchess that she was going to have a baby in August.

This was unfortunately timed. Lady Georgiana's seventeenth birthday fell on 12 July. Arrangements were being made to present her at Court on the King's birthday in June and on 11 July to give a magnificent coming-out ball for four hundred guests, among whom it was hoped there might be one who would prove willing and worthy to take Lady Georgiana for his bride.

Five years earlier Lady Bessborough had assured Granville that there never existed a stricter confidence than there had been for years between the Duchess, Lady Elizabeth and herself. It might have been expected that as an expert in clandestine *accouchements*, Bess would have been called in for advice and aid. But she was not. She knew about lying-in abroad: but suspicious would have been aroused if Lady Bessborough, now restored to health, had absented herself from Lady Georgiana's debut by crossing a Channel blockaded by the French fleet. The two sisters decided to go it alone, perhaps with the assistance of some discreet practitioner such as the Dr G. who had been so useful to Lady Elizabeth at Rouen twelve years before.

The King's birthday presented no sartorial difficulties. Though fashions had changed since the French Revolution, the Court of St James adhered to the great hooped skirts which could be made to conceal *grossesse*. Perhaps an indisposition may have excused Lady Bessborough from attending the coming-out ball. Among a throng so vast, her absence would have passed unnoticed.

She and Lord Bessborough no longer slept together (her conjugal duties were over, the eldest of her four children coming up for nineteen), and when invitations took her husband and the children away for summer holidays she was left to cultivate her garden at Manresa House, Roehampton.* She had many local interests. In emulation of Mama's good works at St Albans, she had started a hostel two years before where unfortunate girls could lie in and, while nursing their babies, learn the rudiments of domestic service before being found positions elsewhere on Lady Bessborough's recommendation.

On 22 August Lady Bessborough reportedly fell downstairs. Though Roehampton is only a few miles from London, none of her usual doctors was called. Lord Bessborough was not informed, nor was the Dowager Countess. But every day the Duchess, who was conveniently at Chiswick House, crossed the River Thames at Barn Elms with presents of fruit to inquire after the health of her sister and of the baby girl, Harriet Arundel Stewart, who had been born on 23 August and, I imagine, stealthily conveyed later to the crèche in the hostel for fallen women.[1]

When Lady Bessborough returned to Cavendish Square, she wrote a letter to Granville (15 September). 'I came to town, as I told you I would. I was taken from the carriage *lifeless*, and poor Frederico [her manservant] storm'd and rav'd like a madman. They could not pacify him till after I was in my room, and a little recover'd, he was brought in to see me alive. . . .'[2] Five doctors were summoned. Her head was shaved. The scalp was scrutinized. They withdrew for a conference (each with his walking stick in the top of which was placed a bottle of smelling salts for use in cases of putrescence). Then they delivered a unanimous verdict. There was no necessity for an operation on the cranium. Lord Bessborough was duly grateful and suggested that it would help his wife's convalescence if the Devonshires' invitation to Derbyshire were accepted.

Next day the Duchess wrote to Lord Granville inviting him to Chatsworth and to ask Lord Ossulton and H. Bennet if they would like to come. 'I think the more Men the better and I would like to have some names to add to our usual list.'[3] There was a plethora of women in the Devonshire household. Could the Cavendish girls have invited H. Bennet, Ossulton's brother, as a possible husband for Miss Trimmer? Lord O. was for Corisande de Grammont. Lord Tankerville, his father, did not approve of French nobility who had been dis-

---

* She had recently taken up horticulture. When she remarked how strange it was with pineapples at a guinea each in the shops people did not grow their own, the head gardener observed that those grown in the Roehampton hothouse cost about three guineas apiece.

possessed, but he might relent. As for Lord Granville, what could Lord Bessborough suspect if his wife met him as a Chatsworth guest?

The great house-party lasted for months. The centre of attention was Lord Morpeth, who had been Lady Georgiana's principal dancing partner at the coming-out and other balls. He was clearly ready to be brought to proposal point and the Dowager Countess Spencer was invited to be at hand to congratulate her grandson-in-law-to-be. The enormous house was filled with relatives like Lord John and Lady 'Jockey' Townshend and old friends like James Hare.

Eyes were so fixed upon the young couple that others who wanted to have fun could do so unsuspected. Lord John Townshend, no longer as infatuated with 'Jockey' as when she had been another man's wife, laid siege to a Mrs Spencer.[4] Lord Granville and Lady Bessborough were able to enjoy one another more easily and longer than in clandestine meetings in Cavendish Square. The Dowager Countess's searchlight eyes, usually scanning the assembly for impropriety, were fastened on the courting pair and, as usual, with disapproval. Lord Morpeth was all that could be desired in a wooer. But Lady Georgiana Cavendish was stand-offish. She was smitten with 'a certain person now in Scotland'. Of course no *pressure* could be put on the girl, but the Duke, whose constitution was feeling the strain of over-eating, over-drinking and compulsory jollity, let it be known that, should Lady Georgiana accept Lord Morpeth, there would be a dowry of £30000 and Londesborough House to live in.[5] Nonetheless Lady Georgiana would not say yes, Lord Morpeth left in a pique, the Dowager Countess retired to her Sunday Schools in St Albans and Lord Bessborough and Lord Granville, who had found they had much in common, apart from Lady Bessborough, travelled up to do business in London in the same carriage.

On their departure it seemed as if the campaign was ended. The Duke of Devonshire was so ill that James Hare suggested accompanying him to Bath to undertake a cure. But the Duke was resolute. He had had to give up stag-hunting, but he was still capable of husband-hunting. Lord John Townshend applauded his resolution. He himself, without relaxing his pursuit of Mrs Spencer, turned his attention also to Lady Bessborough.[6] Those long corridors at Chatsworth were magnificent for hunting women. When Lady 'Jockey' complained, he accused her of flirting with little Lord Ossulton.

The marriage campaign was resumed in December. The Dowager Countess did not feel up to another visit but back came Morpeth, Bessborough and Granville eager for more. Apart from the children, they sat down twenty-three to dinner. In a week they ate twenty-three sheep and two oxen. The Dowager was appalled. How many pounds of meat, she asked, were yielded by a fat ox and a sheep?[7] She seems to have feared that the Devonshires would banquet themselves into bankruptcy before getting Lady Georgiana off their hands. Huge dinners were followed by sumptuous suppers, washed down by gallons of wine. It must have been a nice calculation, to gorge Georgiana into acceptance without stuffing Morpeth beyond proposal point. But on 18 December this gargantuan courtship reached its climax. Morpeth proposed. Lady Georgiana accepted. The Duke relaxed. And dozens of pens scribbled away the momentous news.

On Christmas Day the Prince of Wales sat down and wrote a letter of congratulation as florid as he had grown since he had first written to 'Perdita' Robinson as her Florizel. It might seem strange that in the middle of what we must regard in retrospect as the *first* world war, he should have had the time for such an effusion. But the tragedy of the Royal Family at that time was that though his brothers could be usefully employed by King George III, the Prince of Wales, as heir to the throne, was given no job and afforded no experience which might qualify him to succed his father.

It might seem equally strange that when Lady Elizabeth Foster heard that her mother, Lady Bristol, had died at Ickworth Park, she did not hasten south to join her younger sister, Louisa, for the funeral. But in those days, women never attended a burial. They just wore black and put mourning rings on their fingers and wrote letters, sincere or insincere. So nobody thought Lady Elizabeth unfilial in not going home.[8]

But there was comment after Christmas. Lord Morpeth had to hurry back to London for the New Year. The Duchess and Lady Georgiana had to follow to make preparations for the wedding, the magnificence of which can be judged by Nunn & Barber's bill of £3368 9s 6d, just for lace, muslins, ribbons and handkerchiefs.[9] In previous years Lady Elizabeth had been the centre of all attention. But during Morpeth's courtship, she and her beloved children had been pushed into the background. In the forthcoming marriage celebrations, she knew that she would be equally obscure. 'I have offered to stay with the Duke,' she wrote to the Duke of Richmond, whom she still counted amongst her adorers. 'I am aware how much it may renew old stories, and he has been uneasy about it, but I have told him how little I mind if it does so, and have made him consent to my staying. . . .'[10] It seems unlikely that during their stay together at Chatsworth she again became his mistress

– the gouty Duke was in too much pain for pleasure – but what mattered to Lady Elizabeth was to publicize an intimacy which she hitherto had striven to hide. 'I trust the D. of D. will take courage, and come to town the first moment he can,' James Hare warned the Duchess. 'I dislike the last account of him. The stomach with him is the important part.'[11]

The marriage took place on 21 March and the young couple went to Castle Howard, choosing to live there rather than in Londesborough House. Their marriage, despite its hesitations and delays, was a brilliant success. In temperament Lady Morpeth was as equable as her grandmother, the Dowager Countess, and within a few months she was expecting a 'petit paquet', the first of a dozen she was to present to her husband. When the Devonshires went to stay at Castle Howard, the Duchess must have envied her daughter's life with a man so agreeable in conditions so free from giddy temptation.

December 1801 saw Chatsworth crowded once more. The Duke had gout in both feet and one knee. Lord Granville was once more among the guests, much to his mother's distress. Lady Stafford had heard that he had returned to town the previous year with 'a pale, languid Face – quite the Appearance of a Person out of Health'.[12] So she was pleased to hear that the Dowager Countess Spencer was among the party, to ensure an early retirement. Lady Spencer, she thought, would be a very good 'Guide and Counsellor' to Granville. As for the others, 'I have a real regard for the Duke of Devon., and, I hope, when the Gout leaves him, that he will be quite well; but I am not impatient for that Epoch; a little Gout will do him no great harm, and good Hours will do you much Good; so will they the Duchess and Lady Bessborough. . . .'[13]

Lord Bessborough also had gout, his first attack, which he said was almost worth having to be so lovingly nursed by his Countess. After she had seen Harum tucked up in his bed, Granville slipped into hers. Early nights were enjoyed by all. The Duchess knew that the love her sister felt for Granville was more poignant than anything she had experienced with Grey. Harriet had resisted longer and then fallen more deeply into love. There was no telling where it would end.

When Granville left to join his parents at their country place the weather closed in. Snow covered the Derbyshire Peak. The River Derwent froze and the younger generation came into their own. Caro St Jules dressed up with a brown wig and blackened eyebrows and appeared among the skaters, pretending to be Lady William Russell. Corisande deceived Mr Adair as a weeping housemaid and Duncannon put on a carter's smock and swept the snow. 'Skating makes us very gay,' the Duchess told Mama who had returned to St Albans.[14] She meant 'them'. Georgiana had become a spectator. But it was delightful when William Ponsonby and Augustus Clifford, who had gone straight from Harrow into the Navy, were given leave by Lord St Vincent in anticipation of a negotiated peace with France.*

When the Treaty of Amiens was signed at the end of March, Georgiana exulted: 'Peace! Peace!'[15] Like Fox, who hailed the treaty with 'joy and exultation', she had never approved the war. Addington was nearer the mark: 'a Peace everyone was glad of and no one was proud of'. The Channel was open again. Social interchange began once more, but not without suspicion. The French envoy, M. Otto, was received tepidly. The three sons of Philippe Egalité, who had spent the last four years in a French prison, were cheered by everyone, Whig and Tory alike. The twenty-five-year-old Mme Récamier in full beauty was received enthusiastically at Devonshire House. The Duchess took her to the Opera and introduced her to the Prince of Wales. Her appearance caused such a sensation that she was smuggled out through a private exit before the final curtain.[16]

The London salons buzzed with talk of Paris and Bonaparte. Charles Fox and James Hare were among the first to go to France. Before Fox left, he announced that Mrs Armistead, with whom he had been living for ages at St Anne's, Chertsey, had in fact been his wife for the last eight years. 'Those who were shocked at the immorality of his having a mistress,' observed Lady Bessborough, 'are still more so at that mistress having been his wife for so long.'[17]

When Lady Elizabeth announced her intention of going to Paris with Caro St Jules and Frederick Foster, she was outraged by Sheridan's remarking 'that she went to Paris as most ladies did, under cover of [seeing] the Apollo Belvedere but really to display all the tenderness of her nature'.[18] He would bet anything that she would faint seven times running when first she saw Bonaparte, if nothing else would attract his attention. What an insult to the friend of Marie Antoinette and the Duchesse de Polignac! The Bessboroughs planned to cross the Channel and urged the Devonshires to come too. But before they went, there were social duties to perform and further marriage plans to pursue

Hary-O was to be presented at Court in the following year. To put everybody in good humour and allow more freedom for smaller parties

* When Lady Elizabeth called them 'Our two dear little midshipmen', Hary-O and Caro Ponsonby must have shuddered and giggled with delight at this Lady Liz-ism.

after the presentation, the Duchess planned a 'great breakfast' at Chiswick House in June 1802 to get over all the people she was obliged to entertain.[19] Then in late August the Devonshire family moved down to Ramsgate, together with Lady Elizabeth, Caro St Jules, Corisande de Grammont and Frederick Foster. They were joined there in September by the Bessboroughs. Lady Melbourne was already there with George Lamb, and Frederick Lamb arrived later. For the Duchess and Lady Bessborough it was no rest cure. 'If you were with me at this moment, and many other hours in the day, you would go mad,' Lady Bessborough wrote to Granville. 'On one side I have a boarding school, where various instruments and Voices are playing and solfégeing so loud that it makes perfect discord; on the other side Harriet is practising the Harp with Mdlle Menel, Corisande on the piano forte, Caroline St Jules on the guitar, and my Caro up stairs on the Piano forte – all different music, all loud and all discordant.'[20]

The fond hope was that Hary-O and Duncannon would find each other as desirable partners as their parents imagined. But nothing is more destructive of love than to follow a parent's or an aunt's desire. At nearby Margate was Lady Elizabeth Villiers. Her mother, Lady Jersey, had already caught Duncannon's cousin, John Ponsonby* for her younger daughter, Lady Frances. Now she was out to catch young Duncannon, who kept popping over to Margate. Lady Bessborough urged him not to mistake a *fantaisie* for real love. 'Use a better argument,' he answered, 'and say you dislike it and wish me to avoid Lady Elizabeth.'[21] Off he went to London and did not come back until the Bessboroughs were ready for France.

In October the Ramsgate party broke up. The Bessboroughs and the Fosters sailed to France. The Duke, the Duchess and Hary-O remained in England. The Duke's gout was better, but he was afraid that if he crossed the Channel it might grow worse. The Duchess felt too ill to dissuade him. One can see the failing of her eyesight in the degeneration of her handwriting. The headaches were almost continuous. Sometimes she spent a day or two in bed with a pain in what seemed the intestines. Her letters to Lady Elizabeth were sad. 'My dearest,' Bess cooed from Paris, 'why are 'oo gloomy? Why are 'oo vexed?'[22]

Lady Elizabeth was having the time of her life, on the Duke's money. She did not have to faint seven times to attract Napoleon's attention. Out of loyalty to Marie Antoinette, she could not attend his assemblies,

---

*John Ponsonby, heir of William, first Lord Ponsonby of Imokilly, and brother of Mrs Charles Grey, by then Lady Howick.

but she asked her dear Marshal Berthier if Napoleon would turn his head as he walked past reviewing his regiments. 'The moment that he came to where I was, I only thought of him as a conqueror amid his troops and forgot the Tyrant.'[23]

'*My dearest Bess,*' Georgiana pleaded on Boxing Day 1802. '*Do you hear the voice of my heart crying to you? Do you feel what it is for me to be separated from you,* or do new scenes and occupations obliterate the image of a poor, dull, useless insignificant being such as myself?'[24]

Lady Elizabeth's only response was to suggest that the Duchess should send Hary-O to Paris. The girl might be dumpy, but Lady Elizabeth knew corsetiers who could discipline the most refractory of figures.

Two months later the Duke added his humble pleas. 'I don't make out exactly from your letter in what manner you mean to draw for money, but I assure you that whatever sum you may want will be paid by me with as much pleasure, and I may truly say with more, than I should advance it to answer any purpose of my own. We are very impatient to see you and I hope you will return soon, though I cannot wish you to act contrary to your inclination and your feelings upon this occasion, of which you are the best judge. Yours, dearest Bess, sincerely D.'[25]

The Bessboroughs and the Morpeths came back at the end of February but Lady Elizabeth lingered on, even though it was increasingly plain that the Peace that 'no one was proud of' would be broken by a war that was inevitable. She did not return until the end of April, leaving Frederick Foster, young Duncannon and James Hare trapped by the renewal of hostilities. In fact they would have been interned if Bess had not cajoled Marshal Berthier to give them passports: an infatuated service for which he was 'shockingly scolded' by the First Consul.[26]

Lady Elizabeth's influence over Marshal Berthier made plain that she had become a power in her own right. There was no longer one Devonshire household, but two under the same roof. The Duchess was primarily concerned with Lady Harriet Cavendish and Hartington, now that young Georgiana was married and contentedly breeding. Lady Elizabeth had Caro St Jules and Augustus Clifford whose interests she used every occasion to impress upon the indolent Duke. She also had Frederick and Augustus Foster, whom she regarded primarily as a Hervey responsibility, but she was equally solicitous for both her broods. For example, when news came in July 1803 that the island of St Lucia had been seized from the French, she called on the Duke to rejoice that their son Augustus Clifford had been in actual war, and only thirteen years old.[27] When she heard a week later that her father had died suddenly of 'gout in the stomach' in an outhouse on his way from Albano to Rome,* she immediately enlisted her brother Frederick, now fifth Earl of Bristol,† on behalf of the Foster boys. For Frederick Foster she secured the parliamentary seat of Bury St Edmunds, which the new Earl vacated on his succession: for Augustus Foster the promise of a Secretaryship of Legation as soon as one fell due.[28]

The Duke of Devonshire assured her that the love and friendship that he had felt so long were firmly fixed and unalterable. This was gratifying because now that he had reached his fifties he had started behaving skittishly. His daughter Harriet observed, 'It was ridiculous to see papa and the Duchess of St Albans flirting the whole evening, and as she is terribly deaf, he was obliged to repeat all the little gallanteries and small talk two or three times ... to the amusement of us all.'[29] The news of his carrying-on had even reached Hare in Paris. 'If the pursuit . . . serves to amuse you for an hour or two in public, and still more if now and then for a few minutes in private,' wrote Hare on 2 November 1802, 'I shall rejoice in it as a compleat recovery of health and spirits . . . if you are seriously in love, I am not sure I shall enter into all your lovesick feelings.'[30]

---

* Three months before he had been described as 'sitting in his carriage between two Italian women, dress'd in a white Bed-gown and night-cap like a witch and giving himself the airs of an Adonis'. The Earl-Bishop had expressed the wish to be buried at Ickworth Park. Knowing that sailors were afraid of carrying corpses, the British Minister at Naples put him in a crate labelled ANTIQUE STATUE before loading him on a British man-of-war.

† The elder brother Augustus, Lord Hervey, having made a disastrous failure as British Minister at Florence, had died at sea in January 1796, as a result not of enemy action, but of catching cold.

14

As gratifying to Lady Elizabeth as the Duke's reassurance of his love and friendship was the Duchess's request that in the event of her death Bess would undertake the ordering of her private papers. In 1803 the Duchess was only forty-six, but in September she was stricken with a mysterious and agonizing illness. From time to time she complained of belly spasms. Lady Elizabeth, who merely coughed blood, attributed her dearest friend's attacks to eating and drinking too much,[1] but, whatever the cause, on 13 September the Duchess suffered a seizure more acute and prolonged than ever before.

Even if he had wished, the Duke could not have been much use. A week before he had had a fall at Chiswick House, which his mother-in-law with gloomy satisfaction considered might be fatal in case of hernia.

From London Sir Walter Farquhar, physician to the Prince of Wales, was summoned for his medical opinion, and from Roehampton Lady Bessborough, herself a frequent sufferer from 'dreadful spasms' at moments of crisis, hastened to her sister's bedside. They found the Duchess in agony. Sir Walter was perplexed. According to his textbooks, Her Grace should be suffering from obstructive jaundice, but there was no evidence of yellow, green or orange discoloration. In those days, some surgeons would remove a gallstone without anaesthetics in under a minute and, provided that sepsis did not set in, the patient recovered. But there were no X-rays to identify the seat of obstruction and exploratory surgery would have resulted in certain death. All that Sir Walter could advise was immersion in a warm bath, while blood was let. After this operation, the Duchess either fainted or went to sleep. At any rate she lost consciousness for three hours, leaning on her sister's arm. Immediately she regained consciousness, the pain was as acute as ever.

We know from Lady Bessborough's letters to Granville how agonizing the next seven days appeared to her: at first keeping a twenty-four hour watch at the bedside, reading aloud almost uninterruptedly. The tormented Duchess did not take in the sense, but the sound of a voice penetrated senses deadened by laudanum and reassured her that she was not alone.[2] We know that soon Lady Bessborough's vigil was shared with the Dowager Countess, turn and turn about. Presumably others, the Duke, Lady Harriet Cavendish, Hartington, and Lady Elizabeth tiptoed in to see the patient; but the burden of nursing fell on her sister and mother while Sir Walter remained in constant, if futile, attendance. His Royal patron waived Sir Walter's services for himself, though as the First Gourmandizer in Europe he suffered four days' stoppage of the bowels, followed by sixty motions.[3]

But we can only speculate what the Duchess herself thought as, hovering between life and death, she endured the tortures of hell on earth. Death must have seemed welcome as an end to agony, but her sense of duty reinforced her will to live. She had not set her affairs in order. Probably foremost in her mind was her daughter Hary-O, since until Hary-O was married off and her future secured with an adequate dowry, the Duchess could not feel at peace. Hary-O's cousin, Viscount Duncannon, was the ideal husband for her, but Duncannon was restless, anxious to sow a few wild oats before settling down, and Hary-O was not the easiest of girls: she had not enough beauty and too sharp a wit for most men.

Georgiana's debts were also a worry. There was no hope of their being liquidated in her lifetime and she had not much hope that the Duke, advised by Heaton, would ever repay dear Thomas Coutts, who had always been so generous and patient. She had written that letter to Hartington, begging him when he came of age or when he succeeded to the Dukedom to rescue her good name by paying what was due to the banker in the Strand. But she wanted to live a little longer to fortify the love between herself and her son: as a boy, he had been very withdrawn and she had imagined that he had inherited the unfortunate Cavendish temperament. But two years earlier she had discovered that he was hard of hearing. The reason why he had shut himself off from other people was that he did not know what they were saying. In temperament he was far more like herself than his father, generous, warm-hearted and loving. He adored his cousin Caro Ponsonby and though she was three years older than he, he wanted to marry her when he reached the age of eighteen. That would be in 1808, a little less than five years' time. If only she could live to see that happen, the Duchess felt that she would have rounded off her time on earth.

On 21 September she passed 'a gall stone of amazing size',[4] and though she felt very weak, the pain left her. She was 'well' again.[5] She and the Duke went to Bath, to recuperate and incidentally to see Dr Francis Randolph, Prebendary of Bristol, whom she had taken as her spiritual adviser, so to speak, her Coutts in God.

She was rather frightened of introducing him to the Duke, though gout and the prospect of death had awakened the Duke's interest in religion. Though 'the best and warmest hearted of creatures', Randolph was 'all heart and no head'. 'His want of knowledge of the world,' she confessed to Mama, 'is such that I should not be surpris'd if he thunder'd at a sermon at *us all* today and preach'd against indolence etc.' Perhaps the Duke did not consider that anything delivered from the pulpit could be levelled at His Grace; at any rate, he pronounced Dr Randolph 'in reading and preaching the finest he had heard'.[6]

The Duchess became assiduous in prayer. But the world remained the fatal enemy to her peace; and she did not live to see the fulfilment of any of her hopes. Early in 1805 Lord Melbourne's heir, the Honourable Peniston Lamb, died of tuberculosis and William Lamb, now heir apparent, declared to Caro Ponsonby the love he had long cherished but been too impoverished to avow. The future Prime Minister of Britain did not appear much of a prize. He drank too much, was loose in his morals and could not pronounce his *r*'s. In his cups he had lectured Hary-O on 'the danger of a *young woman's* believing in *weligion* and *pwactising mowality*'.[7] But the Duchess and her sister, unhappy victims of arranged marriages, did not feel justified in opposing a marriage of true love and Lady Bessborough left it to Caro to decide. 'And that decision is in my favour, thank Heaven!' exclaimed William Lamb, and, to Lady Bessborough's embarrassment, embraced her in the foyer of Drury Lane Theatre in front of Mr Canning, who knew, and disapproved, of her affair with Lord Granville.[8]

When the fifteen-year-old Hartington heard the news he went into hysterics, declared he looked on Caro Ponsonby as his wife and swore that she might think it hard to wait for him, but he would have waited any time for her. The Duchess had to summon Sir Walter Farquhar to give him a sedative.[9] And in May 1805 Caro Ponsonby became Lady Caroline Lamb, a blissful bride who was destined to become a disastrous wife.

The plans for Hary-O proved equally fruitless. Childhood friendship might have matured to true love, if its path had not been made so smooth, but Duncannon, feeling cornered, first declared that he was not keen to marry at the moment and then married the heiress Lady Maria Fane in November. Lady Harriet, left on the shelf at the age of twenty, said she wept no tears for her '*ci-devant*' lover, but the Duchess felt sad. Everything was closing in on her and little time was left.

The final monetary crisis had begun when Lady Elizabeth was still in France and the Duke was assuring her that she could spend any money of his that she liked on herself and Caro St Jules. At that time he ignored the Duchess's debts, which were so much greater than the few hundreds or the thousand or two which were necessary for Lady Elizabeth's day-to-day expenses that they could not be compared. We do not know enough about psychosomatic illness to say to what extent, if at all, the stone in the Duchess's gall bladder was caused by her money worries. We know only that she used every excuse, physical and political, to postpone the Final Reckoning. She could no longer discuss finance with the Duke. When he played Heaton as his pawn, she had countered with Coutts. Lady Elizabeth and James Hare had acted as honest brokers between both sides. But in March 1804 James Hare suddenly died at the age of fifty-five.[10] The settled plan for negotiations was disturbed and a new scheme had to be drawn up. In the place of Hare, Charles Fox and Robert Adair were chosen to become future administrators of the Duchess's financial affairs, with Lady Elizabeth remaining as a backstairs negotiator.[11] They all agreed that the Duchess must be bound financially as fast as Lemuel Gulliver by the Lilliputians. She was a mad spendthrift who must be put in a straitjacket. One would not gather from Lady Elizabeth's journals that she had anything to do with this lethal operation. But Lady Bessborough's letters to Granville show that Bess was consulted at every stage.

The disclosures lasted weeks. On 8 November the Duke 'knew everything except the amount'. Two weeks later, 'He expects *five* or *six* – and it comes to thirty-five.' Lady Bessborough had no need to say she was writing of thousands. A fortnight later, she was in high hopes. 'All goes well for Sis . . . it is, alas, past 40, but it is to be done by degrees.'[12]

The Duchess had endured leeches to reduce the congestion which had protruded her eye like a clenched fist; she had suffered the agony of passing a stone of amazing size. But spiritually the pain can have been nothing compared with the humiliation of confessing to borrowing from servants, doctors, friends, relatives and chance acquaintances. 'Make up the account as much against yourself as possible,'[13] urged Charles Fox, who knew the gambler's temptation to ignore those small sums which were most shameful to recall. 'Count up, for God's sake, every debt you have,' Robert Adair pleaded; 'everything which, although not strictly debt, has a tendency to produce debt, and even those things which by bearing an appearance of obligation, might lead people to reasonable expectations of future favour. . . . Remember that you are now drawing out your last stake; you are disposing of the fee simple of your resources and that you are, in a manner, *at your world's end*, beyond which there is no room for hope to live in.'[14] Her sister, Lady Bessborough, saw even further: 'I am extremely anxious as I think it far more than mere relief, but literally a concern of life and death.'[15]

Darkness fell from the air. One day in November 1805 Lady Bessborough set out from Roehampton to meet some people in Queen Street, London. The fog, thick when she started, grew denser and denser. It was so pitchy in Hyde Park that it was impossible to find the way. The footman got down to *feel* the road. The holloing of unseen drivers and muffled screams of pedestrians pierced the murk. It took an hour to find a way out of the Park and Lady Bessborough decided to turn back to Roehampton. Two men carried flambeaux in front of the horses. The coachmen could not see the men. Even the flames were barely visible. Every ten or twenty yards they had to knock at a door to ask where they were. It took three hours to reach Chelsea, at which time the air began to clear a little. Lady Villiers, befogged, rode into the Thames and was near drowned.[16]

Next day a horseman galloped to Chiswick with a despatch. The Duchess read it and ran to Bess who was reading Herodotus with Caro in the gallery. The Duchess looked so pale that Lady Elizabeth thought she had been taken ill again. There had been a battle at Trafalgar, the Duchess said. Lord Nelson was dead. But what about Augustus Clifford on the *Tigre*? asked Lady Elizabeth. What about Robert Spencer, the Duchess's nephew? The Earl Spencer, his father, was First Lord of the Admiralty. He ought to know.

Ropes were tugged. Bells jangled in the servant's quarters. A footman came with decorous speed and then ran to the stables. Horses were harnessed and backed between the shafts of the fast cabriolet. In what, a hundred and seventy years ago, was almost no time, the Duchess and Lady Elizabeth were bowling down the turnpike road to London, accompanied by Hartington, who hero-worshipped Nelson.[17]

As they raced along, Lady Elizabeth kept saying that it was only six weeks before, 6 September to be precise, that she, the Duke and Freddie Foster had dined at 'Fish' Craufurd's to meet Lord Nelson and Lady

Hamilton. Nelson has asked her to drink a glass of wine with him, so that he could tell dear Augustus Clifford he had done so: and after dinner she had given the Admiral a letter, begging Nelson to put it into Clifford's own hand. 'Kiss it then!' said Nelson, 'and I shall take that kiss to him.'[18]

Trafalgar was a victory, but in the streets faces were sad. Exultation was lost in sorrow among the crowds thronging the Admiralty. A messenger, recognizing the Duchess, told her that Robert Spencer had not been in action. 'What about the *Tigre?*' asked Elizabeth. Though the messenger did not know, he took them to an officer who said that the *Tigre* had been sent with Admiral Louis on another service. And Nelson? Dead. Shot by a midshipman from the mainmast of the *Rédoutable*.

Back at Devonshire House, they were drawn close together by the mournful victory. The Duke could talk of nothing else. When a special edition of a newspaper arrived at dinner, the Duchess, wearing her crape eye-shade, read it aloud. Public mourning was to be a black scarf or rosette so that even the poorest could manifest their grief. Lady Elizabeth begged the Duke to pen some lines worthy of the hour.

The Duke laboured through a gouty night and next morning produced what Lady Elizabeth called six 'noble lines', of which the third was a concession to Virtue.

> Oft had Britannia sought midst dire alarms
> Divine protection for her sons in arms.
> Generous and brave, though not from Vices free,
> Britons from Heaven received a mixed decree.
> To crown their merits but to check their pride
> God gave them Victory but Nelson died.[19]

When the *Victory* berthed at Portsmouth, bearing the coffin made from the mainmast of the French flagship *L'Orient* and 'the greatest sailor since the world began', pickled in rum (which incidentally was tapped by the crew en route), Hartington posted down to honour the fallen hero. It was a homage which endeared him to his mother.[20] On the other hand Lady Harriet Cavendish was not won over by Lady Liz's 'despair for Lord Nelson'. 'Her private affectation is enough to destroy the effect of a whole nation's public feelings. While she is regretting that she could not "have died in his defence", her peevish hearers almost wish she had.'[21]

Lord Nelson's body lay in state at Greenwich. Then, even as the bier was borne to the Admiralty and thence to St Paul's, came news that Mr Pitt was ill. He could not attend the opening of Parliament on 21 January 1806. Two days later he was dead. Young Pitt, beginning with his Mincemeat Parliament, had hunted Fox, his senior by ten years, so astutely that the older man never had a chance of power. Yet it was the Foxite Whigs who mourned him most. 'It feels as if something was missing in the world,' lamented Fox, like a prisoner so long incarcerated that he was saddened to see his cell door open. 'It is awful to reflect on a death of such magnitude,' the Duchess wrote to Hartington, who was in the country with his tutor, 'on the death of a man who had so long fill'd an immense space in the universe.'[22] Over twenty years had passed since she had degraded herself for Fox in his fight against Pitt and now the only man to take Pitt's place was Fox himself.

Fox set about forming a ministry with Grenville as Prime Minister, himself at the Foreign Office, Earl Spencer at the Home Office, Charles Grey at the Admiralty and Sheridan Treasurer to the Navy. The Duke of Devonshire was offered any office he wanted. As usual, he preferred none. But the Duchess pleaded in vain for her protégés, the Lords Morpeth and Ossulton. 'I am weary and tired to death,' she wrote to her son. 'I have plagued him [Fox] without knowing his situation, but never will again.'[23] It was prophetic. Neither of them was to live long enough, she to beg, or he to grant, favours.

Her last appearance was at a brilliant assembly and supper which she gave for the new Ministers. Charles Grey was there, but no longer a commoner. He now had the courtesy title of Lord Howick, as his father had just been given an earldom. During the political crisis just over a year before the Duchess had written him a letter ending, 'God bless you. Give my love to my baby.'[24] They were probably also the last words she spoke to him, as he kissed her hand that evening in departure.

When Charles Fox was once more returned as MP for Westminster, the Duchess was too exhausted to see him chaired round Covent Garden 'like Bacchus'. The famous Westminster Election of 1784 seemed a lifetime ago, the huzza-ing progress to Devonshire House, the young Florizel at the head of the stairs, the banner Sacred to Female Patriotism, the triumph at the hustings and the shame of Plumpers sold for Pouting Lips.

She could no longer see to write. She had a crippled little Derbyshireman to act as amanuensis, even for the letters which she poured out to her dearest Hartington. On him, her dying love was focused. 'I live in you again,' she dictated on 9 March 1806. 'I adore your sisters, but I see in you still more perhaps than even in them what my youth was. God grant that you may have all its fervours and cheerfulness without partaking of many of the follies which mark'd with giddiness my introduction to the world.'[25]

Simultaneously she seemed assailed by both her physical ailments. The blinding headaches recurred. It was painful to see bright light. And she felt the griping agony which had preceded the passing of the gall-stone.

But this time Sir Walter Farquhar was reassuring. All she had was jaundice, he assured her, not realizing that jaundice was not an illness but merely the symptom of some obstruction of bile from the liver into the intestinal canal. She dictated a letter to Mama assuring her that as the jaundice had turned from orange to yellow, she feared 'no other consequence from the attack'. And then in the penultimate letter of a correspondence which had been continued almost every day they had been apart since she had left Wimbledon for Chiswick thirty-two years earlier, she made one last request. Could Mama lend her £100 until Lady Day?[26]

It was the last straw. After the Final Reckoning, after Fox's pleas and Adair's awful threats, Georgiana was running up debts again! And pretending to be ill, as a sort of blackmail! The Dowager Countess sent the Duchess £20. But then, because her heart was as soft as her moral principles hard, she despatched to Lady Bessborough the remaining £80, to produce if the emergency was really genuine.

'I am so much better today they think it will pass without stone,' the Duchess dictated in her final letter of thanks. 'They give me a complete holiday without physick.' She was dying of an abscess in her liver. But she did not know it. No one knew it. The trouble with Mama, her daughter Hary-O had remarked, was that she had 'a most unfortunate knack of making everything into a scene'.[27] She had so often been so terrifyingly ill that there seemed no reason why she should not recover. But, as a precaution, the Morpeths came to London and Hartington was summoned to Devonshire House from his tutor's in the country.

Four doctors danced attendance. They cut off her red-gold curls, shaved her head and fixed a blister on the scalp. One day she was bad, the next better, the day after far worse. By 25 March Mr Fox was assured that all danger had passed.[28]

Two of the reasons for continuing to live which had sustained her in 1803 had been cancelled. Duncannon had married Lady Maria Fane, Caro Ponsonby had married William Lamb; thus Lady Harriet

Cavendish and young Hartington would have to find mates for themselves. There was no prospect of the Duchess doing anything to help them. And now that the debt business had started again, she may well have remembered Adair's grim warning: 'You are, in a manner, at *your world's end*, beyond which there is no room even for hope to live in!'

On 27 March she had a relapse. After three days of agony 'more horrible, more killing than human being ever witnessed'[29] she ceased to moan. At the age of forty-nine the private Georgiana, Duchess of Devonshire, was dead. She once had written to Calonne, 'I have opened my heart to you and you have seen that despite all my gaiety, it is often quite tormented.'[30] The end had come at last to torment, to borrowing and lying, to giddiness and desperation, to promises made and broken.

But the public Georgiana, the legendary, the beautiful, the natural, warm-hearted, generous Duchess of Devonshire, Empress of Fashion, lived on. She was caught by Downman's water-colour drawing on the terrace of Chatsworth, a young beauty towering to the clouds with the Derwent valley lying at her feet. Reynolds had immortalized her, the delighted mother holding her first-born baby at arms' length. Angelica Kauffmann had captured her in the miniature which hung from a chain on Lady Elizabeth's neck. Gainsborough enshrined her pensive beside a column. Lady Diana Beauclerk profiled her alone, and Jean Guérin in company with Lady Elizabeth. She had been allegorized by Stothard as Liberty and by Maria Cosway as fair Cynthia, Goddess of the Moon. She had been caricatured for her canvass and pilloried for her plumes. Bartolozzi had engraved her after a dozen originals. She embellished ladies' scrapbooks throughout the United Kingdom and the continent of Europe. In North America and the Indies, West or East, 'the Duchess', unless otherwise specified, was Her Grace of Devonshire, Georgiana.

She had composed her own epitaph, ending in this petition:

And to her God she Offered
　Her deep Contrition
And the Sorrows of her Life
　And her presumptuous Hope
That the all-good, long-suffering and all-seeing Power

　Who best could know the extent of her Errors
Would although dreadful in all his Judgements
　Compassionate and Appreciate
　　Her Repentance.[31]

But this was merely to be carved upon the tomb containing the remains of what had once been young and golden, in the hope of peace and happiness in a future world. What remained on earth after she had drawn her last breath was the fame of a woman who epitomized the great ladies of the late eighteenth century as truly as Pitt and Fox the politicians, Nelson the sailors and Sir John Moore the soldiers. She was a legend even before she died. And for those who stood around her deathbed, her grandeur shone unflickeringly forth, when life was extinct.

Even the Duke, who had always seemed to take his Duchess for granted, was bewildered; especially when the four doctors who had agreed that the crisis had passed on 25 March gave four different reasons why she died six days later.

Interlude Four

The Duchess lay in state from 30 March until Easter Sunday, 5 April. Her children wrote nothing of this time – indeed there was never again a mention of her name in any of their letters that have been published. Even the articulate Lady Bessborough was too choked by grief to do more than make brief references[1] in her notes to Granville who was in Petersberg. We have to rely entirely upon the journal of Lady Elizabeth Foster, which at this point launches into an intensely emotional, if novelettish, narrative in the style she had used when she was carrying Caroline Rosalie Adelaide. The death of the Duchess had not taken her by surprise and she had already drafted a scenario of what should happen. She must take the place of Georgiana, in the same way that Georgiana had promised to take her place if she died in giving birth to Augustus Clifford. She must become a mother to Georgiana's children; and the best way to do this was to marry the Duke.

She knew that it would not be easy in the six days before the departure of the hearse for Derby for herself (and for the Duke with whom I am sure she had discussed this melancholy contingency) to bring the children from the abyss of sorrow for their mother to the acceptance of a step-mother. She was-so convinced that she was Georgiana's equal in fame, beauty, knowledge and appreciation, that she could not imagine that the thought of Georgiana, Duchess of Devonshire, being superseded by Elizabeth, Duchess of Devonshire, would be regarded as an even greater outrage to Georgiana's public image than to their private feelings. She had no idea of the hatred and contempt inspired in the children, especially Lady Harriet, by her kind efforts to descend to their level and teach them how to make the best of themselves. But she did realize that her journal would provide testimony of her good faith in actions malicious persons might construe unfavourably.

There is no evidence in her journal narrative of a deliberate plan which misfired and had to be improvised as it began to go wrong. But this can be inferred from the insincerity of the style and from the significant omissions. She caught the feeling of others, but falsified it. 'We are alive – but stunned, not yet feeling or conceiving of our loss, scarce believing it true. . . . My angel friend – angel I am sure she is now – but can I live without her who was the friend of my existence?' (She did not add 'at Devonshire House'.) The Duke was rather calmer. 'But we are a family of sufferers and my heart feels broken.'[2]

They were not 'a family'. They were two families, which would split apart unless she was careful, or unless the Duke insisted on keeping them as one. 'One night the Duke was hysterical. I stayed late, very late, with him. I then went feebly to my room – when I got there I saw in his anxiety he had followed me. Oh, God bless and support him.'

More bereaved than the children, less hysterical than the Duke, Lady Elizabeth sought journalistic solace in prayer. 'Look down on me, a miserable sinner, with pity and forgiveness. Receive that dear friend into Thy Bosom, pardon her errors, reward her virtues – and O my God *purify my heart and make me a comfort to her husband and children*.'[3] These are my italics. Here was the message to Georgiana's children: the desire to become a comfort to them and to the Duke was a Divine inspiration, following the purification of her heart. Yet if she *had* prayed to God, she would have recorded this as a fact, not a prayer. This was like a sentimental heroine's soliloquy in a third-rate melodrama, more hollow-sounding because when she was sincere Lady Elizabeth could write well.

She observed the children. Time was a great healer. But she did not have enough of it. She moved with them through the darkened house as in a *danse macabre*, of which the centre was the unmoving Duchess lying, chin bound, shaved head covered, at peace at last. She did not dare to speak about the future to the Duchess's daughters until the evening of 4 April. She would have liked to delay longer, but next morning at dawn the Duke and Hartington were following the hearse to Derby. Caro St Jules and Corisande were sent to their rooms and Lady Elizabeth had a conversation with Lady Morpeth and Lady Harriet Cavendish which she described as 'interesting'.[4] From the later correspondence of the two sisters it is plain that they told Lady Elizabeth that no one could take the place of their mother and the last person on earth to be 'a comfort' to them was Lady Liz.

Lady Morpeth left Devonshire House about midnight. Lady Elizabeth retired to her room; and, I think, Lady Harriet stormed off to Hartington, raging against 'that woman's' impertinence. She might have been

Papa's mistress, but in deference to Mama and to society, she must leave the Duke's household now.

We know from Lady Elizabeth's journal that shortly afterwards Hartington tapped on her door, making the excuse that he wanted some ink. Lady Elizabeth asked why he was not in bed. He answered that he did not intend to sleep as the hearse was coming at 4 a.m. (as if Lady Elizabeth did not know already!). 'I felt then,' wrote Lady Elizabeth, 'I could not go to bed.'[5] And as soon as Hartington left, she went straight to the Duke's room. She did not record what Hartington said that made her go to the Duke. But I think it obvious that he told her that he agreed with his sisters and considered that Lady Elizabeth should leave the Devonshire household. Bess's plan as agreed with the Duke had misfired. She had not bargained for resistance so unanimous.

Lady Elizabeth tells us that she stayed as long as she could with the Duke.[6] We can guess what they talked about. If the children united against her, they would certainly enlist the Dowager Countess, their uncle the Earl Spencer and his odious wife Lavinia. With such allies, there was no telling where the opposition would stop. What about the Duke's relatives, Lord and Lady George Cavendish, the Duke of Portland? What would be the attitude of Charles Fox? of Lady Melbourne? Lady Caroline Lamb? the Prince of Wales? If Lady Elizabeth was driven from the Devonshire household, who would console the Duke in his grief? What would happen to Caro St Jules? to Corisande? to Clifford? And finally where could poor Bess go after devoting the best years of her life to her dearest friends?

One can imagine the lethargic Duke at a loss. He was set in his ways. To lose his Duchess was distressing enough. But to have his whole establishment torn apart to satisfy the self-righteousness of Georgiana's children and their pious grandmama was the limit.

Lady Elizabeth had a solution. The children were beside themselves with grief for their mama. Time was the healer. They must all stay together as a family unit. She knew, the Duke knew, that this was the way that dearest Georgiana would have wished it. The children wanted her to leave Devonshire House. She would be only too willing to do so. It was a house of mourning. Every room brought home the absence of her whose presence had made it a house of joy. But the children ought to leave Devonshire House also; go somewhere where they could share their sorrow less poignantly. And where better than Manresa House, Roehampton? Lady Bessborough was the only one of all the family who shared their secrets and understood their plight.

When the Duke agreed, Lady Elizabeth returned to her room. She had not been there very long when there was another tap on the door. This time it was Lady Bessborough, who, I imagine, had been listening to a denunciation of Lady Liz by Hary-O and Hartington. Lady Bessborough could see both sides. The children, brought up in sound moral fashion by Selina Trimmer, were understandably upset at the thought of Bess going on as before. But they did not realize how the situation had arisen and how impossible it would be to unravel it now. Young people, poor dears, could be very hard and priggish.

According to Lady Elizabeth's journal, Lady Bessborough said as she came in, 'Don't be frightened, but I want to speak to a human creature.' This cryptic remark would have puzzled every reader of the journal except Hartington and Hary-O, who would know that their aunt considered them, as a result of their attacks on Bess, *in*human creatures. 'Come in,' said Lady Elizabeth, 'I was wishing to see you.'[7] She did not explain why. Instead her journal went into paroxysms. 'What is this horror that has seized me! We have been every day in her room – tonight again we knelt by the coffin, kissed it, prayed by it – prayed to be a comfort to each other – and I offered up prayers that my heart might be purified by the tears of agony I had shed. We returned to my room – talked of her – we were calmed and soothed; yet now I am no longer calm, no longer soothed.'[8]

This reads like hysterical gibberish. But it implied to the initiated that Lady Elizabeth's plan to be 'a comfort' was approved by Lady Bessborough and Almighty God in the presence of the Duchess as the prompting of a pure heart. Yet when she remembered the cruel words of Hartington and his sisters, she was 'no longer soothed'.

The journal continued with a fine description of the closing of the coffin, the deep sound of the hearse, the grief of Hartington, and the departure through the gates of Devonshire House, 'those gates that seemed to open but for kindness or to gaiety'. It ended: 'The morning just began to dawn – all was reviving to light and life but her – her who was our light and life.'[9]

The tragedy over, comedy began. Bess gave Harriet Bessborough breakfast in her own room. As pangs of grief were assuaged with those of hunger, Lady Bessborough was drawn to propose that they should all come to stay with her at Roehampton. Lady Elizabeth accepted for herself, Caro St Jules and Corisande; and when later Lady Harriet Cavendish said she wished to be with her sister, the Morpeths were added to the party. Family unity had been preserved.

Lady Elizabeth spent little time at Roehampton. She had to fulfil her promise to go through the Duchess's papers. Incriminating letters from, or alluding to, Charles Grey had to be disposed of before the Duke returned from Derby. She invited Lady Bessborough to help. Lady Bessborough would best know what to do with letters referring to herself, Granville, and her other lovers.

They spent days together at Chiswick and Devonshire House. They found 'prayers, prayers everywhere'.[10] But there were dozens of bundles. The Dowager Countess's correspondence covered thirty years. Some letters were even earlier, a screed from John Spencer written from Harrow in 1770 anticipated that Georgiana might publish 'a poetic Epistle from a Young Lady of Quality abroad to her brother at School in England'.[11] There were poems, essays, journals, *jeux d'esprit*. There were letters from the Duchess's legitimate children to be set on one side and those from Eliza Courtney on another. Letters from creditors ran into hundreds. The Duchess had borrowed from the highest in the land to the lowest. These had all to be collected for the scrutiny of William Adam, the Prince of Wales' attorney-general, who had undertaken the ordering of the Duchess's finances. There were letters of thanks for services rendered in money or kind. There were family letters, social letters, political letters, letters of historical interest.

With the years spread on tables before them, Bess and Harriet Bessborough relived the scrapes in which the three of them had shared secrets hidden from everyone else. As they discovered things they had, forgotten, a joke, some occasional verse or things they never suspected, a meditation, some act of charity, they felt drawn closer together and to Georgiana than ever, even in Georgiana's lifetime.

In this accord they considered the future as well as the past. Lady Bessborough agreed that even if Lady Harriet Cavendish and Hartington refused to be comforted, it was Bess's duty to give the Duke solace in his grief and help him order the Duchess's affairs, whatever society might say.

When the Duke returned from Derby, Lady Elizabeth moved back to Devonshire House, leaving the girls at Roehampton. It was up to Lady Harriet Cavendish to decide whether she wanted to abandon her father.

15

Lady Elizabeth behaved as she had when the Duchess was alive. She listened to the Duke's anecdotes as if she had never heard them before. She pointed out the playfulness of the puppies. She asked him to read to her aloud. She brought to him news of the day, especially about Augustus Clifford and the progress of the war at sea. She did not question the political pronouncements which he was as fond of making as he was averse to holding public office.

The most significant entry in her journal was for 7 July 1806. 'Last night D.D. and I talked of the list of my poor G.'s debts which Mr Adam gave in. D.D. asked me what I should do, so circumstanced. I could only speak as my feelings prompted me. He said, with that angelic goodness and simplicity which characterize all his actions "I should not feel comfortable if I did not pay these debts!" '[1] Lady Elizabeth did not mention what her feelings prompted. But from the context it is clear that she said that the Duke was not legally responsible for debts incurred without his knowledge. This was not necessarily disloyal to poor G. With her experience, Lady Elizabeth knew the best way to ensure the Duke's honouring the debts was to tell him he did not have to. What the Duke did was to renew his bond to Coutts and pay nothing.

The Dowager Countess was open in her disapproval of Lady E.F. In returning the Dowager's letters, Lady Elizabeth had asked if there was any memento of Georgiana her mother would cherish. The Dowager replied that the Duchess's possessions were not in Lady Elizabeth's gift. Lady Elizabeth despatched a lock of the red-gold hair which had been cut from the Duchess's head before the doctors applied their blister. It was enclosed in a note which read: 'Dear Madam, The enclosed paper is the only thing that I *can* take the liberty of asking you to accept.'[2]

The Spencer family deliberated what should be done. Should the

Dowager Countess move into Devonshire House to protect Lady Harriet? If she did so, there would be a conflict of management and the Duke would be certain to take sides with his mistress against his mother-in-law. Should Lady Harriet Cavendish go to live with the Dowager Countess at St Albans? In that case, victory would have been conceded to Lady Elizabeth and her offspring. Lady Harriet's marriage prospects depended on the Duke's generosity. If she left home, Lady Elizabeth would argue that Lady Harriet had disinherited herself. There was only one solution. Lady Harriet must return home, stay as close as possible to her father and do everything she could to win him away from Lady Liz.

The convention of the time was that the eldest daughter living at home should act as hostess and sit at the opposite end of the table to her widowed father. But Lady Harriet found that place already occupied by her father's mistress. She had no allies at hand. Hartington was back at his tutor's, vowing that he would not go home while that woman was in the house. The neutral Corisande left to get married to Lord Ossulton when in July his father gave his consent. Caro St Jules could not be trusted. So it was only in letters that Lady Harriet could let herself go. 'Lady E.F. has taken up drawing and places herself in all the most romantic spots,' she wrote to Georgiana Morpeth. 'Thank heaven and summer she is obliged to leave off the mud coloured shawl.'[3]

Lady Elizabeth skilfully ignored enmities. Lady Morpeth, happy in her family and furthest removed from Lady Elizabeth, was the first see reason. She warned Hartington, 'I think from little things Ly E. has said of you not having written and that "surely when so near you will come to see Papa", he might be really hurt with you if you do not.' For his father's sake, Hartington was forced to do what he would have liked to do except for Ly E.'s presence. Lady Harriet had never known her father well, but from this time onwards it was her prime concern to win his affection. Unfortunately he was seldom at home and Ly E. seldom away.

About the time of Corisande's wedding, the Duke of Devonshire, with unusual perception, began to worry about the health of his old friend Charles Fox. With the successive deaths of Nelson, Pitt and his Duchess, his awareness seems to have been quickened. Fox was fifty-nine, and after years of heavy drinking – five bottles of claret at a sitting – his liver was packing up. For weeks he hung on, with immense, quantities of castor-oil applied within and plasters of liverwort without, tapped for the dropsy which made his ample limbs colossal. He was removed to Chiswick House, where he wandered through the gardens and the familiar rooms, clear in speech, gentle in his farewells, but not quite certain of his company.

While Fox fought for his life, Lady Elizabeth had a private conversation with Sheridan on 10 September. According to her, Sheridan said how much he wished to see her married to D.D. She answered that she was still too unhappy to hear such talk. But if Mrs Creevey is to be believed, Sheridan said that Lady Elizabeth 'had *cried* to him, because she felt it her severe duty to be Duchess of Devonshire!'⁴ Lady Elizabeth was certainly planning to marry the Duke when the right time came, but thought that before she did 'her severe duty', it would be better to marry off Lady Harriet Cavendish. Lord Granville had returned from a successful mission to Petersburg. He was still Lady Bessborough's lover. But one evening in November 1806 Bess came up to Lady Harriet just before dinner, a note in her hand, and said with a meaningful smile, 'I suppose you know who is coming tonight.'

'Who?'

'Lord Granville!'

'Will you tell me, my dear G.,' Harriet wrote to her sister, 'why she always talks of him to me as if I was so very much interested (to say the least) about him?'⁵ She had known Granville since she was a child. He was a good-looking joke figure, always in pursuit of one heiress or another, but never far from aunt Bessborough. Lady Elizabeth's assumption that Harriet was attracted to him was upsetting because it was true. It might be just possible that Lord Granville had invited himself that evening because he wanted to see her and not because Lady Bessborough was coming to dinner. But when Lord Bessborough and Willie Ponsonby turned up, but no Lady Bessborough and no Lord Granville, Harriet Cavendish turned all her anger against Lady Liz. She took it as a deliberate plot to humiliate her. She did not realize that Lady Elizabeth was just as disappointed as she. Granville was obviously the ideal husband for Harriet Cavendish, though in November 1806 Lady Elizabeth Foster was the only person to appreciate this.

Lady Harriet's relatives thought differently. Lord Spencer would have liked her to marry his heir Viscount Althorp. Her brother Hartington advanced the claims of his friend Sir William Rumbold. Lady Harriet herself was less interested in marriage than in fighting Lady Liz for her father's attention.

It became a sort of obsession. She went to stay for months at Althorp with the Spencers and later at Castle Howard with the Morpeths. She did not mind leaving her father to Lady Liz at Devonshire House or Chiswick. But if there was talk of his going to Bath, Lady Harriet was ready at a moment's notice to companion him to prove that she, as a daughter, was devoted to her father's health, while Lady Liz was interested only in using his money and position to move in society.

When they were all in London, things were more difficult. The Dowager Countess took a house nearby, in Jermyn Street. Harriet went there before breakfast and spent the day 'looking after grandmama', but slipped back to Devonshire House the moment her manservant came to say the Duke was up and alone. Lady Elizabeth wished to take her into society more. Lady Harriet went into society, but chaperoned by Lady Bessborough.

The most ludicrous situation arose when Lady Elizabeth wanted them all to go to Brighton. Lady Elizabeth's purpose lay in furthering the marriage of Caro St Jules to young George Lamb. George had read for the bar, but then had turned to literature. He wrote for the *Edinburgh Review*, was a good amateur actor and had written a comic opera which had had three performances at Covent Garden. But what he earned was a pittance. Lady Elizabeth hoped to interest the Prince of Wales, who was George's natural father, in the marriage of these two children of love.

Lady Harriet saw it as a diabolical plot to trap her into appearing in public with Lady E. If Lady Elizabeth was old enough or fat enough to please the Prince, she wrote to Georgiana Morpeth, she would be prepared to 'chaperon her into every corner of Brighton, live in the Chinese Apartment of the Pavilion and never rest' until she had fastened Lady Liz 'by hook or by crook upon his royal Highness'. But here was the quandary. 'Am I to go to Mrs Fitzherbert with Lady Elizabeth ten times more commented upon than in London, where I have always avoided being seen with her? On the other hand, how can I let him and her go without me, and what reason can I give for not going into bad company (for surely one need not mince the matter about Mrs Fitzherbert) without her silencing me, with "After all if I do?" One of those questions which would cover me with confusion and gain for her the points she aims at.'[6]

The visit was called off, because Lady Elizabeth fell dangerously ill. Sir Walter Farquhar made her worse, by bleeding her almost to death. She became so enfeebled that Lady Harriet almost liked her. Papa perked up, left alone with two young girls who flattered him even though the only subject of his conversation was puppies. He was in better spirits than Harriet had ever seen him. There could be no question of Ly E. leaving (except in a hearse). But had she not rooted herself by all the ties of habit, Papa would have been ten thousand times happier.[7]

Four weeks later Lady E. rose from her sickbed. Affectations and disputations strengthened with the beat of her pulse. As she had lain near death, she had been planning ahead. She had never revealed to Caro St Jules who her parents were. George Lamb, of course, knew from Lady Melbourne his mother. Lady Elizabeth hinted that George might be wise to tell Caro. She herself could not do so, but once the secret was known, she thought the Duke would be relieved and generous. All that Lady Harriet noticed of this was that Caro became 'excessively reserved ... mentioned Clifford and appeared extremely agitated'. She seemed to dislike talking of George Lamb to Harriet but, though agitated, she had 'the appearance of not being unhappy'.[8]

All previous writers have presented Caro St Jules as a dear, sweet, innocent girl who did not know the identity of her parents until after the death of the fifth Duke.[9] This assumption is insupportable. Unless she was a cretin, Caro must have wondered even before George Lamb spoke to her why she had been received into the Devonshire household. After he had, she must have confirmed her parentage with Lady Elizabeth, even if she never asked the Duke, her father.

To enable his illegitimate daughter to marry the illegitimate son of the Prince of Wales, the Duke settled on her £30000, the same amount he had given for the future Earl of Carlisle to marry his eldest legitimate daughter. The marriage took place on 17 May 1809. But long before Caro St Jules became Mrs George Lamb, the Dowager Countess, Lady Bessborough, Lady Caroline Lamb and all the Duke's legitimate children had been speculating what 'that woman's' next move would be. What they feared seemed impossibly outrageous even for the shameless Lady E. Yet it followed inexorably on what had gone before.

Lady Elizabeth protested dearest D.D.'s generosity, so characteristic of his angelic nature. But the moment the settlement was made, she pointed out the invidious position in which it placed her. In London, Chiswick, Chatsworth, Bath or wherever they might be; in Dublin, Ickworth, France, Italy or Switzerland, wherever she was known; through the town and *ton*, in Grub Street or at Drury Lane, at Carlton House and the Court of St James, the Duke (blinded by his noble nature) had published abroad that she, poor little Bess, was nothing but his w—e or s—t! When Georgiana had been in high Hystericks, Bess's voice had been as soothing as warm oil in an abscessed ear. Now it was like the Chinese water torture: drip drop, drip drop, always in the same place but at different intervals so that the Duke's nerves were always tensed. An engraving shows him at this time, one button of his jacket secured, his paunch busting out below. His head, lean in youth, is now inflated; the once disdainful mouth is now depressed in melancholy, shaped like a seagull planing, the nose like a lump of putty. What the eyes see is nothing pleasant.

In demanding marriage, Lady Elizabeth was doing no more than Mrs Armistead had done of Charles Fox. And she deserved it. Without her, none of the Duke's children might have been conceived. She had served the Devonshires for over a quarter of a century. She had borne the Duke two lovely children, had endured the malice of the Dowager Countess Spencer and every self-righteous busyboy and now, with Caro's marriage, tongues would start wagging again. It was high time the Duke made an honest Duchess of her. She wanted the wages of sin, a marriage settlement.

Throughout the summer of 1809, the Duke fought a losing battle. When he said that the Dowager Countess Spencer would never forgive him if there was a second fifth Duchess of Devonshire, she said she was prepared to waive the title. Lady Bessborough, who was kept abreast of the campaign, told Granville, 'I own I should rejoice at her not taking the name, tho' we have no right to expect it.'[10]

Lady Bessborough went on to give her views of Lady Elizabeth. 'I really love Bess, and think she has many more good and generous qualities than are allowed her, but I think she has the worst judgement of anybody I ever met with; and I begin also to think that she has more Calcul, and more power of concentrating her wishes and intentions, than I ever before believ'd.'

If Lady Bessborough had fully understood Bess's 'Calcul', she would have revised her low opinion of Bess's judgement. Her scheming was more devious even than that of the Marquise de Merteuil and the Vicomte de Valmorin in *Les liaisons dangereuses*. But Lady Harriet Cavendish was quite wrong to think her 'character unparalleled for want of principle and delicacy', 'more perverted than deceitful'.[11] Her motives were self-seeking, but far-sighted. They all thought she was just interested in marrying the fifth Duke whereas she knew that he would die before her and that then her future would depend on the goodwill of Hartington, as the sixth Duke. Hartington, in himself, would be easy enough to manage, but only if Lady Harriet Cavendish was happily married off.

This was why when she had discussed with Sheridan her 'severe duty to be Duchess of Devonshire' she had also been making arch remarks about Lord Granville to Lady Harriet. She was not a scheming villainess. She was a scheming good fairy.

In 1806 her plans for Harriet had been premature. In 1809 Lady Bessborough suddenly became enormously fat.[12] She had only to look in the mirror to see that her charms had become engulfed in *embonpoint*. At the same time, Lord Granville had abandoned his roving diplomatic missions abroad. In July 1809, through Canning's influence, he had become Secretary of War and a member of the Cabinet. For years Granville had combined pursuit of heiresses with enjoyment of his mistress. Now she had blown up, he decided to settle down. Lady Elizabeth proposed her solution. In becoming Granville's aunt, Lady Bessborough could find some compensation for ceasing to be his mistress. Though no beauty, Lady Harriet was an intelligent girl and would mellow with motherhood. Given the example of the Devonshire nursery, she could with a little diplomacy be brought to accept into her home Granville's children by her aunt, and thus give Lady Bessborough opportunities to see them without giving rise to gossip.

Lady Bessborough accepted the idea with resignation. It was even possible that, if she lost weight, Granville could be on with his new love without being off with his old. Lord Granville was enthusiastic. Lady Harriet had the wit he admired in her aunt. At thirty-six a man did not want a raving beauty for a wife. A homely young woman was less prone to temptation.

The only person who did not understand this convenient match-making was Lady Harriet Cavendish. When Lord Granville invited her to stay with his sisters, she was aware that she was being examined for her suitability as his bride. But she imagined that her aunt was intriguing to frustrate her romance and she had no idea that the scheme had originated with Lady Liz who 'hardly knows the difference between right and wrong now. Circumstances have altered her conduct and situation at different times but she has invariably been what even when a child I understood and despised.'[13]

Lady Elizabeth seems to have felt a danger that Lady Harriet would not recognize that the price she must pay for marrying Granville was acceptance of the fifth Duke's second marriage. Lord Granville was told that Harriet intended leaving home if her father married Bess, and though he was more than a little in love with Harriet, he was not such an ass as to propose to her without the assurance of a dowry and the

Duke's consent. He begged Harriet to do nothing foolhardy. She assured him that such an idea had never entered her head. If the Duke chose to marry Lady Elizabeth, she would continue to live at home.[14]

Thus Lady Harriet was drawn to accept a marriage which she had bitterly opposed. The most virulent opposition now came from Lady Caroline Lamb, who wrote from the Dowager Countess's to Hartington, accusing him of being privy to the plan of Lady E.'s marriage. This was untrue. But she was nearer the mark when she denounced her sister-in-law, Mrs George Lamb, 'that emblem of innocence', as being 'all along cunningly and slyly aware of the whole intrigue'.[15]

Deserted by his children, legitimate and natural, the beleaguered Duke surrendered on 17 October. He copied out a letter which Lady Elizabeth had drafted and subscribed his signature. It told the Dowager Countess that he intended to marry Lady Elizabeth. There was no concession that, out of deference to Georgiana, she did not intend to take the title.[16] Two days later they were married at Chiswick House. The solemnizer was the Reverend James Preedy, one of the Dowager Countess's tame parsons, chosen by Bess to give the impression that the Dowager Countess blessed the marriage. The only witness was Lady Elizabeth's companion, Mrs Spencer, of whom we previously heard as being pursued by Lord John Townshend. She was the only Spencer who could be produced to approve the union. Even her husband, Mr Spencer, and Bess's first-born, Frederick Foster, absented themselves though they were at Chiswick House. The first journal entry made by Elizabeth, Duchess of Devonshire, ran: 'So many contradictory emotions agitate my heart and soul that I can say no more on this subject, but may I be as grateful as I ought, and contribute to his happiness as to his children's as much as I wish.'[17]

The Dowager Countess never spoke to her again. The Prince of Wales sent fulsome congratulations and invited her to Carlton House to give her 'advice'. She went, but not before receiving visits from the Morpeths and Lady Harriet, who 'could not have been kinder in their manner'.[18]

The poor Duke felt so guilty that he did not write to Hartington for a week and even then only because the newspapers had announced the news. 'I shall give you my reasons for having taken this step when I see you.' His 'affectionate and dutiful' heir expressed neither surprise nor enthusiasm. He was vague about when he might visit. His step-mother reiterated the invitation by return. 'Nobody was ever kinder than Georgiana and Harriet have been to me.'[19]

Lady Harriet's anger concentrated on her aunt, Lady Bessborough, who brooded over Chiswick House like a hen, afraid her marriage plan would not hatch. 'You can have no idea of the manoeuvring of her conduct,' Harriet wrote to Selina. 'She has acted fairly by no one person – a directly different part to each and then obliged to have recourse to artifice and duplicity to try and reconcile the whole – what shipwreck has she made of honour, dignity and fair renown!'[20] She could not believe that Lady Bessborough and Lord Granville were striving to bring about what she herself (and Elizabeth Devonshire!) equally wanted. She begged Hartington to come and advise her;[21] and having come, at a moment critical for his sister's future, the least Hartington could do was to be charming to his step-mother. 'My heart is now at ease,' wrote Elizabeth Devonshire, 'as his conduct to me is as kind as possible. God bless him and preserve him to us.'[22] She had been acknowledged by all her step-children and could now give Lady Harriet a husband as her reward.

On 14 November Lord Granville nervously proposed to Lady Harriet and was nervously accepted, provided the Duke gave his consent. Lord Granville asked the Duchess if he might have a word with the Duke after dinner. Without waiting for Lord Granville to declare himself, the Duke remarked that Granville was of all persons the one he would prefer for Lady Harriet. When Granville tried to confess his former follies, the Duke said he was already aware of them. Whereupon, as he informed his ex-mistress and aunt-to-be, Granville emphasized that he did not *intend* to persevere in them.'[23]

Three days later Granville explained to Harriet that he had confided every step of his courtship to Lady Bessborough and she had always encouraged him. Harriet's fears and suspicions melted in a moment. Her aunt was not a monster but a true friend.

Granville and Harriet were married on Christmas Eve. Three days later he wrote to Lady Bessborough, 'Every hour I passed with Harriet convinced me more and more of the justice and liberality of her way of thinking, and of her claim upon me for unlimited confidence. She is indeed a perfect angel.'[24]

As Granville had resigned from office in October and the Duke had settled on Lady Harriet £10000, only a third of the jointure made over to Caro St Jules when she married George Lamb, they decided to retire to the country. They first chose Sandon and then Tixall Hall in Staffordshire, where they were joined by Granville's two 'wards', Harriet and George Arundel Stewart. On 25 October 1810 Lady Harriet gave birth to Susan Georgiana, the first of Granville's legitimate children. Henceforward it was only at second hand that they heard of the progress of the former Lady Elizabeth Foster.

During the London Season Elizabeth, fifth Duchess of Devonshire, aimed to outshine the social triumphs of Georgiana, fifth Duchess of Devonshire, at the height of her splendour.* The Hervey in her blossomed. Evening after evening there were dinners or suppers for twenty or more. When the King's malady recurred in 1810 she fancied herself as influential in the Regency proceedings as Georgiana had been twenty-two years before. But unfortunately the Duke disliked the social festivities of his second Duchess even more than those of his first. Given a gout-stool, a bottle of port and a litter of puppies, he was as near as he could come to content.

In July 1811 he fell ill. Chest spasms and difficulty in breathing made lying down intolerable. For five nights he sat upright in a chair, trying to sleep. That arch-bleeder, Sir Walter Farquhar, ministered to him and his Duchess cancelled most of her engagements. The sixty-two-year-old Duke felt so much better that he toddled out on the terrace and then ate a hearty dinner. But next evening he found it hard to breathe. Mr Walker, Sir Walter's attendant apothecary, decided to bleed him again. He bound the Duke's arm, preparatory to lancing a vein. But while he was getting out the lancet, the Duke's head fell back, and in the words of The Gentleman's Magazine, 'he expired without a groan in the arms of the Duchess'.[25]

---

* As Duchess of Devonshire Elizabeth ranked first in order of precedence after members of the Royal Family. As an Earl's daughter Lady Elizabeth Foster ranked twenty-ninth. During Georgiana's lifetime Lady Elizabeth must have been galled on formal occasions at the etiquette which emphasized their difference in public rank, so contrary to the ranks they held in the Duke's esteem.

Interlude Five

The escutcheon over Devonshire House was once more shrouded. The circumstance was the same as five years earlier, the pomp was greater, but the grief was less. Elizabeth, Duchess of Devonshire, watched the massive bier being carried down the steps and loaded on the hearse, covered with a black pall. The doors closed. The six black horses, each with a black cockade, waited on the word of the coachman with his black hat ribboned with black crape which was tied at the back and fell across his shoulders. For the occasion, the Duchess wore her sables as she stood at the head of the stairs. In her delicate hand she held a little handkerchief of the finest black Mechlin lace. She applied it to her eyes from time to time. There may have been tears.

Her marriage to the Duke had lasted only twenty-two months. Hart, as she still called him, though he was now sixth Duke of Devonshire, bent and kissed her upon the forehead. The handkerchief went to her lips, as he went slowly down the stairs and mounted into the coach. The steps were folded, the door closed and the footmen gravely climbed up behind. The driver of the hearse waited for a nod from the driver of the coach. Then he shook his reins and the black horses moved slowly forwards. The hearse passed through the gates, followed by the Devonshire coach-and-six. They disappeared from sight. But the gates were not closed. The Duchess remained where she was at the head of the stairs, in an attitude of incarnate Grief that Lady Hamilton herself could not have bettered. The first of the mourning coaches passed the open gates. The Prince Regent had heaved himself forward to look through the window. He raised his hand and the Duchess bowed her head. As coach followed coach, she bowed again and again, like an admiral on his flagship reviewing his fleet.

There were in all twenty-one Royal and noble coaches in the cortège,[1] which followed the funeral as far as the end of the cobblestones on the

Great North Road. When the last was out of sight of the terrace, the Duchess turned and went inside.

She was not alone. Caro George Lamb and Mrs Spencer had been with her throughout the Duke's illness and Frederick Foster had hurried over from Ireland as soon as he had heard the news. The four of them were together now in a house which could no longer be considered home. While Hartington continued his funeral journey to All Saints', Derby, the Duchess removed her personal possessions to Chiswick House.

Her position was not so insecure as it had been after the death of dearest Georgiana. She had secured a marriage settlement from the Duke. But though she had nagged him to add a codicil in her favour to his will, she was not certain he had done so. She had done well for her children. Caro George Lamb was assured her £30000. Augustus Clifford had been posted Master and Commander, RN, and would surely receive some provision from the Duke. Augustus Foster had been appointed British Minister in Washington. Frederick Foster had his seat in the House of Commons and the patronage of his uncle, the Earl of Bristol. All these she could count as friends. So were George Lamb and the Prince Regent.

But she had her enemies. The Dowager Countess Spencer, the Earl Spencer and his Countess, Lavinia, were implacable. Lady Caroline Lamb was venomous. The Granvilles and the Morpeths were uncertain quantities. *Their* attitudes would be influenced by the head of the family, the arbiter of their fortunes, the twenty-one-year-old sixth Duke of Devonshire.

16

After burying his father, the sixth Duke consulted his trustees. The family was represented by the sixth Duke's uncle, Lord George Cavendish, and the business interests by Mr Heaton. Heaton was now preparing to hand over to his junior partners, Benjamin and Currie, but there was no one on earth who knew as much as old Mr Heaton about the two Devonshire and Clifford estates of which the sixth Duke was now the life tenant. When the fifth Duke had succeeded, the combined incomes had been estimated as £36000 a year. No doubt the sixth Duke's first question was: what had it been reduced to now? His mother's debts were fabulous, his father's unknown. £30000 had been settled on his elder sister, Georgiana Morpeth, £30000 on Caro George Lamb, £10000 on his younger sister, Harriet Granville, and in the two years of her marriage Elizabeth Devonshire had squandered money regardless of what she had secured as her jointure.

Mr Heaton, who like most family lawyers probably liked to take his time, admitted that there was a great debt. How great could not be determined at the moment. The late Duke had not liked to discuss money matters. He liked to give notes of hand and allow the interest thereon to accrue rather than settle his liabilities outright. How many of his first Duchess's debts were still outstanding it was impossible to say immediately. There was also the inequity, as Lord George Cavendish agreed, of Lady Harriet's having received only £10000 as her marriage portion: this could be made up, if His Grace agreed, to £30000 out of the Clifford estate. This was gloomy news, but Mr Heaton was pleased to be able to say that by wise development in coal-mining, building, etc., the income from the combined estates had increased to a sum impossible to state precisely, but about one hundred and twenty-five thousand pounds a year.* The figure so astonished the Duke that he

---

* The equivalent today of about £6 million or $10 million, after tax.

offered to raise Mr Heaton's salary above £1000 a year, and made him a present of £2000 into the bargain.[1]

The Duke then produced two letters from Thomas Coutts, the first of which he had received when he had come of age in May and the second immediately his father died. Both contained copies of the letter that Georgiana had written begging Hartington to establish her good name by paying Coutts £5520 19s due for the years ending 1798, plus interest accruing thereafter. Coutts also pointed out that he held the fifth Duke's bond for £4000 on which neither interest nor principal had been paid.[2]

Heaton swore that he knew nothing of this bond. If genuine then it must be repaid with interest. But as for the sum referred to by Her late Grace, Thomas Coutts had no claim in law. If Her Grace had received any such money it reflected not on her good name but on the business malpractices of the Banker in the Strand. In September the Duke saw Thomas Coutts and on 24 October paid him £4000 plus interest up to September 1811. Coutts did not receive one penny of what Georgiana had requested on his behalf and had to write it off as a bad debt.*

The sixth Duke was not heartbroken over the death of his father, whose health had been deteriorating for years. The marriage to Bess had been the result more of desperate loneliness than of zest for life. As the sixth Duke returned south he was less concerned with his father than with his father's widow.

Lady Bessborough wrote Granville an account of life at Chiswick House on his return. 'Bess supports herself with a degree of fortitude that is really quite wonderful. Her loss is one that, besides the tearing asunder of every tie of long affection, touches her so in every point, that there can be no doubt of what she feels; indeed, her whole appearance bears testimony to it. Yet so far from any display of grief, she quite surprizes me with the composure and even cheerfulness with which she mixes in society (I mean, of course, only what is here or the few people she knows very well that call). She does not dine with us, but excepting that, all morning and all evening is *about*, and in the drawing room; and really, sometimes George Lamb's and dear Hart's

---

* He had, however, benefited in other ways. He had become the Prince Regent's banker. His youngest daughter, Sophia, in 1793 married Francis Burdett (later Sir Francis Burdett, fifth Baronet), the wealthy son of a Derbyshire squire in the Devonshire interest. Georgiana's introduction of the Coutts girls into society (as well as Coutts' wealth) contributed to Susannah Coutts becoming the second wife of George Augustus, ninth Baron North and third Earl of Guilford, in 1796, and Fanny Coutts becoming in 1800 the second wife of John, fourth Earl and first Marquis of Bute.

riotous Spirits would almost oppress one at a gayer time, but she does not seem to mind it – on the contrary, rather encourages. As this must be from consideration to them, I really think it is a very great merit, and one I should feel wholly unequal to. Meanwhile every thing I fear turns against her. She has done herself great harm with Hart by that foolish paper and some other things.'[3]

The 'foolish paper' to which Lady Bessborough referred was a statement of claim which Bess had drawn up while Hartington (as they still all called him) had been in Derby. She maintained that the fifth Duke had promised to add a codicil to his will making over Chiswick House to her, for her lifetime. But Heaton swore there was no codicil. Even so, Bess maintained, the fifth Duke had *wished* her to have Chiswick. This eagerness to gather the profits of her marriage rather than mourn the loss of her husband may have prompted Hartington to display his 'riotous Spirits'. Bess ought to have restrained, rather than encouraged them. Lady Bessborough tried to win Hartington's sympathy by pointing out how ill she looked. 'I see she wears no rouge,' he answered.[4]

The atmosphere at Chiswick House grew tense. Lady Bessborough was deputed to instruct Bess that she could not have Chiswick House, but some other house could be provided. Caro George Lamb told Hartington that instead of a house Bess would prefer more money. When Hartington suggested making up her jointure to £6000 a year, Caro seemed pleased, but next day wrote begging him to do more. 'You cannot think how unpleasant all this is,' Lady Bessborough wrote to Granville. 'Hart comforts me by assuring it was as stormy about Clifford* beforehand, and that she will be as well pleas'd with him afterwards as she was with that, as I know his good nature will induce him (tho' he says not) to help her in fitting up her house etc.'[5]

Another wish Elizabeth Devonshire expressed was to keep the Devonshire jewels until the young Duke married. Lord George Cavendish refused. She had to hand them over to Hart, who returned comparatively worthless pieces as belonging to Bess rather than to the family and gave the rest to Sir Samuel Romilly for apportionment.[6]

An ignoramus in business, Lady Bessborough sympathized with Bess. She was shocked when she heard Hart had raised Heaton above £1000 a year. Why not pay a percentage, as Lord Bessborough had done so successfully to his Irish man of business? When the young Duke pointed

---

* Augustus Clifford's naval pay was supplemented with an allowance from the fifth Duke. The sixth Duke offered to increase the amount, but not by as much as Bess wanted.

out that £1000 a year was only 0.125 per cent of his income, he could have bitten off his tongue. If Bess heard that, she would increase her demands. He swore his aunt to secrecy. Harriet Bessborough gave her word, but could not resist telling Granville.[7]

Since the collapse of her first marriage Bess had been astute in concealing her calculations. But at this stage in her career, greed and ambition confounded her judgement. She protested against having to sign 'releases' on the ground that if she had no legal rights, how could she resign them? She launched a campaign to legitimize her bastard children. The first that Lady Bessborough heard of this was when George Lamb told Lord and Lady Holland that though Caro had long known that Bess was her mother, she had only just learned that the fifth Duke was her father. Lady Bessborough was puzzled until Bess said that since her marriage to the Duke would have legitimized their children by *Scots* law, therefore they were legitimate by *English* law and that this gave them the right to bear the Cavendish arms and strengthened their claims on the sixth Duke's generosity. Lady Bessborough was 'astounded'.[8]

Bess did not leave Chiswick House. She even invited Georgiana Morpeth to come there for her next *accouchement*, saying that she intended staying there for the next twelvemonth. Hartington gave her notice to quit. 'Thank God,' he wrote to his grandmother, 'I have got rid of the Duchess at last.'[9]

Lady Caroline Lamb, Hartington's boyhood love, had not yet thrown herself at Lord Byron, but she was flirting with Byron's pothouse companion, Sir Godfrey Webster, Lady Holland's son by her first marriage. She did not mind Bess's immorality, but abominated her secretiveness. She congratulated Hartington on having 'ferrit'd the maim'd fox out of its last hold'. He answered, 'Dear Cousin, I was almost on my knees to persuade the fox to remain in her den on less wonderful expense than what she had done on, but she wouldn't.' He foresaw that throughout life he would 'much cherish, assist & support the poor body in her old age and crepitude'.[10]

Bess was too angry to realize her step-son's kindness. Banished from Chiswick and Devonshire House, she took a lease on 13 Piccadilly Terrace, overlooking Green Park. Lady Bessborough suggested that, while it was being made ready, Bess should stay at Roehampton but Bess feared this would advertise her eviction. She proposed they should both go to Portsmouth where Augustus Clifford and William Ponsonby were awaiting sailing orders.

Then her Legitimation Campaign became 'in some degree like insanity'.[11] She revealed to Clifford what he must have long suspected, that the fifth Duke was his father. If Clifford was 'deprived' of the Cavendish arms, she would give him those of Hervey. She urged him to assert his position.

In those days tables of precedence were strictly observed. As a bastard, Augustus Clifford had no standing. As an officer of the Navy he ranked seventy-sixth, below barristers-at-law and above Army officers. Now Clifford made a point of entering and leaving rooms ahead of Viscount Duncannon (ranked twenty-sixth) and the Hon. William Ponsonby (ranked thirty-third). Before dining with the Lieutenant Governor of Portsmouth, he sent word he was to be received as a Duke's son (ranked twenty-second). For this breach of etiquette Commander Clifford was reprimanded by his Admiral. Lady Bessborough told Granville that when she taxed Bess with encouraging such folly, she answered that 'it was not intended as a formal message, but merely giving to understand who he was, as he had often been put quite at the bottom of the table etc. in short, she meant Clifford to let the *secret* of his birth, as far as regarded his father, be *guessed at*. He had done more, and told it with a sort of claim that has prov'd both offensive and ridiculous.'[12] Bess was displaying the same sort of misplaced arrogance that had made the Earl-Bishop a laughing stock. But whereas her father had been concerned with self-aggrandizement, she strove to advance her children.

Leaving Portsmouth, Bess moved into Piccadilly Terrace and soon after had a riverside villa built at Richmond overlooking the Petersham water-meadows.* Her thoughts turned to the life hereafter. In Heaven, there was no marriage or giving in marriage. But she wondered if a *ménage à trois* could be arranged for the Duke, Georgiana and herself.[13]

The house at 13 Piccadilly Terrace was much too big for her. Priggish Annabella Milbanke (Lady Melbourne's niece and the future Lady Byron) meeting her at Brocket Hall, the Melbournes' country place, remarked, 'The Dss of Devonshire is a portrait of restless wretchedness. If vanity and dissimulation have been there, misery has chastened the soul from their influence. She has the spiritless look of penitential humility.'[14] The truth was that she was lonely. She cultivated her younger sister, Louisa, whose husband as second Earl of Liverpool became Prime Minister in 1812. She saw the Melbournes and the

---

* Now demolished; it was on the river side of the Petersham Road, close to the Three Pigeons inn.

Bessboroughs, until the latter had to take Lady Caroline Lamb to
Ireland after the Byron scandal. But she drifted away from the Hollands
because they were Bonapartists and partisans of the raffish Caroline,
Princess of Wales. For her, the Prince Regent and dear old England.

She was a woman who could never be happy without a man. During
the years she was waiting for the interminable war against Bonaparte
to end, the man closest to her was the sixth Duke. She encouraged him
when he fell in love with the Prince Regent's daughter, Princess
Charlotte. When the Regent gave his daughter a coming-out ball, Bess
noted, 'The Duke danced with her a great deal, was quite at ease and
the Princess seemed to enjoy it very much.'[15] Princess Charlotte was
the opposite of Caroline Lamb: a bouncy Betjemanesque girl to whom
the Duke sent pheasants from Chatsworth. But when he wanted to
give her more than game, the Prince Regent put his foot down. The
heiress presumptive to the throne of the United Kingdom was reserved
for a princeling. Bess was dotty to have encouraged his presumption,
but it showed a good heart.*

In her statement of claims and her Legitimation Campaign, she had
made mistakes, which she now redressed. The enchantress of the Dukes
of Dorset, Richmond and the fifth Duke of Devonshire set out to
captivate the sixth Duke. As interested in public life as his grandfather
had been, he might have held high political office if his increasing deafness
had not cut him off. No. 13 Piccadilly Terrace was just down the road
from Devonshire House and the Duke's habit was to walk across Green
Park from the House of Lords to take a meal with Bess before going
back to the Chamber. We do not know what they talked about apart
from public affairs. But we may speculate on what led to an intimacy
between Bess and the sixth Duke far greater than she enjoyed with any
of her children. It is, I emphasize, mere conjecture.

Bess had publicized the paternity of Caro George Lamb and Augustus
Clifford. The sixth Duke must surely have asked her what had really
happened. The whole of his childhood had been passed in the company
of others whose position in life was ill-defined, genealogically speaking
'sinister'. Apart from Bess's acknowledged bastards, there were Harriet
and George Arundel Stewart, whom his sister Harriet Granville had
taken into her home as Lord Granville's 'wards'. There was Eliza
Courtney, his mother's child by Charles (now the second Earl) Grey.
Eliza Courtney was ostensibly the child of the first Earl Grey – which

---

* When Princess Charlotte died in childbirth in 1817, Bess reconciled the Regent and
the Duke.

made her the apparent sister of her real father. And, to make it all the more complicated, in 1814 she married Colonel Robert Ellice, brother of Edward Ellice who had married the second Earl Grey's sister. So Eliza Ellice was actually her father's sister-in-law, but only ostensibly his sister!

This was clearly a very puzzling situation even in those family trees which showed legitimate relationships with straight lines and illegitimate with dotted lines. But the sixth Duke must have been interested not merely in genealogical tables, but also in the emotional entanglements which led to them. 'My God! what a set!' Matthew Arnold remarked, contemplating the complications of Shelley and his women. The sixth Duke might have thought the same, reflecting on the two fifth Duchesses of Devonshire and Lady Bessborough.

The one person who could enlighten him was Bess. She knew everything about those shadowy figures who had peopled his childhood. But she also knew a great deal more. She was a fascinating talker, when he could follow what she was saying by sitting opposite her and reading her lips. He himself was a child of the French Revolution and the wars that had followed. The Bastille had been stormed before he was even conceived. Bess had been at Versailles when the Duke of Dorset had said that Marie Antoinette should have another son. 'Why should I?' the Queen asked. 'So that M. d'Orléans should have him killed?' Bess had stories which made it clear that the Revolution was not an inexorable progress, but touch-and-go. Wit could turn a trick. When a mob was threatening to burn the house of a certain M. d'Espremenil with his wife and children inside, a citizen shouted, 'Messieurs, in my opinion we ought not to burn the house of M. d'Espremenil, because it is not his and only the poor landlord would suffer; nor children, who are not his either; nor his wife, who is everybody's.'[16] So they were all saved.

Such an anecdote – and there were hundreds of them – might have prompted the sixth Duke to say, 'But you must write this down', and his step-mother to answer, 'I already have.' And so began, I imagine, the lending of Bess's journals. The Duke took them one by one to Devonshire House, discovering the truth about events which had puzzled him, or of which he had no knowledge.

The truth? Well, not exactly. As we have seen, Bess, whether as Lady Elizabeth Foster or Duchess of Devonshire, had her particular slant. The Duke must have sought elucidation. His step-mother gave it, again with her particular slant. The whole business had stemmed from the marriage laws. As dear Dr Johnson had remarked, 'Our marriage service is too refined. It is calculated for the best kind of marriages; whereas we should have a form for marriages of convenience, of which there are many.'[17] Both Bess and Georgiana had both been victims of marriages of convenience; so indeed had the sixth Duke's father. Then they had been trapped by the terrible law of entail, whereby all the daughters suffer unless a male child is born. So when the Duke fell in love with Bess, and Georgiana with Charles Grey, they could do nothing until the sixth Duke was born. Perhaps she excused her own 'sins' by pointing out that Caro and Augustus Clifford had been born before he had been, but Eliza Courtney afterwards. We only know that thereafter there was a stronger bond between Bess and her step-son than between herself and her own children. She made him the executor of her will.

As soon after the Battle of Waterloo as travelling was possible, the Duchess went abroad, first to Paris and then to her beloved Italy. She had borrowed £1000 from Lady Bessborough and begged the sixth Duke if, even though she had set aside half her jointure to repay debts, she die abroad without having liquidated them, he would continue half her jointure for a year. To Lord Byron, who declared, as he was separating from his wife Annabella, that he wanted 'space', she let 13 Piccadilly Terrace for £700 a year. But she received no rent until he had sold his ancestral estate, Newstead Abbey. She had grown to hate Regency London; the flippantly dissolute world of Harriette Wilson, the brazenly amoral philandering of Lord Byron and the Shelleys, drunk on the Free Love preached but not practised by Mary Wollstonecraft and William Godwin. If de la Rochefoucauld was right that hypocrisy was the homage which vice pays to virtue, Elizabeth, Duchess of Devonshire, was all for hypocrisy. It was so much seemlier.

She settled in Rome, where she was already well-known as the daughter of the eccentric Earl-Bishop and as the enchanting companion of the adorable Georgiana Devonshire. Now, as Elizabeth, fifth Duchess of Devonshire, she set out to emulate her father in patronage of the Arts, living in almost royal magnificence. Sir Thomas Lawrence made a drawing of her in her sixties. Wearing a splendid hat with osprey feathers embracing her curls and tumbling to meet the billowy lace on her left shoulder, her eyes pensive, nostrils delicate and lips made to be kissed, she looks a noble lady half that age. Of all the fashionable English portrait painters, Lawrence was the greatest flatterer (having in youth made the error of painting King George III's consort, Queen

Charlotte, as she really was). This was not how Elizabeth looked in 1819. But it was *how she felt she was*. It is a happy contrast with a miniature made ten years before, just after her marriage to the fifth Duke; the eyes larger but more calculating beneath Medusa-curls, nose long and pronounced, mouth curling up not in happiness but triumph. The restlessness detected by Annabella Milbanke at Brocket Hall vanished in Rome. 'The Duchess is adored,' Lord Gower wrote from Rome to Harriet Granville, in 1817. 'She protects all the artists and employs them magnificently, and all along the road, the innkeepers are asking, "Connaissez-vous cette noble dame?" '[18] Guided by her friend Cardinal Consalvi, she had the Forum excavated, employing paid (not convict) labour. In gratitude for her benefactions the Romans had a medal struck in her honour.

Of course her enemies thought nothing that she did right. 'That witch of Endor, the Duchess of Devon,' remarked Lavinia, Countess Spencer, 'has been doing mischief of another kind to what she has been doing all her life by pretending to dig for the public good in the Forum.' She had unearthed 'nothing but a quantity of dirts and old horrors' and was making herself 'the laughing stock of all Rome by her pretensions to Maecenasship'.[19] Lavinia was referring to errors which scholars had found in an Italian translation of Horace's poem '*Iter ad Brundisium*' ('Journey to Brundisium', Satires I, 5), which Bess had commissioned. But the Duchess promptly had another translation made by Consalvi's secretary and supervised by the Cardinal himself. It was published by the famous Bodoni Press with illustrations by Caraccioli and was followed the next year by Anibal Caro's translation of the *Aeneid* in two volumes, with engravings by Marchetti after drawings by Sir Thomas Lawrence.

Lawrence also painted Consalvi in his cardinal's robes. The face has a vague resemblance to that of the Earl-Bishop in the portrait by Mme Vigée Le Brun, but is more spiritual and sensitive, less self-indulgent. Ercole Consalvi, like Bess, had been born in 1757. Chamberlain to Pius VI and Secretary of State to Pope Pius VII, the Cardinal was not a fully ordained priest. A wise statesman, he had resisted alike Napoleon during the wars and Prince Metternich at the Peace Treaty of Vienna. He was virtually governor of Rome and as ardent as the Duchess in the restoration of the city. He loved the English in general and Elizabeth in particular.

They had passed the age of physical love, but they became united in spirit. Cardinal Consalvi was more worthy of regard than Count Axel

Fersen or the fifth Duke of Devonshire. But her raptures over this final friend made her and him slightly ridiculous. Presentation copies of her magnificent volumes were sent to the crowned heads of Europe, to the Duke of Wellington and of course dear Hart, accompanied by letters singing the praises of the dear Cardinal.

Consalvi advised her over the crisis which followed the suicide of Sir Richard Croft in 1818. In 1817 Croft had taken full responsibility for the *accouchement* of Princess Charlotte. He was rightly blamed when the Princess and her baby died. Faced with a similar case next year, he went out and shot himself. That was not sensational enough for *The Gentleman's Magazine* and *Galignani's*. They recalled that it was Croft and not Dr Denman who had attended Georgiana, Duchess of Devonshire, in Paris in 1790. The story was put about that Elizabeth, Duchess of Devonshire, converted to Papism by Cardinal Consalvi, had confessed to a priest that the man claiming to be the sixth Duke of Devonshire was her child, not Georgiana's, and that she had written to the Prince Regent acknowledging the deception. When Bess begged Consalvi what she should do, he wisely told her 'Nothing!'

Prompt action was taken by the Duke himself. Ann Scafe, the Dowager Countess's companion, made a deposition from her journal of May–August 1790 and this was witnessed by Heaton's successors on 3 February 1818.*[20] If I am right in conjecturing that Bess had already shown the sixth Duke her journals when at Piccadilly Terrace, this may explain his expeditious confidence in refuting the rumour. That it could arise must have brought home to him how lucky he was in his birth and how misfortunate by comparison his half-brother Augustus Clifford. He had already given Clifford a sumptuous banquet on his marriage to the daughter of Lord John and Lady 'Jockey' Townshend, and they were to remain close friends for life.

As death picked off her old relatives and friends, Elizabeth Devonshire drew closer to her step-son. Lady Hervey, the widow of her elder brother John Augustus, died in 1818. Her younger sister, Lady Liverpool, died in June 1821 and Lady Bessborough five months later.[21] In August 1822 Lord Castlereagh was driven to slit his throat and in September of the following year the death of Pius VII stripped Cardinal Consalvi of political power. He retired to his villa of Porto d'Anzio. He was given the honorary office of prefect of the college *De Propaganda Fide*, but to console her spiritual lover Elizabeth Devonshire begged her

* This should have killed the *canard*. But garbled versions of the story circulated for more than a hundred years. See Markham, *Paxton and the Bachelor Duke*.

royal 'brother', now King George IV, to send his portrait to the Cardinal. Even before it was despatched, Consalvi was dead.[22]

It was Consalvi who had had a medal struck in her honour. Now the Duchess ordered that five hundred bronze medals should be struck of him. In a frenzy of grief, she wrote off to five hundred of his admirers, requesting a subscription of one *louis de France*. To the sixth Duke, whose letters during all these years had been 'such a comfort and such a pleasure', she wrote, 'God bless you, dearest D. I know you will feel for me.'[23] The poor body was at last 'in crepitude'.

The moment the Duke heard that the Duchess was failing, he made speed to Rome. He found her 'recovering her spirits which had almost left her since the great loss she had in Consalvi'.[24] Her rally was caused by pleasure at seeing him. She lingered for a week, suffering little pain.

An English clergyman, Dr Nott,* was anxious to hear her confess the sins which had kept gossips guessing for forty years. 'I have long endeavoured to fix my thoughts wholly on God,' she answered firmly 'and am perfectly resigned to His will whatever it may be.' Dr Nott hinted he would like to administer the Last Sacrament. The Duchess chose not to take his meaning.

Looking at the Duke kneeling on the other side of the bed, Dr Nott observed what a blessing it was that she had one part of her family who watched over her with such care and tenderness. It may have been intended as a comment on the absence of her own children.

'I am indeed most truly sensible of the goodness of God towards me in this particular,' the Earl-Bishop's daughter replied, 'and am most sincerely thankful for his blessing.'

The baffled cleric made a further offer of comfort or consolation. 'I thank you,' she said faintly, 'but not now.'

She was so weak that the doctors intervened. Dr Nott and the Duke withdrew to an adjoining closet. The Duke calmed the importunate parson by assuring him that the Duchess would oblige if she had the strength. But the doctors ruled that taking the sacrament 'might remove the small remaining hope there was of a recovery.'[25]

Elizabeth Devonshire died on 30 March 1824, eighteen years to the day after her dearest friend Georgiana. Her body was taken, as her

---

* Dr George Frederick Nott, one-time sub-preceptor to Princess Charlotte, one-time friend but later enemy of Lord Byron, had apartments in the same house as the Shelleys. When Mary Shelley came on three consecutive Sundays at his request to the English church in Pisa, he had preached on each occasion against atheism. Byron called it 'a shabby example of priestly malice', adding that the doctor had revised the ninth commandment to read 'Thou shalt, Nott, bear false witness against thy neighbour.'[26]

father's had been, to be laid to rest in England. Since Europe was at last at peace, there was no reason to hoist her aboard a man of war, labelled ANTIQUE STATUE. She travelled overland and after lying in state in Devonshire House, from which she had been ferreted twelve years before, she was laid according to her wishes beside her friends in All Saints', Derby, as near as she could come to *sarcophage à trois*.

Lady Harriet Granville was in The Hague when she heard the news of the Duchess's death. Now an ambassador's wife and the mother of five children, she had forgotten the hatred she had felt for Lady Liz before she married. 'It has shocked us very much,' she wrote to her sister, Georgiana, Lady Morpeth. 'She had so much enjoyment of life.'[27]

Note on the eye trouble of Georgiana, Duchess of Devonshire

Though it is difficult to diagnose at this distance of time, the opinion of Dr Raymond Greene, the endocrinologist, and Mr Henry E. Hobbs, the ophthalmologist, is that Georgiana was suffering from a 'unilateral exophthalmos of endocrine origin'. Dr Greene writes: 'Endocrine exophthalmos is still not understood but we do know that it may be unilateral and that it may not be associated with thyrotoxicosis.' This thyroid disorder is often accompanied by violent bursts of temper, such as the Duchess confessed to, apologizing to Selina Trimmer (7 April 1797), 'Surely you must know the infirmity of my nature, that with a heart not bad (I humbly trust) I have an instability of nature that is sometimes madness. The only alleviation of this to my friends is that it is only to those I love I have ever shewn these odious destructive paroxysms.'

Mr Hobbs observes: 'The gross swelling of the eye-lids and periorbital tissues with severe proptosis may well have developed from that in 1779; no suggestion of a sudden evolution appears in the account and, once again, although an ulcer is mentioned, severe pain is not. It would, therefore, appear unlikely that the condition was an acute inflammatory one – orbital cellulitis, for example; but more probable that it was congestive, of severe degree and perhaps complicated by corneal exposure from the protrusion of the eye. The fact that it resolved, at least partially, either spontaneously or from the decongestive effects of the leeches would support this view.'

Notes on sources

When Lady Elizabeth Foster and Lady Bessborough went through the papers of Georgiana, Duchess of Devonshire, there must have been a considerable destruction of letters and other documents. For example, the Duchess's correspondence to and from Grey has almost completely vanished. In the Durham University Department of Palaeography and Diplomatic there survives one letter in the second Earl Grey's papers, from the Duchess to Charles Grey, dated 10 November 1804. Primarily concerned with politics, it ends, 'God bless you my love to my baby'. Miss Eliza Courtney was at that time aged twelve. On 17 May 1809, when her father had become the second Earl Grey, we find the seventeen-year-old Eliza writing to him as 'My dearest Charles' and subscribing herself 'believe me, dear Charles, yours most affect E. Courtney'. It is possible that the Georgiana–Charles Grey letters exist somewhere but I think it is unlikely.

Among the Chatsworth papers (Fifth Duke's Collection) the most obvious gaps in the Duchess's correspondence, apart from references to Grey and Lady Bessborough's relations with Granville, are the silences which followed the publications of the 'Tête à Tête' article and of *The Sylph*. Another omission, so vast that it is almost invisible, is the absence of letters to and from the fifth Duke. It is as if he was as reluctant to take a place in history as he was to take public office. Is it possible that in some forgotten chest the Duke's own correspondence and private papers survive?

I confess that I have not gone out of my way to find new manuscript material. To make sense out of what has already been published appears to me more important. The trouble up to date has been that selections of original documents have been published without any satisfactory attempt to correlate them.

It began in 1898 when Vere Foster, Lady Elizabeth Foster's grandson, published *The Two Duchesses*, a selection from a mass of family letters relating to 'memorable contemporary events and subjects of public interest'. Apart from the two Duchesses the correspondents included the Earl-Bishop, the Countess of Bristol and a number of others. It was followed in 1899 by selections from Georgiana's correspondence in the *Anglo-Saxon Review* (June and September). In 1909 Walter Sichel appended to his two-volume *Sheridan* twenty-eight pages of the Duchess of Devonshire's Journal of the King's Illness, 20 November 1788–12 January 1789, and fifteen letters by Sheridan to Georgiana and her sister, Lady Bessborough.

In 1916 Castalia, Countess Granville, produced *The Private Correspondence of Lord Granville Leveson Gower, 1781–1821*. Fantastic as it may seem, Castalia, Countess Granville, was Lord Granville's daughter-in-law.* A large part of her two bulky volumes was devoted to letters from Lady Bessborough to Lord Granville. From these she deleted what was of a purely personal nature (i.e. referring to Harriet and George Arundel Stewart). After her death much of the correspondence was deposited with the Public Record Office. But a large number of Lady Bessborough's letters from which she had quoted extracts were withheld from the PRO – these would throw more light on the dark places in their love story. The letters from Granville to Lady Bessborough, which she kept in a cedarwood box, were destroyed after her death.

In 1920 Ernest Hartley Coleridge produced *The Life of Thomas Coutts, Banker*. In it he printed a number of letters to Charles Fox, the Duchess of Devonshire and the fifth Duke which revealed details of the Duchess's gambling debts hitherto imprecise.

In 1940 two books appeared. Sir George Leveson Gower and his daughter Iris published *Hary-O, the Letters of Lady Harriet Cavendish, 1796–1809*. His father had already, in 1894, published a two-volume selection of Lady Harriet's letters, written after her marriage to Lord Granville. But *Hary-O* dealt with tensions in the Devonshire household before and after the death of Georgiana. Lord Bessborough's *Lady Bessborough and her Family Circle*, with its introduction by A. Aspinall, brought out skeletons which had been kept in cupboards by Castalia, Countess Granville; and prepared the way for Iris Leveson Gower's *The Face Without a Frown* (1944), a fictionalized biography useful chiefly for its account of the Westminster Election and extracts from the Duchess's letters written from exile to her children.

After another gap two books appeared in 1955. *Georgiana, Duchess of Devonshire*, edited by Lord Bessborough, was an extensive selection from the Duchess's correspondence, derived mainly from Chatsworth, and Miss Dorothy Margaret Stuart's *Dearest Bess* did the same thing by Lady Elizabeth Foster, drawing for the first time on Lady Elizabeth's journals in the Dormer Collection.

Apart from these books, each drawing on new and only slightly over-lapping material, three books tried to cover what Hugh Stokes called *The Devonshire House Circle* (1917). This first was a lively if inaccurate book;

* Her husband, born May 1815, married first Marie, daughter of the Duc Dalber and widow of Sir Frederick Acton, who died March 1860, and second Castalia Rosalind Campbell in September 1865.

more satisfying than either *A Regency Chapter* by Ethel Colburn Mayne (1939) or *The Grand Whiggery* by Margery Villiers (1939).

My task has been to draw upon this mass of published material in order to understand the relationships of the Duke and his two Duchesses, as seen by themselves and others. In the 'Notes on sources' I have used abbreviations for the most common sources. Where the Manuscript source is Chatsworth I use (C), where Dormer (D). But since most of the material has been published (see Bibliography) I also give the following abbreviations.

G   *Georgiana, Duchess of Devonshire*, ed. the Earl of Bessborough

DB   *Dearest Bess*, D. M. Stuart

HO   *Hary-O, the Letters of Lady Harriet Cavendish, 1796–1809*, Sir G. Leveson Gower and I. Palmer

GLG   *Private Correspondence of Lord Granville Leveson Gower, 1781–1821*, Castalia, Countess Granville

LB   *Lady Bessborough and her Family Circle*, ed. the Earl of Bessborough and A. Aspinall

TFWAF *The Face Without a Frown*, I. Leveson Gower

TC   *The Life of Thomas Coutts, Banker*, E. H. Coleridge

TD   *The Two Duchesses*, Vere Foster

Where material is drawn from Chatsworth but appears in a book there will be a double entry such as (C) G. Similarly there may be (D) DB.

CHAPTER ONE *(pp. 11–20)*

1. Horace Walpole, *Letters*.
2. (C).
3. *Town and Country Magazine*, 'Tête à Tête', March 1777, p. 121.
4. 'I begin to think that the Duke of Devonshire will certainly marry Lady Betty Hamilton. After there has been so much talk about it, he would undoubtedly not choose to go constantly to the Duchess of Argyll's box at the Opera, nor do I think, as a Man of Honour, it would be consistent to give her so much reason to flatter herself, if he did not intend it.' Lady Mary Coke, *Letters and Journals*, vol. 4, p. 158.
5. Stokes, *Devonshire House Circle*, p. 54.
6. *Town and Country Magazine*, 'Tête à Tête', March 1777, p. 122–3.
7. The Earl of Bessborough (G. p. 1) states without giving his authority that the Duke met Georgiana for the first time at Spa after 1772. In view of the friendship between the two families this is unbelievable.
8. LB, p. 1, footnote 3.
9. GLG, vol. 1, p. 312.
10. LB, pp. 18–30.
11. (C) G, p. 11.
12. TFWAF, p. 20.
13. G, p. 12.

14. Described by Mrs Delany, 14/17 January 1756, quoted in Maclean, *Memoir of the Family of Poyntz*, p. 216.

15. (C) G, pp. 12–13.

16. Boswell, *Life of Johnson*.

17. Georgiana, Duchess of Devonshire, *The Sylph*, vol. 1.

CHAPTER TWO *(pp. 21–32)*

1. (C) G, p. 165, Hare to the Duchess: Lady Derby 'appears to have totally lost the use of her legs, speaks so slow that the D. of Devonshire would repeat the Lord's Prayer whilst she says Jack Robinson'. Walpole used the Duke in a different comparison (*Letters*, 9 September 1780): 'our freeborn weather, that on Monday and Friday was as hot as Lord George, is now as cold as the Duke of Devonshire.'

2. *Recollections of the Table Talk of Samuel Rogers*, ed. A. Dyce, 1856, pp. 192–3.

3. (C) G, p. 13.

4. *Ibid.*, p. 15.

5. *Ibid.*, p. 16.

6. *Ibid.*, p. 18.

7. *Ibid.*, p. 15.

8. *Autobiography and Correspondence of Mary Granville, Mrs Delany*, ed. Rt. Hon. Lady Llanover, vol. 5, p. 98.

9. (C) G, p. 32.

10. Hobhouse, *Fox*, p. 5 ff.

11. *Autobiography and Correspondence of Mary Granville, Mrs Delany*, ed. Rt. Hon. Lady Llanover, vol. 5, p. 114.

12. Le Marchant, *Memoir of John Charles, Viscount Althorp, third Earl Spencer*.

13. Stokes, *The Devonshire House Circle*, pp. 60–1.

14. Bleackley, *The Beautiful Duchess*, p. 199.

15. (C) G, p. 20.

16. LB, p. 20.

17. (C) G, p. 20.

18. *Ibid.*, p. 21.

19. *Ibid.*, p. 22.

20. *Ibid.*, p. 23.

21. *Ibid.*, p. 24.

22. *Autobiography and Correspondence of Mary Granville, Mrs Delany*, ed. Rt. Hon. Lady Llanover, vol. 5, p. 115.

23. (C) G, p. 26.

24. *Ibid.*, p. 27.

25. *Ibid.*, pp. 27–8.

26. *Ibid.*, p. 30.

CHAPTER THREE *(pp. 33–41)*

1. (C) G, p. 242.

2. Stokes, *The Devonshire House Circle*, pp. 93–6.

3. (C) G, p. 31.

4. *Ibid.*, p. 32.
5. *Ibid.*, p. 36.
6. Bleackley, *The Beautiful Duchess*, p. 210.
7. (C) G, p. 39.
8. Diary MSS (Berg), p. 1040, quoted by Hemlow, *History of Fanny Burney*, p. 101.
9. *Morning Post & Daily Advertiser*, 30 September 1779, in G, Appendix III.
10. (C) G, p. 41.
11. *Ibid.*, p. 45.
12. G, p. 46.

CHAPTER FOUR *(pp. 42–9)*

1. G, Appendix II.
2. Walpole to the Earl of Strafford, *Letters*, 1 September 1780.
3. Le Marchant, *Memoir of John Charles, Viscount Althorp, third Earl Spencer*.
4. (C) G, p. 52.
5. Fothergill, *The Mitred Earl*, p. 47.
6. (C) DB, p. 6.
7. TD, pp. 83–4.
8. (C) G, p. 53.
9. TD, p. 200.
10. (C) G, pp. 56–7.
11. *Ibid.*, p. 58.
12. (C) DB, p. 8.
13. Walpole to Sir Horace Mann, *Letters*.

CHAPTER FIVE *(pp. 50–7)*

1. DB, pp. 8–9.
2. (D) DB, p. 9.
3. *Ibid.*, p. 13.
4. *Ibid.*, p. 12.
5. Fothergill, *The Mitred Earl*, pp. 67–8.
6. DB, p. 12.
7. (C) G, p. 59.
8. *Ibid.*, p. 62.
9. DB, p. 15.
10. (C) DB, p. 13. Bess envied those who were Lady Georgiana's godmothers, 'But I am to be the little Mama, Canis said so!'
11. (C) G, p. 62.
12. *Ibid.*, p. 64.
13. DB, p. 17.
14. *Ibid.*, pp. 19–21.
15. *Ibid.*, p. 16.
16. (C) G, p. 60.
17. *Ibid.*
18. (C) DB, p. 14.

19. (C) G, p. 77.
20. *Ibid.*, p. 81.

CHAPTER SIX *(pp. 58–68)*

1. TD, p. 100.
2. (C) G, p. 61.
3. *Ibid.*, p. 66.
4. *Ibid.*, p. 67.
5. *Ibid.*, p. 68.
6. *Ibid.*, pp. 78–9.
7. *Ibid.*, pp. 80–1.
8. See TFWAF, chap. 8.
9. (C) G, p. 84.
10. *Ibid.*, pp. 85–7.
11. DB, p. 2.
12. (C) G, p. 81.
13. *Ibid.*, p. 91.
14. *Ibid.*, pp. 92–3.
15. DB, p. 23.

INTERLUDE ONE *(pp. 69–71)*

1. DB, p. 19. The Duchess was already discussing their passing a happy old age together. If the Duke became Lieutenant-Governor of Ireland perhaps he could persuade little f to allow his two sons to join the Devonshire household.

CHAPTER SEVEN *(pp. 72–80)*

1. (C) G, p. 93.
2. *Ibid.*, p. 94.
3. (D) DB, pp. 23–4.
4. *Ibid.*, p. 25.
5. *Ibid.*, p. 24.
6. *Ibid.*, p. 27.
7. *Ibid.*, p. 28.
8. *Ibid.*, p. 29.
9. Lady Elizabeth's dramatic account is reprinted from (D) in DB, pp. 1–33.
10. (C) G, p. 99.
11. *Ibid.*, p. 100.
12. *Ibid.*, pp. 100–1.
13. (D) DB, pp. 34–5.
14. *Ibid.*, p. 35.
15. *Ibid.*, p. 36.
16. *Ibid.*
17. Fothergill, *The Mitred Earl*, p. 114.

18. (C) TFWAF, p. 130.
19. Doran, 'Mann' and Manners at the Court of Florence, 1740–86.
20. (D) DB, p. 37.

CHAPTER EIGHT (pp. 81–9)

1. Yarde, The Life and Works of Sarah Trimmer.
2. Hibbert, George IV, Prince of Wales, chap. 15.
3. (C) G, pp. 101–3.
4. Ibid., p. 106, Lady Elizabeth from Naples to the Duchess: 'Why won't you tell me if all I hear of dear Harriet and Harum is true? I suppose and swear always it is not.'
5. Ibid., p. 55.
6. TC, vol 1, pp. 251, 259–65.
7. (C) G. p. 113.
8. Ibid., p. 112.
9. Ibid., pp. 122–3.
10. Ibid., p. 125.
11. (D) DB, p. 39.
12. (C) G, p. 111.
13. DB, p. 39.
14. (C) DB, p. 40.
15. (C) G, p. 126.
16. (D) DB, p. 41.
17. Ibid., p. 42.

CHAPTER NINE (pp. 90–7)

1. (C) G, p. 133.
2. Ibid.
3. Ibid., p. 145.
4. Ibid., p. 135.
5. Ibid., p. 136.
6. TC, vol. 1, p. 216, Fox to Coutts, 1 August 1787.
7. Ibid., pp. 243–6.
8. Ayling, George the Third, pp. 329–45; Hibbert, George IV, Prince of Wales, pp. 75–81.
9. TC, vol. 1, pp. 260–1.
10. (C); (C) G, p. 138.
11. Sichel, Sheridan, vol. 2, pp. 399–426.
12. Ida Macalpine and Richard Hunter, King George III and the Mad Business.
13. (C) G, p. 139.
14. G, pp. 142–4.
15. (C) G, p. 145: 'Si je suis grosse je n'hésiterais pas à tous dire au Duc, puisque la naissance d'un fils serait probablement le fin de tous nos embarras.'
16. (C) G, p. 146.
17. Ibid., p. 147.

INTERLUDE TWO *(pp. 98–100)*

1. TFWAF, p. 174–5.
2. (C) G, p. 46.
3. *Ibid.*, p. 47.
4. *Encyclopedia Britannica* (1945 ed.), vol. 9, p. 804.

CHAPTER TEN *(pp. 101–8)*

1. (D) 23 June. Lady Elizabeth Foster's journal for the period 22 June 1789 to 14 August 1790 is a most vivid, if somewhat bewildering account of the way the revolution in France struck her – and incidentally the Devonshires – on the spot and in Belgium. DB makes greater use of this than I have done, because I am concerned with historic events only in so far as they affected the Devonshire House circle.
2. (C) G, p. 148.
3. (D) 25 June.
4. (C) G, p. 149.
5. *Ibid.*, p. 160, letter from James Hare to Lady Elizabeth, 15 September: 'It was not necessary to desire me to make a visit to the little Norman [Augustus Clifford], I had seen him before I received your last letter, and found him perfectly well. He promises to be a giant. He is uncommonly shy (how happens this?) and would not take much notice of me. The woman seems to be very fond of him, and made all sorts of excuses for his not receiveing me kindly. She enquired how my friend [the Duke of Devonshire] did, when she should see him, and whether the little boy's mother [Lady Elizabeth] would return at the same time. I was so surprized, confounded and puzzled that I said yes, and am now as surprized at my answer as I was at her question. I asked her how she passed her time, and whether she was not a little *ennuiée*. She said that certainly it would be much pleasanter if she could be placed near the child's mama, but that she did not complain.'
6. *Ibid.*, p. 149.
7. *Ibid.*, p. 154.
8. *Ibid.*, p. 149.
9. *Ibid.*, p. 150.
10. *Ibid.*, p. 151.
11. *Ibid.*, p. 153; (D) 12 July, 10 a.m.; 13, 14, 15 July.
12. (C) G., p. 153; (D) 16 July.
13. (D) 15, 16 July.
14. (C) G, p. 154.
15. *Ibid.*, p. 162.
16. *Ibid.*, p. 160. In a letter to the Duchess written on 8 September Hare, by then in London, had said, 'I am really very glad to hear that you intend taking Charlotte and the little girl from Nagels. . . . It is a pity there should be any obstacles to your taking little Caroline more immediately under your own care, for she is the prettiest child I ever saw.' This implies that there had been previous discussion on the subject.
17. *Ibid.*, p. 163.
18. *Ibid.*, p. 170.
19. *Ibid.*, pp. 163–4.

20. *Ibid.*, p. 166.
21. (C) The Duchess to her mother, 17 March.
22. (D) 21 July.
23. *Ibid.*, 26 July.
24. *Ibid.*, 21 July.
25. (C) Ann Scafe's journal, deposed February 1818.
26. (D) 6 May 1790.
27. *Ibid.*
28. *Ibid.*, 14 May.
29. *Ibid.*, 20 May.
30. (C) Ann Scafe's journal.

CHAPTER ELEVEN *(pp. 109–20)*

1. (C) G, p. 173.
2. *Ibid.*, p. 174.
3. *Ibid.*, p. 175.
4. *Ibid.*, p. 176.
5. *Ibid.*, p. 176.
6. *Ibid.*, p. 178.
7. *Ibid.*, p. 177.
8. *Ibid.*, p. 181.
9. LB, p. 60.
10. Fanny Burney's Diary MSS (Berg), pp. 4399–420. In August Lady Elizabeth and Caro St Jules arrived. The latter was introduced as '*la petite Caroline*, a French orphan'. But, as Joyce Hemlow remarks (*The History of Fanny Burney*, p. 223), she was believed to be, 'as Fanny's brother would have put it, "a little orphan between the Duke and Lady Elizabeth" '.
11. (C) G, p. 182.
12. G, pp. 183–4, based on Melbourne correspondence in the British Library.
13. TFWAF, p. 144.
14. *Ibid.* In chap 14 Miss Iris Leveson Gower based her account of the Duchess's exile on the journals sent to the children, now in Chatsworth. Hers is the fullest published account.
15. (C) LB, pp. 66–7 gives the full text as 'To an unknown correspondent'.
16. G, pp. 185–6; DB, p. 63. They left Aix on 3 February, called on the St Juleses, where the Comte was very seriously ill, and reached Montpellier on 10 February. Eliza Courtney was born on 20 February.
17. (C) G, p. 187.
18. *Ibid.*, pp. 187–8.
19. *Ibid.*, pp. 189–90.
20. *Ibid.*, p. 190.
21. *Ibid.*, p. 191.
22. *Ibid.*, p. 189.
23. *Ibid.*, p. 192. Coutts must have been sceptical. On 15 February Mary Noel, Lady Melbourne's relative, wrote, 'It seems to be very certain that the D. & Dss of Devonshire are never to meet again' (Elwin, *The Noels and the Milbankes*, pp. 413–14).

24. G, p. 191, based on Melbourne correspondence in the British Library.
25. (C) G, p. 191.
26. *Ibid.*, pp. 192–3.
27. *Ibid.*, pp. 194–5.
28. *Ibid.*, p. 196.
29. *Ibid.*, pp. 196–7.
30. (C) TFWAF, p. 179.
31. *Ibid.*, p. 184.
32. See Connell, *Portrait of a Whig Peer*, p. 285. Lady Palmerston's diary for 26 May 1793 (in Rome): 'The Duchess certainly returns to England this summer. The Duke has written a most affectionate letter to desire her to return.' It is possible that Lord Bessborough was able to discuss the Duchess with the Duke in a way that James Hare did not dare to.
33. (C) G, p. 199.
34. *Ibid.*, p. 201.

CHAPTER TWELVE (pp. 121–7)

1. (C) G, p. 203.
2. GLG, vol. 1, pp. 82–3.
3. *Ibid.*, pp. 98–9.
4. (C) G, p. 210.
5. *Ibid.*, p. 220.
6. *Ibid.*, pp. 220–1.
7. GLG, vol. 1, pp. 125–6.
8. (C) G, p. 222.
9. GLG, vol. 1, p. 134.
10. *Ibid.*, p. 142.
11. (C) G, p. 224.

INTERLUDE THREE (pp. 128–30)

1. TD, p. 131.
2. *Ibid.*, pp. 130–1.
3. DB, p. 76.
4. TD, p. 132.
5. DB, p. 77.
6. TD, p. 132.

CHAPTER THIRTEEN (pp. 131–9)

1. GLG, vol. 1, p. 281. Castalia, Countess Granville, remarked of 1800 that 'The letters this year were very numerous, but so largely concerned with private matters and details of Lady Bessborough's long and serious illness, that only a few are of general interest.' The Countess's reticence was due to the fact that though she was writing 116 years after the birth of Lord Granville Leveson Gower's illegitimate

daughter, Castalia Granville was his daughter-in-law! She was careful to exclude all the correspondence referring to the pregnancy from the Granville Papers which she deposited with the Public Record Office. But she included a letter written by Lady Harriet Granville to Harriet Arundel Stewart referring to the latter's birthday as being 23 August. It is possible that Lady Bessborough did in fact fall on the stairs and sustain a concussion. Even if she did, the reason why her doctors were not called in remains the same. The labour pains had started.

2. *Ibid.*, p. 284.

3. *Ibid.*, p. 283. On p. 282 there is a letter from the Duchess to Lord Granville Leveson Gower while Lady Bessborough was still at Roehampton. Castalia Granville omitted the earlier part of the letter which may have referred openly to Lady Bessborough and the baby. The part which she does print is of such 'idiotism' (to use the word the Duchess employed of Mrs Crewe) that one suspects a use of code, similar to that which Lady Bessborough had employed to 'Mr Black' in her letter from Hyères.

4. *Ibid.*, p. 284.

5. (C) G, p. 237.

6. GLG, vol. 1, pp. 286–7.

7. (C) G, pp. 237–8.

8. The news came in a letter from her younger sister Louisa (see (D) DB, p. 90). At the bottom of one page she read 'our sad loss' and the top of the next 'our Mother'. She noted, 'I could no more. I lost my reason – almost my life.'

9. (C) G, p. 238.

10. *Ibid.*, p. 239.

11. *Ibid.* In the same letter Hare told the Duchess, 'I agree with you in every word you say of Ly Elizabeth, there cannot be a warmer, steadier, more disinterested friend: she shews perhaps too great a distrust in her natural graces, for I never will be brought to say that she is not affected, tho' I allow it is the most pardonable sort of affectation I ever met with and is become quite natural.'

12. GLG, vol. 1, p. 313.

13. *Ibid.*, p. 312.

14. (C) G, pp. 246–7.

15. *Ibid.*, p. 248.

16. G, p. 248.

17. GLG, vol. 1, p. 344; (D) DB, pp. 96–7.

18. HO, p. 30.

19. (C) G, p. 249.

20. GLG, vol. 1, p. 366.

21. *Ibid.*, p. 365.

22. DB, p. 99.

23. (D) DB, p. 107.

24. (C) G, p. 258.

25. *Ibid.*, p. 260.

26. DB, p. 109.

27. *Ibid.*, p. 110.

28. *Ibid.*, pp. 110–11.

29. HO, p. 79.

30. (C) G, p. 255.

CHAPTER FOURTEEN *(pp. 140–9)*

1. DB, p. 140.
2. GLG, vol. 1, pp. 433–4.
3. (C) G, pp. 261–2.
4. *Ibid.*, p. 264.
5. Ibid., p. 262.
6. *Ibid.*, p. 264.
7. HO, p. 44.
8. GLG, vol. 2, p. 68.
9. *Ibid.*, p. 69.
10. TD, pp. 199–201. Georgiana and Bess composed a poem on the death of their 'lov'd Companion and a Friend sincere'.
11. (C) G, p. 267.
12. GLG, vol. 1, pp. 472, 481, 419.
13. (C) G, p. 269.
14. *Ibid.*, pp. 270–1.
15. GLG, vol. 1, p. 491.
16. *Ibid.*, vol. 2, p. 131.
17. (D) DB, p. 126.
18. *Ibid.*, p. 125.
19. *Ibid.*, pp. 126–7.
20. *Ibid.*, p. 128.
21. HO, p. 133.
22. (C) G, p. 276.
23. *Ibid.*, p. 277.
24. University of Durham Department of Palaeography and Diplomatic, Grey (second Earl) papers.
25. (C) G, p. 279.
26. *Ibid.*, p. 280.
27. HO, p. 136.
28. GLG, vol. 2, p. 185.
29. *Ibid.*
30. (C) G, p. 135: 'Je vous ai bien ouverte mon coeur et vous avez vu que malgré toute ma gaieté il est souvent tourmenté.'
31. *Ibid.*, p. 281.

INTERLUDE FOUR *(pp. 150–4)*

1. GLG, vol. 2, pp. 185–6.
2. (D) DB, p. 142. I have in the text related events as they occurred in chronological order. This, however, is not the order in which they appear in Lady Elizabeth's journal. Her entries reached a climax in the early hours of 5 April, beginning with the talks with the Duke and then Lady Bessborough. What had happened before that in time is related after that in the journal: confirmatory evidence that Lady Elizabeth wished to put the record right for her subsequent readers. This entry was made on 31 March, the day after the Duchess's death. In notes 3 to 9 I append the approximate time of the journal entry.

3. *Ibid.*, p. 144, after 5 a.m., 5 April.
4. *Ibid.*, p. 143, after 5 a.m., 5 April, but this and 5 were entered before 3.
5. *Ibid.*, see note 4.
6. *Ibid.*, p. 142, 3 a.m., 5 April.
7. *Ibid.*, immediately following 6.
8. *Ibid.*, p. 143, immediately following 7.
9. *Ibid.*, 5 a.m., 5 April, prior to 4, 5 and 3.
10. *Ibid.*, p. 144.
11. (C) Letter from John, Viscount Althorp, to Lady Georgiana Spencer.

CHAPTER FIFTEEN *(pp. 155-64)*

1. (D) D5, p. 146.
2. (C) DB, p. 146.
3. HO, p. 154.
4. (D) DB, p. 149-50.
5. HO, pp. 167-8.
6. *Ibid.*, pp. 238-40.
7. *Ibid.*, pp. 249, 261-2.
8. *Ibid.*, p. 282.
9. DB, pp. 147-8.
10. GLG, vol. 2, p. 345.
11. HO, pp. 329-30.
12. *Ibid.*, p. 261: 'My aunt is grown immensely large; I never saw so great an increase in size in so short a time and I hear from Lady Elizabeth that she frets herself about it and cannot bear to have it observed' (1 December 1807).
13. *Ibid.*, p. 330.
14. *Ibid.*, p. 328.
15. LB, p. 192.
16. (C) DB, pp. 168-9.
17. (D) DB, p. 170.
18. DB, p. 170.
19. *Ibid.*, p. 171.
20. HO, p. 332.
21. *Ibid.*, p. 333.
22. (D) DB, p. 171.
23. GLG, vol. 2, p. 348.
24. *Ibid.*, p. 350.
25. DB, p. 180.

INTERLUDE FIVE *(pp. 165-6)*

1. DB, p. 181.

CHAPTER SIXTEEN (pp.167–78)

1. GLG, vol. 1, p. 396: 'Heaton is in great favour with Hart; he means also to increase his salary, which seems to me ample now – a thousand a year.' Cf. p. 359: 'Hart gave old Heaton 2000, which tho' I do not love the man, I am glad of . . . this generosity – I suppose unexpected by Heaton – drew Iron tears down Pluto's cheeks. He quite sobb'd and cried like a child. I should have been tempted to say like Lear: "Be your tears wet?" for he wept at what came home to himself, but could not find one tear for the kind Master who had shewn him unlimited confidence and friendship for more than forty years.' Lady Bessborough perhaps misjudged Heaton. The fifth Duke seems to have treated Heaton with coldness as an employee and with fear as the Devonshire trustee. Heaton's tears may have sprung not only from gratitude but from relief at discovering the sixth Duke prepared to discuss business like a human being.

2. G, Appendix 1, pp. 286–8.

3. GLG, vol. 2, pp. 389–90.

4. *Ibid.*, p. 390.

5. *Ibid.*, p. 391.

6. *Ibid.*, pp. 392, 394, 395.

7. *Ibid.*, p. 405: '125 thousand a year, charg'd with a great debt, certainly, but debt and all a very pretty *competency* as times go.'

8. *Ibid.*, p. 402.

9. DB, p. 183.

10. LB, pp. 217–18.

11. GLG, vol. 2, p. 416.

12. *Ibid.*, pp. 422–3.

13. (D) DB, p. 190: 'Two such friends as I had no one ever had before – all that has extended comfort under the severity of their loss I still owe to them. O, dear, adored husband and friend, may Heaven grant my prayer and suffer me to be reunited to you both in another world!'

14. Elwin, *Lord Byron's Wife*, p. 107.

15. (D) DB, p. 194.

16. *Ibid.*, p. 48.

17. Boswell, *Life of Johnson.*

18. Leveson Gower, *Letters of Harriet, Countess Granville*, vol 1, p. 110.

19. *Letter of Sarah Spencer, Lady Lyttelton*, ed. Hon. Mrs Hugh Wyndham, p. 217.

20. (C) Ann Scafe's journal.

21. Lady Harriet Granville forwarded a letter from Lady Duncannon announcing the death of Lady Bessborough to Harriet Arundel Stewart, without making any mention that Lady Bessborough was Harriet Arundel Stewart's mother. Lady Granville remarked that it was not until Lady Bessborough died that she realized how much she liked her. *De mortuis nil nisi bonum.*

22. 24 January 1824.

23. DB, p. 237.

24. *Ibid.*, p. 241.

25. (C) Dr Nott's account, written for the sixth Duke.

26. DB, p. 237.

27. Leveson Gower, *Letters of Harriet, Countess Granville*, vol. 1, p. 269

Bibliography

Manuscripts

CHATSWORTH MSS (Fifth Duke's Collection)
DORMER PAPERS (Lady Elizabeth Foster's journals)
PUBLIC RECORD OFFICE (Granville Papers)
UNIVERSITY OF DURHAM DEPARTMENT OF PALAEOGRAPHY AND
  DIPLOMATIC (Earl Grey Papers, second Earl)

Printed material

ANDREWS, C. B. and F., *The Torrington Diaries*, 1954
ASPINALL, A., *Correspondence of George, Prince of Wales (1770–1812)*,
  1963–71
AYLING, STANLEY, *George the Third*, 1972
BERGER, MORROE, *Madame de Staël on Politics, Literature and National
  Character*, 1961
BESSBOROUGH, EARL OF, and ASPINALL, A., *Lady Bessborough and her
  Family Circle*, 1940
BESSBOROUGH, EARL OF (ed.), *Georgiana, Duchess of Devonshire*, 1955
BINGLEY, J. M., *Life and Memoirs of HRH Princess Charlotte*, 1818
BLACK, CLEMENTINA, *The Linleys of Bath*, 1971
BLEACKLEY, HORACE, *The Beautiful Duchess* (Elizabeth Gunning, Duchess
  of Argyll and Hamilton), 1907
BOSWELL, JAMES, *Life of Johnson*
    Boswell's Column, ed. M. Bailey, 1951
BUTLER, IRIS, *Rule of Three*, 1967
CALDER-MARSHALL, A., *The Grand Century of the Lady*, 1976
CASANOVA, G., *History of My Life*, vol. 9, 1970
CECIL, LORD DAVID, *The Young Melbourne*, 1965
CHEVENIX-TRENCH, C., *The Royal Malady*, 1964
COKE, LADY MARY, *Letters and Journals (1756–74)*, 4 vols., 1889–96,
  repr. 1970

COLERIDGE, E. H., *The Life of Thomas Coutts, Banker*, 2 vols., 1920

CONNELL, BRIAN, *Portrait of a Whig Peer* (2nd Viscount Palmerston (1739–1802)), 1951

CRESTON, DORMER, *The Regent and his Daughter*, 1932

D'ARBLAY, MME (Fanny Burney), *Diary and Letters*, ed. C. F. Barrett, 6 vols., 1904

DELANY, MRS, (Mary Granville), *Autobiography and Correspondence (1700–88)*, ed. Rt Hon. Lady Llanover, 3 vols., 1861, 3 vols., 1862

DEVONSHIRE, GEORGIANA, DUCHESS OF, *The Sylph*, 1779

DEWES, SIMON, *Mrs Delany*

DORAN, JOHN, *'Mann' and Manners at the Court of Florence, 1740–86*, founded on letters of Horace Mann to H. Walpole, 2 vols., 1876

Dictionary of National Biography

ELWIN, MALCOLM, *Lord Byron's Wife*, 1962
    The Noels and the Milbankes, 1967

FOSTER, VERE, *The Two Duchesses*, 1898

FOTHERGILL, BRYAN, *The Mitred Earl*, 1974

GALBRAITH, GEORGIANA, *The Journal of the Reverend William Bagshaw Stevens*, 1965

GOWER, LORD RONALD, *Stafford House Letters*, 1891

GRANVILLE, CASTALIA, COUNTESS, *Private Correspondence of Lord Granville Leveson Gower, 1781–1821*, 2 vols, 1916

GROSVENOR, CAROLINE, and BEILBY, CHARLES (Lord Stuart of Wortley), *The First Lady Wharncliffe and Her Family*, 2 vols, 1927

HALSBAND, ROBERT, *Lord Hervey*, 1973

HEMLOW, J., *The History of Fanny Burney*, 1958

HERVEY, LORD, *Memoirs of the Reign of George II*, ed. R. Sedgwick, 1952

HIBBERT, CHRISTOPHER, *King Mob*, 1958
    George IV, Prince of Wales, 1972
    Regent and King, 1973

HOBHOUSE, CHRISTOPHER, *Fox*, 1947

HOWE, BEA, *A Galaxy of Governesses*, 1954

HYDE, H. MONTGOMERY, *The Strange Death of Lord Castlereagh*, 1959

ILCHESTER, COUNTESS OF, and STAVORDALE, LORD, *Life and Letters of Sarah Lennox*, 2 vols., 1902

ILCHESTER, LORD, *Lady Holland's Journal, 1791–1811*, 1908
    Lady Holland to her Son, 1821–1845, 1946

JESSE, CAPTAIN, *Life of Beau Brummell*, 2 vols., 1927

LEAN, TANGYE, *The Napoleonists*, 1970

LE FANU, W., *Betsy Sheridan's Journal*, 1960

LE MARCHANT, SIR DENIS, *Memoir of John Charles, Viscount Althorp, third Earl Spencer*, 1876

LEVER, SIR TRESHAM, *Letters of Lady Palmerston* (Emily Lamb), 1957

BIBLIOGRAPHY

LEVESON GOWER, HON. F. L., *Letters of Harriet, Countess Granville, 1810–1843*, 2 vols., 1894

LEVESON GOWER, IRIS, *The Face Without a Frown*, 1944

LEVESON GOWER, SIR GEORGE, and PALMER, IRIS, *Hary-O, the Letters of Lady Harriet Cavendish, 1796–1809*, 1940

LOOMIS, STANLEY, *Paris in the Terror*, 1964

MACALPINE, I., and HUNTER, R., *Porphyria, a Royal Malady*, 1968
    King George III and the Mad Business, 1969

MACLEAN, SIR JOHN, *Memoir of the Family of Poyntz*, 1886

MARCHAND, LESLIE A., *Byron's Letters and Journals*, vols. 1–5, 1973–76

MARKHAM, VIOLET, *Paxton and the Bachelor Duke*, 1935

MAXWELL, SIR HERBERT, *The Creevey Papers*, 1905

MAYNE, E. C., *A Regency Chapter: Lady Bessborough and her Friendships*, 1939

PAIN, NESTA, *George III at Home*, 1975

PALMER, ALAN, *George IV*, 1972

PRINCE, P. A., *Parallel History*, 1843

QUENNELL, PETER, *Memoirs of William Hickey*, 1960

ROBINSON, MRS 'PERDITA', *Memoirs*, 1801

SICHEL, WALTER, *Sheridan*, 2 vols., 1909

STOKES, HUGH, *The Devonshire House Circle*, 1917

STUART, DOROTHY MARGARET, *Molly Lepell*, 1936
    Daughter of England, 1951
    Dearest Bess, 1955

STUART, LADY LOUISA, *Letters, 1778–1834*, 1926

Town and Country Magazine, March 1772

VILLIERS, MARJORIE, *The Grand Whiggery*, 1939

WALPOLE, HORACE, *Letters*, ed. Paget Toynbee, 19 vols., 1918–25

Westminster Election, The History of the, 2nd ed., 1785

WILSON, HARRIETTE, *Memoirs of Herself and Others*, 1829

WRAXALL, SIR N. W., *Historical and Posthumous Memoirs*, 5 vols., 1884

WYNDHAM, HON. MRS HUGH, *Letters of Sarah Spencer, Lady Lyttelton*, 1912

YARDE, D. M., *The Life and Works of Sarah Trimmer*, 1972

CAVENDISH FAMILY

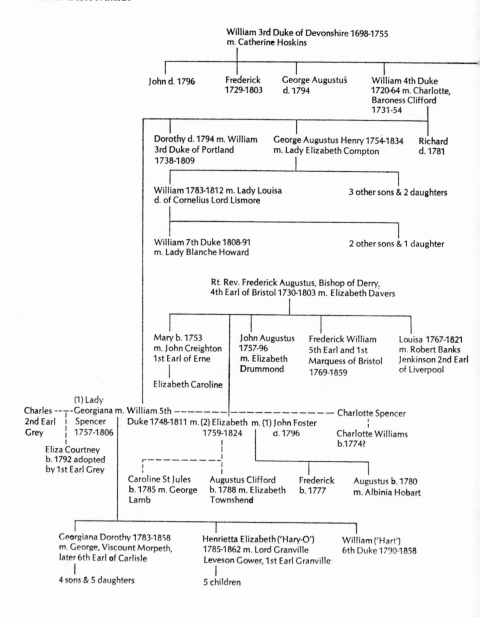

William 3rd Duke of Devonshire 1698-1755
m. Catherine Hoskins

John d. 1796 — Frederick 1729-1803 — George Augustus d. 1794 — William 4th Duke 1720-64 m. Charlotte, Baroness Clifford 1731-54

Dorothy d. 1794 m. William 3rd Duke of Portland 1738-1809 — George Augustus Henry 1754-1834 m. Lady Elizabeth Compton — Richard d. 1781

William 1783-1812 m. Lady Louisa d. of Cornelius Lord Lismore — 3 other sons & 2 daughters

William 7th Duke 1808-91 m. Lady Blanche Howard — 2 other sons & 1 daughter

Rt. Rev. Frederick Augustus, Bishop of Derry, 4th Earl of Bristol 1730-1803 m. Elizabeth Davers

Mary b. 1753 m. John Creighton 1st Earl of Erne — John Augustus 1757-96 m. Elizabeth Drummond — Frederick William 5th Earl and 1st Marquess of Bristol 1769-1859 — Louisa 1767-1821 m. Robert Banks Jenkinson 2nd Earl of Liverpool

Elizabeth Caroline

(1) Lady
Charles - - - - Georgiana m. William 5th - - - - - - - - | - - - - - - - - - - - - Charlotte Spencer
2nd Earl | Spencer   Duke 1748-1811 m. (2) Elizabeth m. (1) John Foster
Grey | 1757-1806   1759-1824   d. 1796   Charlotte Williams b.1774?

Eliza Courtney b. 1792 adopted by 1st Earl Grey

Caroline St Jules b. 1785 m. George Lamb — Augustus Clifford b. 1788 m. Elizabeth Townshend — Frederick b. 1777 — Augustus b. 1780 m. Albinia Hobart

Georgiana Dorothy 1783-1858 m. George, Viscount Morpeth, later 6th Earl of Carlisle

4 sons & 5 daughters

Henrietta Elizabeth ('Hary-O') 1785-1862 m. Lord Granville Leveson Gower, 1st Earl Granville

5 children

William ('Hart') 6th Duke 1790-1858

PONSONBY FAMILY

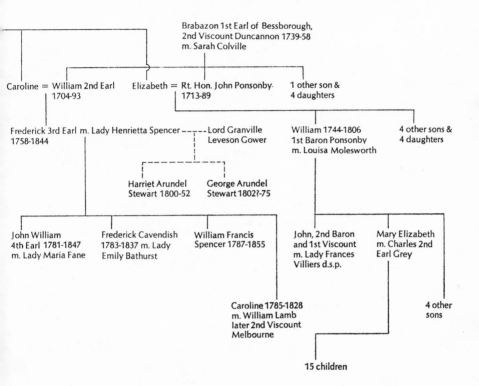

Brabazon 1st Earl of Bessborough,
2nd Viscount Duncannon 1739-58
m. Sarah Colville

Caroline = William 2nd Earl
1704-93

Elizabeth = Rt. Hon. John Ponsonby
1713-89

1 other son &
4 daughters

Frederick 3rd Earl m. Lady Henrietta Spencer ----- Lord Granville
1758-1844   Leveson Gower

William 1744-1806
1st Baron Ponsonby
m. Louisa Molesworth

4 other sons &
4 daughters

Harriet Arundel   George Arundel
Stewart 1800-52   Stewart 1802?-75

John William
4th Earl 1781-1847
m. Lady Maria Fane

Frederick Cavendish
1783-1837 m. Lady
Emily Bathurst

William Francis
Spencer 1787-1855

John, 2nd Baron
and 1st Viscount
m. Lady Frances
Villiers d.s.p.

Mary Elizabeth
m. Charles 2nd
Earl Grey

Caroline 1785-1828
m. William Lamb
later 2nd Viscount
Melbourne

4 other
sons

15 children

SPENCER FAMILY

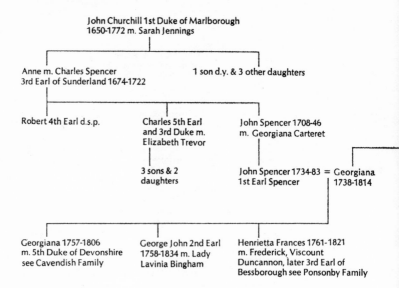

John Churchill 1st Duke of Marlborough
1650-1772 m. Sarah Jennings

Anne m. Charles Spencer
3rd Earl of Sunderland 1674-1722

1 son d.y. & 3 other daughters

Robert 4th Earl d.s.p.

Charles 5th Earl
and 3rd Duke m.
Elizabeth Trevor

John Spencer 1708-46
m. Georgiana Carteret

3 sons & 2
daughters

John Spencer 1734-83 = Georgiana
1st Earl Spencer   1738-1814

Georgiana 1757-1806
m. 5th Duke of Devonshire
see Cavendish Family

George John 2nd Earl
1758-1834 m. Lady
Lavinia Bingham

Henrietta Frances 1761-1821
m. Frederick, Viscount
Duncannon, later 3rd Earl of
Bessborough see Ponsonby Family

POYNTZ FAMILY

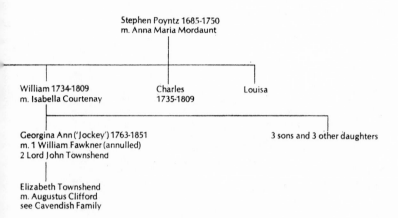

Stephen Poyntz 1685-1750
m. Anna Maria Mordaunt

William 1734-1809
m. Isabella Courtenay

Charles
1735-1809

Louisa

Georgina Ann ('Jockey') 1763-1851
m. 1 William Fawkner (annulled)
2 Lord John Townshend

3 sons and 3 other daughters

Elizabeth Townshend
m. Augustus Clifford
see Cavendish Family

Index